The International
Sub-Saharan

THE INTERNATIONAL RELATIONS OF SUB-SAHARAN AFRICA

by
Ian Taylor

continuum

NEW YORK • LONDON

2010

The Continuum International Publishing Group Inc
80 Maiden Lane, New York, NY 10038

The Continuum International Publishing Group Ltd
The Tower Building, 11 York Road, London SE1 7NX

www.continuumbooks.com

Library of Congress Cataloging-in-Publication Data
A catalog record for this book is available from the Library of Congress.

ISBN: 978-0-8264-3490-6 (Hardback)
         978-0-8264-3401-2 (Paperback)

Typeset by Newgen Imaging Systems Pvt Ltd, Chennai, India
Printed in the United States of America

Contents

Chart

Acknowledgments

This book is based on my readings and observations of sub-Saharan Africa's international relations over the last 15 years or so. Conducting research in and/or visiting over 30 African countries has also helped. Teaching African politics and international relations to African students at African universities has been an undoubted privilege and I have been fortunate enough to have taught at Dalhousie University (Canada), Mbarara University of Science and Technology (Uganda), Renmin University of China (China), the University of Botswana, the University of Hong Kong, the University of Stellenbosch (South Africa) and the University of St. Andrews (Scotland). I thank my students at all these places for their feedback and insights on many of the topics covered in this book. Equally, discussing ideas and thoughts with colleagues at the institutions where I have taught and at numerous academic conferences in Africa and elsewhere has been highly educational.

I would like to thank, in particular, two people who have always been willing to share their thoughts and provide advice: Fredrik Söderbaum of the University of Gothenburg, Sweden and Paul D. Williams of George Washington University. Both have really helped me over the years, and I am lucky to count them as both collaborators and friends.

This book was written while a visiting professor at Renmin University of China, the Chinese University of Hong Kong, the University of Gothenburg and the University of Stellenbosch. I am really grateful to my hosts for facilitating excellent writing conditions.

I would also like to express my gratitude to the following for their various insights which have helped sharpen my thoughts: Daniel Bach, Morten Bøås, William Brown, Fantu Cheru, Christopher Clapham, Scarlett Cornelissen, Kevin Dunn, Kenneth Good, Anthony Leysens, Pamela Mbabazi, Gladys Mokhawa, Mpho Molomo, Xenia Ngwenya, Francis Nyamnjoh, Cyril Obi, Adebayo Olukoshi and Tim Shaw.

Finally, I would especially like to thank my wife, Joanne, and my two children, Blythe and Archie, for their love and inspiration and for accompanying me on numerous travels around Africa. This book is dedicated to them.

Abbreviations

AAF-SAP	African Alternative Framework to Structural Adjustment Programs for Socio-Economic Recovery and Transformation
AASM	Associated African States and Madagascar
ACBF	Africa Capacity Building Foundation
ACP	Africa, the Caribbean and the Pacific
ACSA	Airports Company South Africa
AFRICOM	United States Africa Command
AGOA	African Growth and Opportunity Act
AML	Anti-money laundering
APPER	Africa's Priority Program for Economic Recovery
ASSOCHAM	Associated Chambers of Commerce and Industry of India
ATT	Arms Trade Treaty
AU	African Union
BAE	British Aerospace
BBC	British Broadcasting Corporation
BRIC	Brazil, Russia, India and China
CAP	Common Agricultural Policy
CAR	Central African Republic
CCA	Corporate Council on Africa
CFA	*Communauté Financière Africaine*
CFSP	Common Foreign and Security Policy
CHOGM	Commonwealth Heads of Government Meeting
CJTF-HOA	Combined Joint Task Force-Horn of Africa
CNOOC	China National Offshore Oil Corporation
COMESA	Common Market for Eastern and Southern Africa
CPC	Communist Party of China
CPLP	*Comunidade de Paises de Lingua Portuguesa*
CSR	Corporate Social Responsibility
CVRD	*Companhia Vale do Rio Doce*
DFID	Department for International Development
DPA	Development Partnership Arrangement
DRC	Democratic Republic of the Congo
DTI	Department of Trade and Industry
EACTI	East Africa Counterterrorism Initiative
EC	European Community
ECGD	Export Credit Guarantee Department
ECOWAS	Economic Community of West African States
EDF	European Development Fund
EEC	European Economic Community
EPA	Economic Partnership Agreement
ESAF	Enhanced Structural Adjustment Facility

EU	European Union
EUFOR	European Union Force
FAO	Food and Agriculture Organization
FCO	Foreign and Commonwealth Office
FDI	foreign direct investment
FICCI	Federation of Indian Chambers of Commerce and Industry
FIEO	Federation of Indian Export Organizations
FOCAC	Forum on China-Africa Cooperation
FSA	Financial Services Authority
G-20	Finance ministers and central bank governors of Argentina, Australia, Brazil, Canada, China, the European Union, France, Germany, India, Indonesia, Italy, Japan, Mexico, Russia, Saudi Arabia, South Africa, South Korea, Turkey, the United Kingdom and the United States of America
G-7	Forum involving Canada, France, Germany, Italy, Japan, the United Kingdom and the United States of America
G-8	G-7 plus Russia
G-77	Coalition of developing states at the United Nations
GATT	General Agreement on Tariffs and Trade
GDP	gross domestic product
GNP	gross national product
GNPC	Ghana National Petroleum Corporation
HIPC	heavily indebted poor countries
HIV/AIDS	human immunodeficiency virus/acquired immunodeficiency syndrome
IBSA	India-Brazil-South Africa Dialogue Forum
IEPA	Interim Economic Partnership Agreement
IFF	International Finance Facility
IFIs	international financial institutions
IMF	International Monetary Fund
IOC	*Indian Oil Corporation*
LDCs	least developed countries
LIFE	Leadership and Investment in Fighting an Epidemic
LPA	Lagos Plan of Action
MCA	Millennium Challenge Account
MDGs	Millennium Development Goals
MEND	Movement for the Emancipation of the Niger Delta
MFA	Multi-Fiber Agreement
MFN	most-favored nation
MOUs	Memoranda of Understandings
MTV	Music Television
NAFTA	North American Free Trade Agreement
NAM	Non-Aligned Movement
NARC	National Rainbow Coalition
NATO	North Atlantic Treaty Organization
NEPAD	New Partnership for Africa's Development
NGOs	nongovernmental organizations

NIEO	New International Economic Order
OAU	Organisation of African Unity
ODA	Overseas Development Administration
ODI	Overseas Development Institute
OECD	Organisation for Economic Co-operation and Development
ONGC	Oil and Natural Gas Corporation Limited
OPEC	Organization of the Petroleum Exporting Countries
OVL	ONGC Videsh Limited
PEPFAR	President's Emergency Plan for AIDS Relief
PIO	People of Indian Origin
PRC	People's Republic of China
PRSP	Poverty Reduction Strategy Paper
PTA	Preferential Trade Agreement
SACU	Southern African Customs Union
SAF	Structural Adjustment Facility
SAP	Structural Adjustment Program
SAR	*Société Africaine de Raffinage*
SSA	Sub-Saharan Africa
STABEX	Stabilization of Export Earnings
SYSMIN	Stabilization Scheme for Mineral Products
TSCTI	Trans-Sahara Counterterrorism Initiative
UN	United Nations
UNAMSIL	United Nations Mission in Sierra Leone
UNECA	United Nations Economic Commission for Africa
UNODC	United Nations Office on Drugs and Crime
UNOSOM	United Nations Operation in Somalia
UN-PAAERD	United Nations Program of Action for Africa's Economic Recovery and Development
UNSC	United Nations Security Council
USAID	United States Agency for International Development
WDM	World Development Movement
WTO	World Trade Organization

Introduction: Africa's International Relations

Despite the myth of marginality and irrelevance, sub-Saharan Africa (SSA) has always been inextricably linked to the global stage and has long played an important role in international politics. The slave trade, the Scramble for Africa and the subsequent colonial period; the proxy wars of the Cold War; and the increasing importance of the continent's natural resources, all demonstrate how significant Africa has been to the wider global political economy (Taylor and Williams, 2004). Obviously, it would be a gross error to begin with the arrival of the Europeans as the starting point for Africa's international relations; there has been a constant flow of ideas, material goods and political contacts between Africa, Europe and Asia since ancient times and the continent's extra-African political and economic ties were mature long before European people began "discovering" Africa (see Diop, 1987; Nöthling, 1989; Smith, 1973, 1976).

Yet within the commonsense parameters that have been constructed (particularly in the West), Africa was devoid of any real identity or history. Implicitly, any biography it possessed was developed by Europeans. Hugh Trevor-Roper's comments that "perhaps, in the future, there will be some African history to teach. But at present there is none: there is only the history of Europeans in Africa" captures this mind-set (cited in Hale, 2005: 7). This of course was a reinscribing of Hegel's own comments that Africa was "an unhistorical continent, with no movement or development of its own" (Hegel, 1975 [1822]: 142). And Durkheim's sociology was built on an implicit (and explicit) distinguishing between those "the great civilized societies of the West" and the "barbaric and savage" societies of the non-West, particularly Africa (Durkheim, 1982 [1907]: 209).

Undoubtedly, racism against Africans accounts for much of these foundational and subsequently dominant readings of the continent's place in the world (see Allimadi, 2003). As Kevin Dunn (2003) demonstrated in his study of the Congo and identity, SSA is a place where the West has long projected characteristics, images and meanings in its attempt to define and delineate what constitutes "Africa," invariably in negative terms (see also Mudimbe, 1988). And as Césaire (1972) pointed out, such discursive effects were developed through the categories of particular post-Enlightenment European social sciences, something that carries on today. Thus if and when the continent does not measure up (in Western terms), even respectable journals feel confident enough to write off the entire continent (i.e. nearly one billion people) as "hopeless" (*Economist*, May 13, 2000).

Certainly, much Western studies of Africa have "perpetuated the sense that the history of Africa was the history of White activity there" (Prior, 2007: 2). Correspondingly, there is a substantial trope of work on Africa's contemporary international relations that defines the continent's global linkages with how non-Africans behave(d) in Africa.

This advances the entirely erroneous notion that Africa is a passive bystander, devoid of agency and acted upon. It is crucial to reject the idea that Africa is a victim (Taylor, 2004a). In such thinking, vulgar structuralists unite with the likes of Trevor-Roper to cast an image of Africans as marginal and perpetual victims, incapable of writing their own history. Yet as William Brown notes (2006: 129):

> [N]ot only was the course of colonization shaped by the interaction between Africans and Europeans but decolonization and the foundation of independent states was a process in which Africans were actors, not simply acted upon. The critics' account also grossly over-simplifies the complex processes which have gone to shape the international system. It is as if the basic structure of the system was erected in seventeenth century Europe and has remained untouched and unchanged by the passing years of war, revolution, social transformation, state collapse and formation, international expansion and revolt.

Consequently, as Jean-François Bayart has asserted, "the discourse on Africa's marginality is a nonsense" (2000: 267). Africa has *never* existed separate from the world but rather has been inextricably entwined in world politics and has continually exercised its agency. In substantial terms, SSA cannot be seen to pursue a relationship with the world as "Africa is in no sense extraneous to the world" (Bayart, 2000: 234). The continent is globally dialectically connected and both determine and are determined by myriad developments, actors and structures, both internal and external, if such an artificial separation is to be cited.

Equally erroneous is the unwillingness to acknowledge that the state-society complex evident across many parts of SSA have critical implications and a vital—possibly decisive—influence upon many aspects of the continent's international relations. Toyin Falola writes that grasping the "nature of the patron-client system in a country is necessary to understand the behavior and activities of members of the political class and warlords" (2006: 181). Critically analyzing the modalities of governance in large parts of SSA and how they combine with external processes is essential if we wish to comprehend the diplomatic practices, global interactions and broad international relations of Africa's elites *and* ordinary citizens. By doing so, the differences between the "shop window" of the external diplomatic image and the actuality of the smoke-filled rooms where decisions are *really* made, the differences between the grand pronouncements of the air-conditioned conferences and the actuality of the decisions made on the verandah, and the gap between rhetoric and reality can be more readily understood (see Kelsall, 2002).

The State-Society Complex of Africa

Obviously, in discussing something as broad as "the African state," generalizations are necessary, and the applicability of general conceptual frameworks to each individual SSA country is contingent and dependent upon myriad factors. Having said that, it cannot be denied that a great deal of postcolonial African countries, bounded by formal frontiers and with an international presence at various international institutions, function quite differently from conventional understandings of what a formal essentialized *Western* state is and should do. In fact, many African states are not institutionally functional (see Taylor, 2005a).

That African states should not conform to Western models is, of course, not surprising—"before the state is a thing it is a social relation" (Rosenberg, 1990: 251) and the history of African social relations and states have their own historical contexts. In order for Africanists to understand the politics of the state on the continent, the concept of neo-patrimonialism has largely become the standard tool of analysis (LeVine, 1980; Jackson and Rosberg, 1982; Medard, 1982; Callaghy, 1984; Sandbrook, 1985; Callaghy, 1987; Crook, 1989; Bayart, 1993; Bratton and van de Walle, 1994; Chabal, 1994; Bratton and van de Walle, 1997; Tangri, 1999; Chabal and Daloz, 1999). This feature of politics in many parts of SSA has profound implications for any attempt to situate and appreciate the proper context and behavioral patterns of Africa's international relations. Ignoring such realities, however politically incorrect they may be, also results in a distinct naïveté in evaluating how and why many African elites behave on the international stage. As Chabal (2009: 179) has noted:

> [I]t is incumbent upon social scientists to explain what they witness, however unpalatable that explanation . . .[I]t is not the analyst who creates the realities of poverty, violence and illness found in Africa today. To deny the validity of an interpretation merely because it is derived from a generalization is to deny the very essence of research-based analysis.

Under a neo-patrimonial system the separation of the public from the private is recognized (even if in practice only on paper) and is certainly publicly displayed through outward manifestations of the rational-bureaucratic state—a flag, borders, a government and bureaucracy, etc. However, in practical terms the private and public spheres are habitually not detached and the outward manifestations of statehood are often facades hiding the real workings of the system. In many African countries, the official state bureaucracies inherited from the colonial period, however weak and ineffective, have become dysfunctional and severely constrained in their official, stated duties. Many postcolonial African leaders have rather relied on effected control and patronage through capturing power over the economy, rather than through the state in the form of a functioning administration. "What matters for members of the networks is less how politicians come to hold office and with what probity they occupy it than how they discharge their obligations under existing systems of reciprocity" (Chabal, 2009: 51–2). In a good number of states postindependence, this swiftly degenerated into outright personal dictatorships (Decalo, 1989), something that the much-heralded waves of democratization has only partially moderated. Emblematically, the acronym for the National Rainbow Coalition (NARC) in Kenya is wryly said to also stand for "Nothing Actually Really Changes."

Of course clientelism and patronage are *not* unique to Africa (see Lemarchand and Eisenstadt, 1980; Clapham, 1982; Fatton, 2002), nor are neo-patrimonial regimes. Ukraine, the Central Asian republics, Indonesia, various Latin American nations, etc. have all been described as fitting into the neo-patrimonial mode of governance. Categorizing SSA states as neo-patrimonial is certainly not to exoticize them, nor even to place a normative value on their dynamics. Nor is it to romanticize or de-historicize the Western state experience, as if the West somehow represents "normality"—the "Western state has neither been 'unproblematic' nor 'taken for granted' at virtually any point in its history. It is perhaps useful to remind oneself that what might be taken for granted as the 'European state system' today was, as recently as 1945, in a condition of near total collapse" (Brown, 2006: 127–8).

Yet it is vital to understand that many African bureaucracies are "patrimonial-type administrations in which staff [are] less agents of state policy (civil servants) than proprietors, distributors and even major consumers of the authority and resources of the government" (Jackson and Rosberg, 1994: 300). Handing out bureaucratic posts has become an important way in which leaders can secure support. This support stems from the fact that "being appointed into the government is tantamount to being given the opportunity to fill one's pocket with state-owned wealth and also the opportunity to develop one's part of the country if the appointee has any sense of loyalty to his people" (Fru Doh, 2008: 40). And so the patronage networks spread from the capital outwards.

The composition of Africa's diplomatic corps is a graphic example of this, with fierce competition and pressure on the patrons to deliver the best jobs (at the United Nations, in the developed world's capitals, etc.). In many African countries, those who hold the highest diplomatic ranks are not the best qualified—they are just the best connected. This of course has often grave implications for the competency of Africa's representation overseas. Nigeria's diplomatic corps, for instance, has seen numerous appointments that have been "absurd and sometimes disastrous" (Fafowara, 2008: 90). "Appointment of heads of mission is at the discretion of Nigeria's head of state, who is often under strong pressure to offer such appointments to political hacks and discarded military officers" (ibid.).

Such clientelism is central to neo-patrimonialism, with widespread networks of clients receiving services and resources in return for support. This is well understood and expected in many African countries, reflecting the mutual benefits that neo-patrimonialism confers to both patron and client. Indeed, the exercise of personalized exchange, clientelism and corruption is internalized and constitutes an "essential operating codes for politics" in Africa (Bratton and van de Walle, 1997: 63). This is "accepted as normal behavior, condemned only in so far as it benefits someone else rather than oneself" (Clapham, 1985: 49).

Those not in the loop may resort to appeals to "democratization" or even insurrection as a means of accessing the resources and power that accrues to those who have captured the state. As one Congolese official put it in commenting on the overthrow of long-time dictator Mobutu Sese Seko, "You know, in the fight against Mobutu, not everyone shared the same objectives . . . Some people wanted to change society. Some just wanted to replace him. It's the principle of '*Ôte-toi de là, que je m'y mette*' (Get out of the way, so I can take your place)" (quoted in Wrong, 2000: 291).

In many countries, corruption, working the system and subverting the state is "a firmly established practice . . . to the point where citizens no longer realize it is a wrongdoing. Because corruption is now the norm, anyone trying to do the correct thing by serving [the people] without stealing or asking for bribes can lose his job . . . as his colleagues accuse him of snatching the morsel from their mouths" (Fru Doh, 2008: 141).

Sovereignty and "Development"

As outlined above, control of the state serves the twin purposes of lubricating patronage networks *and* satisfies the selfish desire of elites to self-enrich themselves, in many cases, in a quite spectacular fashion. That is what lies at the heart of the profound reluctance by African presidents to hand over power voluntarily and why very many African regimes end messily (Decalo, 1990). In most cases the democratic option is either absent or is not respected by the loser—"no party will accept to be unsuccessful and so form the opposition, which according to Africa's political trend, would be deprived of power and the means to those favors for their camp" (Fru Doh, 2008: 51). Politics in Africa thus tends to be a zero-sum game.

National development and a broad-based productive economy is far less a concern '(in fact, might stimulate opposition) to elites within many such systems than the continuation of the gainful utilization of resources for the individual advantage of the ruler and his networks. For instance, in Kenya "So few Kenyans [identify] with any overarching national project, their leaders [feel] free to loot state coffers" (Wrong, 2009: 60). This has serious implications for the efficacy of international developmental assistance—something that most donors refuse to confront or even acknowledge, however unpalatable it may be. Even where elites may not actively block progress, such international notions of "development" have to be mediated through African expectations. As Chabal (2009: 83–4) points out:

> "Development" translates in practice into the material advantage sought and obtained by the various groupings to which the politicians belong or to which they are beholden. This does not mean that there is no effort on the part of government to devise, and implement, policies that benefit the country as a whole. What it does mean is that the implementation of such policies is subjected not just to the greed of local demand but also, and more problematically, to competing notions of public good that politicians find almost impossible to resist . . . [There are] systemic contradictions inherent in the translation of the local ethics of public virtue into a more coherent and long-term vision of the public good.

In short, the nature of the state-society complex in Africa has critical implications for the continent's local political and economic structures, development, international relations and its interactions with external players. This is particularly so in the context where "African leaders . . . are saddled with a strategy that hardly any of them believes in and that most of them condemn . . . Lacking faith in what they are doing and caught between their own interests, the demands of their external patrons, and their constituents, African leaders tend to be ambivalent, confused and prone to marginalize development and even their role in its pursuit. The development of Africa will not start in earnest until the struggle over the development agenda is determined" (Ake, 1987: 41).

In his book, *Africa and the International System* (1996a), Christopher Clapham discusses how complex local, regional and international processes incorporate SSA. A starting point for Clapham is the argument that many African states only possess quasi-statehood, i.e. while they enjoy recognition and support from the international system of states, many are unable to sustain themselves internally and practice the neo-patrimonial forms of governance discussed above, which are antithetical to broad-based development (ibid.: 271). Clapham argues that African independence saw an international regime of juridical sovereignty incorporating (and then maintaining) weak states that lacked empirical sovereignty and that would almost certainly not have survived in previous historical periods. The effects of the Cold War in stimulating this milieu cannot be underestimated.

The response from African elites presiding over such entities was to pursue a policy of extraversion—the utilization of external resources and political support to maintain power and sustain their patronage networks. Subsequently, "Sovereignty has been elusive for most African states and that . . . one can talk of a crisis of legitimacy. This results from the tensions and polarization between state and society, as well as being the result of globalization. As such, the concept of sovereignty that deals with state-building processes has become increasingly alien and has increasingly been replaced by a notion of sovereignty arising from an international regime external to . . . state borders" (Weiss and Hubert, 2002: 364).

It might be argued that acknowledgment of the sovereign status of many African state formations, however dysfunctional and fictitious, has allowed and even encouraged the current situation whereby many African citizens are materially worse off than they were under colonialism. Gaining control of an African state immediately supplies recognition and prestige from the outside world and provides external diplomatic backing and access to aid, which then further lubricates the patronage networks on which the state is predicated. In addition, assuming office automatically leads to membership in an elite club of African rulers who, as has been repeatedly demonstrated, band together for mutual support and protection against both external threats and domestic opposition to their rule. Such recognition, be it external or intra-African, is based on a concept of sovereignty that grants opportunities to rulers of even the most dysfunctional and weakest states. The use and abuse of the notion of sovereignty also allows an assortment of non-African actors to successfully construct commercial and military alliances with state leaders and their courtiers, as well as with private corporations.

In short, many state elites in Africa use the mantle of sovereignty not to promote the collective good but to bolster their own patronage networks and to weaken those of potential challengers. The international system is complicit in such a charade (see Taylor and Williams, 2001). Malgovernance is aided—even perpetuated—on the continent by the doctrines of sovereignty and noninterference, and it is no coincidence that Africa's elites are among the most enthusiastic defenders of these principles. This remains the case, despite the African Union's ostensible claim to provide an increased scope for intervention.

Contra to the notion that Africa is a passive bystander to global processes, African elites have generally proven themselves excellent arch-manipulators of the international system. The continued flow of resources in the form of development assistance, even to countries where the ruling elites manifestly do not care about development, bears testament to this. Even allegedly omnipotent international agencies such as the International Monetary Fund (IMF) and the World Bank have failed in achieving meaningful results in most SSA countries vis-à-vis their reform projects, as African governments have fought tooth and nail to protect their sinecures and prebends.

Subversion has led to partial reform. Indeed, there are considerable gaps between stated and actual commitments to reform across much of SSA. This is because donor-supported reforms have within them measures that would cut considerably the opportunities for informal manipulation over economic resources, rent-seeking and the ability to show favor to clients by state actors. Thus what occurs is the partial reform syndrome where aid-recipient administrations manipulate the reform process in order to protect their patron-client bases (van de Walle, 2001). Although Western governments "have not renounced their self-proclaimed right to influence the course of events" on the continent (Bayart, 2000: 239), the politics of resistance to attempted neoliberal reconfiguration is very much alive in Africa (Harrison, 2002).

For instance, Daniel arap Moi of Kenya was a "master in running rings around the donors" (Wrong, 2009: 185). "He would fiercely resist a suggested change throughout months of negotiations, then appear to give way, only to implement it in a way that made a mockery of the entire process . . . [T]he Kenyan government promised the same reform—of its maize marketing system—to the World Bank at least five times over a fifteen-year period in return for aid, only to reverse it on each occasion" (ibid.). As Paul Collier put it, "The amazing thing is that the money kept coming. How did Kenyan government officials manage to keep straight, sincere faces as for the fifth time they made the same commitment? How did officials of the agency manage to delude themselves into thinking that adherence this time was likely?" (Collier, 2007: 109). The answer is that African elites know that their mistakes or inappropriate behavior will almost always be covered by the ambiguous efforts of international organizations and nongovernmental organizations (NGOs) (see Tangri and Mwenda, 2001).

Implications for Africa's International Relations

As the processes outlined above have unfolded since independence, many African states have increasingly succumbed to modes of governance where the elites (in alliance with non-African partners) have effectively undermined the formal and institutionalized structures of their own states. The informalization of politics and institutional processes has resulted in the multiplying of informal markets, popular survival strategies (increasingly operationalized through emigration), forms of privatization that depend on the patronage and largesse of diverse global actors and, in some extreme cases, the criminalization of the very state itself. Often, such a "rolling back of the state" has gone hand in hand with the privatization strictures of the international financial institutions (IFIs), though such outcomes are no doubt quite different from what the donor community had envisioned when it promoted liberalization as the way to "set the market free."

An international relations of questionable statehoods across SSA is of profound importance for any discussion of the continent's dialectical interactions with the world. Yet many analyses of Africa's place in world politics suffer from an inability to conceptualize processes, events and structures that fall within the realm of what is usually considered private, illegal or worse, mundane and apolitical. Rectifying these inadequacies would require, according to Bayart, paying close attention not only to what transpires within government structures, but also at "the trading-post, the business-place, the plantation, the mine, the school, the hospital, and the Christian mission-station" (2000: 246).

In fact, while the Western-derived (and approved) state model has increasingly foundered, Africans, through a dialectic of structural pressures and their own political agency, have continually interacted with the world in ways that accommodate ideas of personal and communal progress and order. Although these concepts are defined in ways that do not necessarily resonate with dominant liberal approaches (Chabal and Daloz 1999), they nonetheless represent African agency and are rational and careful responses to the irresponsibility of the continent's elites and the stress placed on SSA by global pressures.

Problematically, many previous studies ignore such dynamics. Depending upon frameworks that are exclusively state-centric in both their ontology and approach, such analyses fail to pay due attention to the critical roles played by non-state actors in the continent's international relations, particularly the IFIs, development and humanitarian

NGOs and multinational/transnational corporations. Private (and occasionally public) corporations, diasporic communities, sportsmen and women, musical collaboration and criminal networks all flourish next to, together with and "beneath" the more readily observable state-to-state interactions that generally make up most studies of SSA's international relations.

Furthermore, history and location profoundly influences an African's engagement with the mundane aspects of the continent's international relations. The linguistic and/or religious dimensions of this are fascinating. For instance, an average Cape Verdean will likely be intimately knowledgeable about Brazilian soap operas, the Portuguese national football team and may know about the *Comunidade dos Países de Língua Portuguesa* but perhaps not the Commonwealth. Meanwhile, a Kenyan may play cricket, drink Guinness and listen to the BBC. These may appear humdrum, but they are in fact quite telling insights into the continent's varied global interactions and the quite different worlds that Africans insert themselves into.

Equally, other influences may come to bear that shape Africans' different worldviews and understandings of the international. In Dar es Salaam, for example: "There's a world centered around Oyster Bay. This is the financial district that looks towards London and New York and Europe. And then we have another world with its centre around the market area of Kariakoo and this world has Dubai and Saudi Arabia at its centre of information" (Vilby, 2007: 37–8).

Obviously, the society of states and the international organizations that its members have established and are members of remain important contexts for appreciating Africa's global place. There can be no serious argument advancing the notion that the African state should be dismissed as a foundational element in studying the international relations of SSA. However, the society of states itself exists beside and in a mutual relationship with a global political economy which increasingly demonstrates alternative, non-state sites of authority and where actors engaged in business more and more bypass formal political boundaries (either legally or illegally). Equally, the very nature of the state-society complex in SSA is central. Mature analyses of Africa's place in the world necessitates an understanding how in these contexts, state-society relations, the society of states *and* the non-state world interacts with the global political economy and influences the affairs of SSA's peoples and communities.

Sport, Music, the Diasporas, Criminals

As mentioned above, Africa's international relations are obviously not just state-led or limited to the IFIs and NGOs. The international flows associated with sport, music, diasporas, criminality and religion are but a few of the myriad aspects of Africa's interrelationships with extra-African spheres and locations. Of course, these processes often come together, such as when Afropop music founder Papa Wemba was imprisoned in France for illegally smuggling into Europe thousands of Africans, mostly Congolese, who posed as musicians and dancers working for his musical troupe. But they also arguably represent a notion of SSA's place in the world that has more resonance for the "average" African than the high politics of diplomacy, African Union (AU) conferences and state visits.

Sport

Sport has granted an extremely high international profile to Africa and Africans and has often been the gateway for Africans of humble backgrounds to internationalize. So extensive has Africa's contribution to international sport been that is difficult to delineate a sport where Africans have not made contributions. Africa does not as yet have a bobsleigh team (unlike Jamaica), but a South African *did* compete in the skeleton sledding event at the 2006 Winter Olympics.

Football is probably the sport that represents the extent of this particular aspect of Africa's international relations. "African football players have become more accessible as a result of the growing commercialism of the football industry and the compression of time-space that brings potential professional labor closer than ever to the global markets for its employment" (Darby, 2002: 23). At the World Cup in Germany in 2006, 75 percent of the African squad's players were plying their services in Europe. It can be said that Africans playing in Europe (and elsewhere—the Middle East most notably) is increasingly "a reflection of pre-existing social, political and economic power arrangements in sport" (Maguire and Stead, 1998: 60), but this is not new. The greatest player ever to play for Portugal was, after all, Eusebio, a black Mozambican.

Until the 1980s, however, Africans actually playing for European national sides was a rarity. This is no longer. France is probably the most notable country in this regard—its squad at the time of writing includes four players physically born in Africa and another eight of immediate African descent. Their familial links are a veritable register of Francophone Africa—Cameroon, Senegal, Benin, Mali, Algeria and Côte d'Ivoire—and are a most graphic representation of both *Françafrique* and contemporary African diasporic networks (see Maguire and Pearton, 2000). Of course, it is not only France that reflects the diaspora's growing presence—the 2009 Under-21 squad of Germany had five players of African descent. And such public symbols of African football's internationalization are not just one-way: Angola and South Africa regularly field white players of European descent.

African countries are also increasingly seeking to host global sport mega-events—the 2010 football World Cup's hosting by South Africa is a graphic example. The desire to play host to such events is connected to both internal (domestic) and external (international) elements and is invariably entangled in legitimating narratives for extant regimes (Cornelissen, 2004). Yet within the context of a generally negative global position vis-à-vis organizational reputation and the overbearing preeminence the developed world enjoys in the control and replication of international sport, Africa has by and large failed to secure sporting mega-events (given the costs involved, this is perhaps a good thing). The competitions to host mega-events occurs on an unequal basis for sure, but the tenacity of African countries bidding for such occasions represents an insertion into the global sporting arena unthinkable even 20 years ago.

Music

Music is also another aspect of Africa's international relations that usually slips beneath the radar screen but is no less an important element and symbol of the continent's global integration (see Franklin, 2005). In fact, music is arguably central as a motif for the transnational identities and global intersections that make up the complexities of the African diaspora and the continent's international relations. Certainly, African music is increasingly global vis-à-vis artists' location, production and distribution. Artists such as Senegal's Youssou N'Dour or Benin's Angelique Kidjo maintain successful artistic careers within the standard parameters of world music and can certainly not be restricted to the "African music" box. Of course, the diversity of sound has always been the reality of Africa's music—it is however now that the continent's music has emerged to stake its place globally. An important element of this is the role of the African diasporas (see Monson, 2003). As Somali-born, Toronto-based hip-hop artist K'Naan asserts:

"African music" can't be contained by any one definition—and not even by the boundaries of the continent itself . . . I think there is no real start and stop between being African and being an immigrant. My spirit is obsessed with movement, and the distance that is caused by the movement. (quoted in *Los Angeles Times* [Los Angeles], March 22, 2009)

Obviously, the fundamental links among African music and its American incarnations such as jazz, blues, samba, etc. were forged through the slave trade and in this sense African music has long been international (Kidjo for one has explored such realities—her album *Black Ivory Soul* was a celebration of the Afro-Brazilian culture found on Benin's coast while another album (*Oyaya!*) was largely inspired by Afro-Latin and Afro-Caribbean music). Of course, the music of Cape Verde, made famous by Cesária Évora, is a mix of African, Brazilian and Portuguese music.

Yet arguably it was the embrace of African music in the 1980s by Western artists such as Paul Simon and Peter Gabriel that served to reintroduce African music *from Africa* to the (Western) world. Artists such as Miriam Makeba had long enjoyed a measure of success outside of Africa (in Makeba's case, not by choice), but the anointment of African musicians by Western pop stars in the mid-1980s was probably the defining moment. Naturally, this in itself was problematic, particularly when music from Africa became "World Music" and the (temporary) fashionable accessory of Western liberals (see Agawu, 2003).

Now, however, much African music is truly global, is independent of Western patronage and increasingly mirrors the contemporary processes associated with the internationalization of Africa's peoples. For instance, a large percentage of albums recorded by African artists are recorded in Paris, London or New York. Unlike most Western artists, many African singers are truly global—Côte d Ivoire's Alpha Blondy has sung in Dioula, Malinke, Arabic, French, English, Ashanti, Hebrew and Wolof, among others and he is not particularly unique in this regard.

While Africa gives to the world in musical terms, the reverse is also true. Both reggae and hip-hop are immensely popular on the continent, and music often represents a reverse African migration in many ways. Some artists literally symbolize this—Mali's Salif Keita, for instance, moved to Paris to reach a wider audience, built up an international profile and incorporated European and American musical styles into his music, before returning to Mali to live and record. Indeed, Impey (1998) has argued that we need to acknowledge that popular music in Africa represents the interaction between foreign ethics and styles. It is thus therefore a site for adaptation, assimilation, appropriation, experimentation and hybridity and demonstrates Africa's international relations in a nutshell.

The explosion of African music worldwide can be traced to processes stemming from the late twentieth century that not only broke down national boundaries but also facilitated the (relatively) free movement of African musicians. Taking advantage of technological developments pioneered in the developed world, such African artists have truly expanded the reach of "African" music. Nigeria's Femi Kuti's voice even features in the videogame *Grand Theft Auto IV*, as the DJ of a radio station, International Funk 99. His voice is in the game as the DJ of the station and he is described as "playing a great selection of classics from West Africa, the US and elsewhere."

Music *must* be seen as an important cultural force intimately associated with SSA's international relations. Of course, the expansion of World Music as a genre exemplifies the deterritorialization of cultures implicit in globalization and certainly mirrors the real life experiences of many Africans. It also throws up how African cultural commodities can be quickly commodified and marketed by Western capitalism as commercial phenomena. But equally, such processes could not have occurred without the active construction and contestation of discourses of place and otherness by African agency (see Connell, 2004). In short, African music discloses insights and various elements of the continent's communities, politics and cultural interactions that are vital for tracing Africa's global insertions.

The diasporas

A vital aspect of Africa's international relations these days is the presence and activities of the African diasporas. African actors have constructed numerous transnational networks linking African localities to commercial centers such as Brussels, Guangzhou, Lisbon, London, New York and Paris. According to one analysis, these networks can be understood as part of a broader phenomenon of transboundary formations that connect global, regional, national and local actors through diverse networks and narratives that have widespread effects on Africa, as well as on the wider international community (see Callaghy, Kassimir and Latham, 2001). Such formations have proactively developed extant commercial activities that have existed for years between, for example, Central Africa and Europe (see MacGaffey and Bazenguissa-Ganga, 2000; Bayart, 2000).

It might be said that the existence of the diasporas recasts questions around what constitutes African cultures, identities and the continent's international relations. Indeed, the diasporas exemplify the globalization of Africa. Crucially, the very existence of the diasporas are now seriously considered by African states (and international development agencies) as important developmental assets. Ghana is perhaps the most enthusiastic African state to embrace the diasporic communities (at least rhetorically and commercially). "Taking Israel as its model, Ghana hopes to persuade the descendants of enslaved Africans to think of Africa as their homeland—to visit, invest, send their children to be educated and even retire . . . 'We want Africans everywhere, no matter where they live or how they got there, to see Ghana as their gateway home', J. Otanka Obetsebi-Lamptey, the tourism minister, said" (*New York Times*, December 27, 2005).

The potential of the diasporas are something that is often remarked upon. After all, "Between \$4 and \$6 billion per year flows back into Sub Saharan Africa as a result of remittances from Africans living outside the continent, according to a 2005 World Bank report" (World Bank, 2007). In May 2003, the African Union Executive Council directed the AU to actively engage the diasporas in the development efforts of the organization. In turn, there is a growing consciousness on the part of the diasporas and the potentialities to act as transnational lobbies on behalf of the continent.

Historically, the black Atlantic model of *the* Diaspora has dominated, focusing on those Africans taken from West Africa to the Americas during the period of industrialized slavery (e.g. Gilroy, 1993). Given the size of the diasporas in the Americas this is not altogether surprising—the AU estimates that the African diasporas are about 112.6 million people in South America; 39.2 million people in North America and 13.5 million people in the Caribbean, compared to about 3.5 million people in Europe (World Bank, 2007). Yet, in fact, there are at least three sets of African diasporas, the trans-Atlantic, the trans-Indian Ocean, and the trans-Mediterranean. Each have their own origins, and though they share some similarities, the differences are compelling (Zeleza, 2005).

Furthermore, the Atlantic model is increasingly problematic given the growing presence of Africans elsewhere in the world and, critically, the construction of "new" voluntary diasporas which have left Africa post-abolition and particularly since decolonization and the failure of many independence projects (see Koscr, 2003). According to many studies, more African migrants have been arriving in the United States than during the Atlantic slave trade:

> Since 1990, according to immigration figures, more have arrived voluntarily than the total who disembarked in chains before the United States outlawed international slave trafficking in 1807. More have been coming here annually—about 50,000 legal immigrants—than in any of the peak years of the middle passage across the Atlantic, and more have migrated here from Africa since 1990 than in nearly the entire preceding two centuries. (*New York Times*, February 21, 2005)

How this will impact upon the long-established diasporas in the United States will be of great interest, as will how this may influence Washington's relations with the continent.

It does, however, have to be said that other than the remittances that the diasporas send home, outward migration from Africa is generally negative to the continent. Despite the self-justification of some Africans abroad (mostly academics) who claim that their sojourns abroad are temporary, there is very little evidence of significant numbers of Africans returning to the continent. Given the political and economic conditions in many countries as well as the fact that most African states do not allow dual citizenship (i.e. there is no insurance policy if one does return) then that is not particularly surprising. More problematic, the evidence of skills transferal from the diasporas back "home" needs questioning. Many emigrants have pretty much abandoned Africa; certainly we must be cautious about the commitment of their offspring to the continent.

Sadly, there are more Ethiopian doctors practicing in Chicago than in Ethiopia (World Bank, 2007) while there are more Malawian nurses in Birmingham, England than there are in Malawi (*Independent* [London], June 1, 2005). Notably, magazines such as *New African* are full of letters from people from the diasporas urging others about their obligations to the continent, even suggesting returning to help facilitate Africa's renewal, but the overwhelming majority of these letters are of the "you go first" type. In fact, as Mercer, Page and Evans (2008) show, it is vital to critically engage with the current enthusiasm among policymakers (and diasporic academics) who treat the African diaspora as an untapped resource for development. By focusing on diasporic networks (rather than remittances) Mercer et al. expose the challenges diasporas face in acting as a coherent group. Not least of these is the problem in mobilizing members of the diaspora to actually fulfill their obligations back "home."

Having said that, the African diaspora is an important element of the continent's international relations and reflect inventive patterns of "globalization from below" whereby individuals and groups (rather than transnational corporations) profit from and utilize the opportunities offered up by globalization processes. Rethinking what we mean by the African diasporas beyond its Atlantic fixation is critical. After all, with over 20,000 Africans now living in Guangzhou alone, focusing only on the traditional sites of the diasporas makes less and less sense. Placing the diasporas and their dynamics and unfolding networks into the wider context of Africa's interactions with the world is vital in order to include an increasingly important (and vibrant) element of Africa's place in the world.

Criminals

How various types of criminal activities involving Africa fit into the continent's global interactions is another part of the bigger picture of Africa's international relations. The criminological aspects of Africa's extraversion, such as smuggling, corruption, money laundering, natural resource exploitation, etc. are of course controversial; many analysts prefer not even to discuss them (Castells, 2001: 170–1). But they are very much real and in recent years have been enlarged under conditions associated with globalization, transcending formal national borders and taking on intensified international dimensions (see Green and Ward, 2004).

One of the first studies to tackle the subject was Jean-François Bayart, Stephen Ellis and Béatrice Hibou's *The Criminalization of the State in Africa* (1999). Of note, the authors included state-supported criminal activities, something which is to a degree a taboo subject in African Studies. Focusing on the role played by the state and state elites in aiding and abetting corrupt and criminal activities, they went so far as to argue that in some African countries, it was possible to observe a "criminalization" of the state where in some cases African states have become effective vehicles for organized crimes. According to the authors, "politics in Africa is becoming markedly interconnected with crime" (1999: 25) and while this cannot be said to be true for the whole of SSA, there are definitely parts of the continent where this is the case.

The phenomena of warlordism is certainly a feature of some areas of Africa and these spaces cannot survive without—in fact are interdependent with—the global economy (Reno, 1999; Taylor, 2003). For instance, Equatorial Guinea has been described as a "criminal state," where one may observe "the extreme personalization of authority and the government's relationship with a wide range of legal, quasi-legal and criminal supporting enterprises" (Wood, 2004: 553–4). Yet the "President" of this criminalized entity was described by Condoleezza Rice as a "good friend" of the United States (*Washington Post*, April 18, 2006). This highlights the difficulties in defining "state crime" when it is states themselves that determine what activities are considered criminal, or not (Green and Ward, 2004).

The study of Africa's international relations must thus include the study of the linkages between government and institutionalized crime. Certainly, the entanglement of parts of Africa in a web of internal and international crimes is noteworthy and elemental to any coherent study of the continent's insertion into the global political economy. This is not to single Africa out—since the early 1990s global crime has exploded. This is partly due to neoliberalism, something which some African elites have bought into (see Taylor and Nel, 2002). As Naím (2005: 20) puts it, "economic reforms have benefited illicit traders by weakening their enemy. Governments simply have less latitude to act, enforce and spend as they please. Fiscal restraint has become the paramount value by which to judge a government's performance . . . So while traffickers saw their markets grow global and their revenues soar, funding for the agencies in charge of containing them either declined or stagnated." It is ironic that the "global village" within its "borderless world" so celebrated by neoliberal ideologues has actually facilitated such pathologies.

Though some African criminals (notably Nigerians) have been active in smuggling networks exporting heroin from Thailand overland to Malaysia or via Taiwan or Hong Kong for diffusion into Europe and North America, these are generally individuals and not really different from the myriad number of Europeans, North Americans, Asians, etc. who are involved in the global drug trade. This is not to say that Nigerian criminals have not been extremely active and global in their goings-on: "In 2002, Dutch customs officers, in a controlled experiment, for a period of ten days searched every Nigerian arriving in Amsterdam from Aruba and the Dutch Antilles, a route used by many of the 1,200 drug couriers arrested annually at Schiphol airport. They found that of the 83 Nigerian passengers using this route during that period, no fewer than 63 were carrying drugs" (UNODC, 2005: 21). A breakdown of Nigerians in prison across the world in 2008 revealed 1,500 in Libya; 391 in India; 1,461 in Britain; 550 in China, 15 in Nepal; and, incredibly, 8 in Afghanistan (for drugs smuggling) (*Daily Trust* [Abuja], August 4, 2008).

However, qualitatively differently, West Africa has in the last decade or so emerged as a major transit point in the trafficking of narcotics, particularly cocaine, from Latin America and, crucially, this has occurred with the active connivance of elements within the official structures of many West African states. Here, the manipulation of state sovereignty in the furtherance of crime is indeed noteworthy. The United Nations Office on Drugs and Crime (UNODC) estimates that roughly a quarter of Europe's annual consumption of cocaine, worth about US$1.8 billion, annually transits via West Africa (UNODC, 2007: 3). The trade ties together Latin American and African drug dealers, corrupt African officials, criminals and, often, the diasporas (see Akyeampong, 2005).

Crucially, there has been fairly conclusive evidence that elements within the Guinean government have been allied to Colombian drugs barons. After President Lansana Conte died in December 2008, a military government has sought to address such criminality. Indeed, around 20 people from the Conte regime have recently been charged with drug trafficking, including the former army chief, an ex-head of the Marine Corps and an officer who until his arrest was the serving head of the Marine Corps. Ousmane Conte, the son of the former president, admitted on state television in February 2009 to drug trafficking (*BBC News*, June 13, 2009).

Next door in Guinea-Bissau, drug trafficking is so rife that some have labeled the country Africa's first "narco-state." For instance, in April 2007, an estimated 2.5 metric tons of cocaine were flown into a military air-strip in the country while in 2006, 674 kg of cocaine, worth about US$39 million, or 13 percent of the country's total annual income, was found in the capital, Bissau, after a gun battle. "For safekeeping, it was put in the treasury vaults, where it 'disappeared'. The then Prime Minister Aristides Gomes . . . sought to allay fears it had returned to drugs gangs, by saying that he had ordered it to be burnt . . . [but] there is no evidence that it was actually destroyed" (*BBC News*, July 9, 2007). The BBC report goes on:

Large shipments—2.5 tons seems to be a common amount—are either flown or shipped across the Atlantic Ocean. Bags are sometimes dropped from the air onto some of Guinea-Bissau's 70-odd uninhabited islands, where they are picked up by local smugglers on speedboats. The large shipments are then either broken into smaller quantities and taken to Europe by plane or boat, or sailed in bulk straight up the coast to Portugal and Spain.

Problematically, after the only prison was destroyed in a civil war, there is nowhere to hold suspected or convicted drug traffickers. Besides, "If a cell is found somewhere, top military officials often turn up and insist they are freed" (ibid.). As Ellis (2009: 173) points out, "Not only is West Africa conveniently situated for trade between South America and Europe, but above all it has a political and social environment that is generally suitable for the drug trade. Smuggling is widely tolerated, law enforcement is fitful and inefficient, and politicians are easily bribed or are even involved in the drug trade themselves." Even in Ghana, usually praised as politically stable and somehow very different from its Anglophone neighbors such as Nigeria and Liberia, "many of the country's politicians have interests in the drug trade, and some of Accra's impressive building boom is being financed with the proceeds of drug deals" (ibid.: 193).

What is extremely interesting about such criminalized states is the manipulation of sovereignty by both African and non-African actors. Formal international recognition of entities that call themselves the *República de Guinea Ecuatorial* or *République de Guinée*, etc. exist and are members of the international society of states grants enormous benefits to criminals. Immediately, protection from prosecution, diplomatic immunity, "legitimate" export licenses, etc. are readily available as tools to lubricate criminal activities. The colonial-imposed borders, long lamented as dividing Africa, actually serve in some cases as priceless assets to be managed and utilized for the furtherance of illicit accumulation. This cannot occur without international compliance. As Reno (2009: 76) points out:

> [R]ulers and those who support them need others to recognize the existence of these states in order to sustain a boundary between an ostensible state realm and a supposedly private realm that can be manipulated in the interests of maintaining their power. Once important actors in the international community decide such arrangements are "criminal" and question the sovereignty of these states, a key support for this system of authority starts to crumble.

In this regard, definitions of international crime are highly flexible and depend upon constructions made by the globally powerful. This is a lesson that Liberia's Charles Taylor is learning the hard way, while Equatorial Guinea's Teodoro Obiang Nguema continues to be courted. Moral outrage in the developed world about criminality emanating from Africa thus needs to be treated with some skepticism. After all, until various NGOs pressurized governments and the diamond industry to address the issue (culminating in the Kimberley Process) there was a distinct lack of corporate accountability or state interest in the global trade in diamonds, where the buying and selling of diamonds from conflict-ridden spaces in Africa was commonplace (see Taylor and Mokhawa, 2003; Grant and Taylor, 2004). The international community of states quite simply did not care about such criminality until shamed into doing so.

Similarly, the community of states still does not take money laundering and illicit capital flight from Africa seriously. In a study of 30 sub-Saharan African countries, Ndikumana and Boyce (2002) estimated that total capital flight for the period from 1970 to 1996 amounted to US$187 billion. Adding imputed interest earnings, the stock of Africa's capital flight stood at US$274 billion, i.e. equivalent to 145 percent of the debts owed by those countries. Indeed, in 2007 SSA's total foreign debt was "only" (in comparison to the amount shipped out of Africa through capital flight) US$195 billion (World Bank, 2009: 2). As far back as 1990 the Lagos *National Concord* reported that Nigerians held US$32 billion in foreign bank accounts, equivalent to Nigeria's then foreign debt (Ayittey, 1995: 6). In one study, nearly 40 percent of SSA's private wealth was estimated to be held outside the continent (Collier, Hoeffler and Pattillo, 2001). Not all of this money has been criminally accumulated, of course. But a lot of it has and has been stashed abroad with almost total silence from the guardians of financial probity in the West.

Even in spectacular—and obviously—criminal financial transfers the international banking system (and its state regulators) do not seem to be particularly observant. For instance, in the late 1990s, US$242 million went missing during a 419 scam (see below). Nigerian confidence tricksters persuaded an employee of a Brazilian bank (*Banco Noroeste*) to transfer millions of dollars into overseas accounts, ostensibly to invest in the construction of a new airport in Abuja. During this process, money went through "dizzying circuitous routes in the United Kingdom, Switzerland, Hong Kong and the United States. In Nigeria alone, seventeen different banks were used to shuffle and disguise the money. But despite the huge sums and their unusual passage around the world, nobody thought fit to raise the much-hailed red flags of the Western banking system" (Glenny, 2009: 193). "[W]hile accounts were haemorrhaging, whilst huge sums of obscure origin were chugging from bank to bank, and while audits were being merrily signed, nobody noticed a thing—not in Brazil, the Caymans or the US; not in the UK, Switzerland or Nigeria. *Nada*" (ibid.: 197). Indignation is (rightly) directed against unscrupulous African criminals, but this is only part of the story. As Naím (2005: 6–7) puts it: "What about bankers in Manhattan or London who take home big year-end bonuses as a reward for having stocked their bank's vaults with the deposits of 'high-net worth individuals' whose only known job has been with a government in another country?"

No doubt all readers of this book have at one time been cordially invited to take part in another criminalized aspect of Africa's international elations—the 419 scam. The 419 is a type of fraud, named after an article of the Nigerian penal code under which it is prosecuted (see Smith, 2007). The common modus operandi is to convince the victim to send money upfront by promising them a larger amount in return if they cooperate. The criminals receive the money using wire transfer services (the recipient cannot be traced once the money has been picked up). "Ultrascan Advanced Global Investigations . . . which specializes in uncovering 419 frauds, has reported that citizens in thirty-eight developed countries admitted to losses of more than $3 billion in 2005 alone. These estimates are necessarily low because they exclude all those victims who did not confess their gullibility to law-enforcement agencies" (Glenny, 2009: 196).

There are increasing criminal activities initiated in Africa by private citizens, employees of parastatal organizations and state bureaucrats at both the national and continental level. Crucially, very often this is facilitated by the role of non-African actors, who serve to further internationalize criminal activities. Indeed, it is very important to recognize that external actors, including some officials in economically and diplomatically powerful states, do not always support the suppression of various illicit networks nor even seriously seek to help construct strong states (Reno, 2009: 67).

Today, international drug trafficking, money-laundering, currency counterfeiting, credit card fraud, the conversion of cash of dubious origin into legal goods and the theft of international food aid, etc. all make up a part of the continent's international relations. While certainly not wishing to romanticize these activities, it is true that some Africans see them "as the only way to redistribute wealth from the North to the South, arguing that mainstream commercial channels are effectively occupied" (Shaw, 2001: 66). As one Nigerian put it, "If Europeans get ripped off, they deserve it. They are greedy and trying to make money out of African people" (quoted in Glenny, 2009: 198). As the ongoing global economic crisis continues, how SSA reacts may, in part, continue some of the extraversion strategies outlined above.

The Global Economic Crisis and SSA

Although the ongoing global economic crisis traces its origins in the North, developing countries—including those in SSA—are severely affected. Crucially, many SSA states lack the capacity to counter the effects. SSA is affected through two different levels: trade and finance. Regarding trade, 2009 saw a dramatic fall in manufacturing exports and, more seriously, a fall in demand, prices and the concomitant export earnings for commodities. This affected especially low-income commodity-dependent countries. According to *The Economist* (March 17, 2009), it's commodity-price dollar index for all items fell by 40 percent against 2008 prices, with a 56 percent decline in metal prices.

On the ground, this was witnessed in a myriad of ways. For instance, in February 2009, more than 40 Chinese-run copper smelters were abandoned "after their owners fled the country without paying taxes or compensating staff at the end of the commodity boom" (*Financial Times* [London], February 20, 2009). "When global commodity prices tumbled, the result in Katanga was painful: in the space of weeks luxury house-building projects and freshly imported Jeeps vanished to be replaced by unemployment and rising crime" (ibid.). The smelters in the Congo were able to produce a tonne of copper for about US$3,500, giving the operators enormous profits when copper price was at its peak of nearly US$9,000 a tonne in August 2008. But when the price fell to US$3,200 a tonne in early 2009, the industry collapsed.

Although SSA accounts for less than 2 percent of global trade, many of its economies are deeply reliant on trade in very few primary commodities, something which has long been regarded as a bane for the continent. Thus such economies are being hit hard by the decline in prices. In fact, due to the global economic downturn, the African continent can expect only 2.8 percent growth in 2009, less than half of the 5.7 percent predicted before the crisis (*Business Day* [Johannesburg], May 10, 2009).

The finance sector is also impacting negatively on SSA as the economic crisis continued. As Moss (2009: 3) noted:

Private capital is already falling and faces serious risks over the medium term. As credit tightens and risk aversion sets in, African countries may be hit even harder than developed economies. It is ironic that Africa could be disproportionately affected, considering that Africa never touched the complex financial derivatives that sparked the financial crisis. The surge in inflows over the past few years has been driven by new debt issuance, foreign investment in mining and heavy infrastructure, and some new foreign interest in South African and Nigerian banks. Ghana and Gabon had each successfully issued new sovereign bonds in late 2007, but plans for more issuances by Kenya, Nigeria, Tanzania, and Uganda are being shelved for now.

The impact of the crisis will be mixed. However, some countries are likely to suffer quite serious contractions in their economies. The World Bank has stated that the South African economy will probably contract 1.5 percent in 2009, the first drop in 17 years, while Nigeria's government revenues of Nigeria, Africa's primary oil producer, declined by 32 percent below target in the first three months of 2009. Small and open economies such as Botswana and Seychelles were predicted to be the hardest hit, with some predictions stating that the gross domestic product in Botswana and Seychelles may fall by 8 percent and 10 percent respectively (*People's Daily* [Beijing], July 1, 2009).

Which Actors?

A common issue facing studies of the continent's international relations is the often-erroneous treatment of states as unitary actors involved in Africa. In looking at Africa's global interactions and particularly when examining the activities of non-African players, it is crucial to ask what we mean by "China," or "the United States," or "India," etc. In many countries now active in Africa, the central government, diverse ministries, even substate and provincial bureaucracies all have an input into relations with the continent. Private corporations obviously have to be sensitive both to general government policies and proclamations, but often more importantly, to the profit motive. Thus while states such as "China" or "France" or "the United Kingdom" may have a stated policy on a particular African issue, this has to be mediated via the economic interests of separate corporations and the political and economic motivations and aspirations thereof. These may or may not share the enunciated central foreign policy vision (British companies continuing to invest in Mugabe's Zimbabwe would be but one example).

Foreign policy made at in the capitals of external actors is ever more malleable to the parochial organizational, economic and political goals of different actors. What is clear is that the willingness by Indian or Chinese or French actors to perform activities willy-nilly at the behest of their home governments is constrained, to say the least. This applies even to "centralized" states such as China. Ever-changing combinations of forces make and remake foreign policy and across the continent there exists a diverse and pluralistic range of actors and decision makers whose varied interests are reflected in the playing out of non-African actors' behavior on the continent. Competition and compromise in policy formulation as well as execution is largely the norm. Consultations, conferences and public policy debates, NGOs and the media all influence non-African engagement with the continent. In short, bureaucratic interests, economic motives, domestic politics and public opinion, as well as the increasing diversity of actors involved abroad all coalesce to undermine the notion of unitary states relentlessly pushing forward their agendas in Africa. Certainly the idea of the strategic use of economic relations by external actors as a means of achieving power politics objectives needs to be treated with caution. It is important not to overestimate the degree to which foreign states can wholly control and direct the evolution of their international economic relations, particularly in the context of ongoing liberalization.

Yet the degree to which studies are inclined to aggregate such complexity into a unitary "France" or "China" or "United States," with a single attendant interest is remarkable. It is commonplace in the literature on external engagement with Africa to talk of "China" or "France," and while heuristically this may make sense, it does have the potential effect of obfuscating what processes are unfolding and why. Ontologically, such labels are problematic and it is not plausible to speak of states as monolithic entities.

Equally, however, it is not credible to seek to throw the state out of an analysis of Africa's international relations. As Brown notes, "So long as one is prepared to integrate an understanding of 'what goes on within states' with 'what goes on between them', it would be possible to knit together a variety of accounts of these and other developments which get beyond the idea simply that the state doesn't 'fit' in Africa. Indeed, it is not just that it is hard to see how an account could be given which doesn't have the state as one of its building blocks, but in many ways the nature of statehood and the control of the state are what these conflicts are actually *about*. The analytical focus on the state is therefore not simply an academic affectation" (Brown, 2006: 135). This is why the methodology of this book is to start with each selected state or organization(s) and then investigate their relations and interactions with SSA *in toto*. In doing so, the aim is to provide an impression of "outside looking in" regarding African agencies in the global political economy.

Conclusion: Beyond the Usual Suspects

Of course, what is problematic for a book of this type is the selection of what actors to include or, more importantly, what to *exclude*. There are various players that, if space allowed, really should be included as chapter-length studies. These would include, at a minimum, Brazil, Japan, Russia and the Scandinavian countries, as well as the United Nations' various arms (peacekeeping and refugee agencies, for instance), and some of the topics that are touched on earlier in this chapter. Given the inherently global nature of the problem, a chapter on climate change would also be not amiss.

Brazil, for instance, is increasingly active in Africa. This is perhaps natural given that Brazil has the second largest black population of any country in the world, after Nigeria. Solidarity has been presented as central to Brazil's efforts toward intensifying its links with Africa as well as with the rest of the developing world. According to Brigagão (2009: 2), "South-South relations are viewed as having great international potential for Brazil's diversified foreign policy. The foreign policy of Lula da Silva's government stresses the importance of South-South relations as strategic axes and as factors in the diversity of Brazil's international insertion."

Indeed, it was with the change of government and the assumption of President Luiz Inácio "Lula" da Silva on January 1, 2003, that kick-started the deepening of relations with Africa, not only at the rhetorical level but also with practical policies. Lula has now made eight trips to Africa at the time of writing, covering 20 nations. In fact, within a few months of Lula's presidency, the first Brazil-Africa Forum was inaugurated at Fortaleza in June, 2003. The topics covered (commerce, political and social affairs, culture and education) reflected the policy priorities of Brazil's relaunched African engagement. Representatives from Angola, Cape Verde, Gabon, Ghana, Morocco and South Africa attended.

Later that year and reflecting the seriousness in Brazil's new Africa policies, Minister of Foreign Affairs Celso Amorim visited Mozambique, São Tome and Principe, Angola, Ghana, Namibia, Zimbabwe and South Africa, while in November 2003 President Lula, alongside ten ministers, visited São Tome and Principe, Angola, Mozambique, Namibia and South Africa. The tour resulted in about 40 cooperation agreements being signed (Lechini, 2005).

Importantly, Brazil has one of the strongest economies among developing countries and, according to Soares de Lima and Hirst (2006), the key foreign policy aspiration of Brazil is to achieve international recognition as a major power in world affairs. As part of this, Brasilia seeks to assert an independent voice within international affairs (see de Arimatiia da Cruz, 2005). Developing close ties with other developing nations is central to this—as the India-Brazil-South Africa Dialogue Forum demonstrates (see Chapter Five). Of course, Brazil is deeply involved in the *Comunidade de Paises de Lingua Portuguesa* (Community of Portuguese-Speaking Countries), an eight-member organization of which the majority (five) are African.

Africa is now seen "as the most important experiment of South-South cooperation" by Brasilia, "accompanied by an increase in bilateral trade. Fifty-two percent of all Brazilian technical cooperation actions is taking place in Africa" (Visentini, 2009: 5). Trade and investment is central to Brazil's new interest in Africa. In fact, according to Brazilian government figures, trade between Brazil and Africa quadrupled between 2003 and 2008 from US$6.11 billion to US$26 billion (*Namibian* [Windhoek] June 11, 2009). Interestingly, the trade is massively in Africa's favor; Brazil's imports from Africa increased by 39 percent between 2007 and the end of 2008, while exports to Africa increased by only 18 percent during the same time period. Mineral products make up 86 percent of Brazil's imports from Africa. In 2008, the major African trading partners with Brazil were Nigeria (32 percent of total Afro-Brazilian trade), Angola (16 percent), Algeria (12 percent), South Africa (10 percent) and Libya (7 percent) (TRALAC, 2009: 1).

Although there are thousands of Brazilian companies now investing in Africa, two key corporations play a leading role in Brazil's commercial engagement with SSA: Petrobras, the Brazilian oil and energy company and *Companhia Vale do Rio Doce* (CVRD), one of the biggest mining companies in the world. Petrobras has operational activities or offices in 23 countries and is the world's 14th largest oil company. The company has oil exploration and production activities in Angola, Equatorial Guinea, Libya, Mozambique, Nigeria, Senegal and Tanzania. CVRD is a global leader in the production and exportation of iron and an important global producer of copper, bauxite, aluminum, potassium, gold, manganese and nickel. CVRD is present in Angola, South Africa, Gabon and Mozambique (Bermann, 2007). Emblematically, CVRD has a 25-year concession at Moatize, in the Mozambican province of Tete, which it paid US$122.8 million dollars for in 2004. CVRD aims to start exporting coal from Moatize in late 2010/early 2011. The concession holds 2.4 billion tonnes, allowing the extraction of coking and thermal coal (*SteelGuru* [New Delhi], October 15, 2008).

Processes that are both particular to Brasilia and that are reactive to external developments currently propel the upsurge in Brazil's engagement with Africa. As Visentini (2009: 5) notes:

This turn in the Brazilian foreign policy is thus justified, on one hand, for the government's better understanding of the importance of turning to the African continent to enlarge the country's international significance in the global balance of power, as a strategy of international insertion, fulfilling its aspirations as a medium size power. On the other hand, by the African Renaissance, since Africa has been gaining a new relevance in the international scenery, led, in great part, by the valorization of the commodities exported by the African nations and by the Chinese growing investments in the region.

Either way, the continuing intensification of Brazilian-African interaction is something that will continue to stake out the continent's international relations.

Russia is another actor that is increasingly important on the continent. In 2009, President Dmitry Medvedev paid his first official visit to Africa (and the first by a Russian head of state for more than three years), visiting Egypt, Nigeria, Angola and Namibia. During the Soviet era, Africa was obviously an important element in Moscow's foreign policy calculations. This changed under Gorbachev (see Matusevich, 1999), and although Russia never left SSA, the post-Soviet period was marked by a certain disengagement, particularly under Boris Yeltsin's chaotic regime (see Shubin, 2004). Consequently, "Russia is far behind Western and Chinese companies when it comes to securing a share of the continent's natural wealth" (*BBC News*, June 23, 2009). This seems to be now changing (Matusevich, 2006).

Moscow and Cairo have already signed a nuclear cooperation agreement, possibly to facilitate Russian companies' construction of nuclear power stations in Egypt. During Medvedev's tour, Russia's energy giant Gazprom signed a US$2.5 billion deal with Nigeria's state-operated oil company to invest in a new joint venture. The new firm, to be called Nigaz, aims to build refineries, pipelines and gas power stations in Nigeria. As one analyst remarked "Part of the agenda [of Medvedev's tour] is to push Russia's credentials as a representative of commodity-rich developing countries with such forums as the G-8 and the G-20" (*BBC News*, June 25, 2009). Rosneft, the largest Russian oil company, has specifically declared its intention to expand its operations in Africa, while various Russian corporations are involved across the continent in the spheres of diamonds, metals, hydrocarbons and uranium (Alrosa, Russia's state diamond corporation, has worked in Angola for 20 years or so). Currently, Russo-African trade is not significant—trade with Nigeria, for instance, is only US$300 million per year at present, compared to China's US$11 billion (*BBC News*, June 23, 2009).

Although the commercial attractions of SSA are clear for Russian corporations, the political dimension cannot be ignored. A newly assertive Moscow is now actively seeking to project itself as a global player, increasingly in regions far from its traditional spheres of influence. Indeed, Moscow's foreign policy is dominated by efforts to reverse the decline of the 1980s and 1990s. This entails promoting international conditions conducive to facilitating Russia's reconstruction as a major power (MacFarlane, 2006). Moscow favors a multipolar world, with several strong regional centers. The notion of the BRICs (Brazil, Russia, India and China) is part of this and Moscow has been enthusiastically pushing such a configuration (Armijo, 2007). Africa will fit into such considerations as a site where Russian corporations can seek out contracts, particularly in the energy realms, and as a place where more and more Russian investment will likely be located. Of course, competition with Chinese commercial interests is part of this. But what is certain is that Russian involvement in the continent will be increasingly important as another aspect of Africa's international relations.

Of course, there are others actors who, in the future, may be deemed vital for a book on Africa's international relations. Iran, for instance, is stepping up its contacts in Africa, to the extent of offering to host an Iran-Africa summit. This is part of President Mahmoud Ahmadinejad's assertive foreign policy. Thus, in 2008, Foreign Minister Manuchehr Mottaki attended the African Union summit held in Ethiopia and met with the leaders of Sudan, Djibouti, Burkina Faso, Algeria, Mauritania, Mali, Zimbabwe, Lesotho, Namibia, Tanzania, as well as the foreign ministers of Ghana and Chad. Mottaki declared that Iran was determined to boost cooperation with African countries, calling 2008 "the year of expansion of relations between Iran and Africa" (*Tehran Times* [Tehran], February 3, 2008).

Tehran has forged particularly strong ties with Senegal, and President Abdoulaye Wade has traveled twice to Tehran (in 2006 and 2008). During Wade's 2008 visit, Supreme Leader Ayatollah Ali Khamenei declared that developing unity between Islamic countries (including Senegal) would weaken the United States. Ahmadinejad has himself visited Senegal. While Tehran is probably most interested in expanding an Islamic bloc to embrace African states—especially one that might displace the supremacy of Sunni Arab states—African elites are more likely more interested in economic advantages. Iran can deliver on this: in 2007 Tehran agreed to build an oil refinery and petrochemicals plant in Senegal and also promised to speed up the development of an US$80 million car assembly plant in Senegal for state-owned carmaker Iran Khodro (*BBC News*, August 3, 2007). Later that year it was agreed that Iran would supply crude oil for a year to the refining company *Société Africaine de Raffinage* (SAR), in which Dakar holds a majority share. The National Iranian Oil Refining and Distribution Company also planned to buy more than a 34-percent stake in SAR (*Fars News Agency* [Tehran], August 28, 2007).

The fact is that Africa is increasingly important in international relations and is more and more attracting interest from a huge array of actors at a scale perhaps not witnessed since the original Scramble for Africa. When nations such as Turkey host a Turkey-Africa Cooperation Summit, as they did in August 2008, the scale of this upsurge of interest is clear. Demonstrating its commitment, Ankara covered the full expenses of each attending head of state or government and of the 53 members of the African Union, only Mozambique, Swaziland and Lesotho were not represented. Turkey has in fact increased its trade with Africa from US$5.4 billion to US$ 13 billion in under three years, with a target to reach US$30 billions by 2010 (*Mail and Guardian* [Johannesburg], August 18, 2008).

Similarly, Mexico's "foreign policy strategy towards Africa [now] seeks to build a new and much closer relation with this region. Through a wider and more efficient diplomatic presence, the promotion of mutual understanding, the enhancement of co-operation, trade and investments, Mexico wishes to strengthen its links with the African nations" (Mexican Foreign Secretary Patricia Espinosa, quoted by *Reuters* [Cape Town], February 19, 2009). Since 2005, Mexico has been an Observer at the African Union and opened an Embassy in Addis Ababa in 2007 while establishing embassies in Nigeria and Angola in 2008 and appointing Honorary Consuls in Cape Town and Mauritius in 2009. In fact, there does not seem to be a major or middle-ranking power that is not clamoring to deepen ties with SSA.

Thus as Africa's international relations diversify and intensify to include new actors as well as old players and to cover increasingly varied processes and dynamics involving both state and non-state actors, the study of the continent's extraversion is more and more apposite. How external actors and processes encounter the neo-patrimonial regimes of SSA will continue to be fascinating, as will the increasing role of African citizens around the world. I believe that despite its historic neglect by International Relations, Africa is likely to become more and more central to the discipline. This book is but one contribution to such unfolding global realities.

CHAPTER ONE

The Times They Are(n't) A-changing: American Policies in Africa

Over the past ten years or so, American policies toward Africa have been grounded on two main goals: to advance global economic integration under conditions of neoliberalism and to counter perceived threats to American security interests. In 1997, the then assistant secretary of state for African Affairs Susan Rice spelt out this twin-track approach by asserting that the United States had "two clear policy goals: a) integrating Africa into the global economy through promotion of democracy, economic growth and development, and conflict resolution; and b) combating transnational security threats, including terrorism, crime, narcotics, weapons proliferation, environmental degradation, and disease" (Rice, 2000).

Even with the securitization of all conceivable government policies under the George W. Bush administration, and in the context of a post-9/11 world, Washington's approach toward Africa was altered but somewhat. Obviously, 9/11 considerably impacted upon American foreign policy and international society in general, but it is noteworthy that in general US-African relations were only affected modestly. For Africans, a renewed focus on their continent post-9/11 by Washington meant in fact a continuation of well-established policies that predated the Bush government's tenure (Copson, 2007).

It is in policy domains deemed to be particularly apposite to American national security national interests where Africa has enjoyed a resurgence of attention from Washington (Hentz, 2004). This has been interpreted by some as being novel: as one commentator asserted, post-9/11 "Africa has assumed a new, strategic place in US foreign policy and in the definition of vital US national interests" (Africa Policy Advisory Panel, 2004: 2). This has been linked to two interlinked factors: oil and potential terrorist threats. With regard to counterterrorism, military training and policing, American interests and involvement have multiplied post-9/11, with Washington's Africa Command (AFRICOM) being but one example of this redefinition of the strategic place Africa occupies in American policy-making calculations. Yet, referring back to Susan Rice's comments in 1997, it is apparent that Washington's assessments of the main challenges to American-defined interests that Africa presents has remained largely unchanged.

In seeking to demonstrate some of the continuities in US-African ties, four key issues in American policies toward Africa will be examined: security and counterterrorism, energy, HIV/AIDS, and "good governance." Demonstrating how policy calculations post-9/11 contextualized the strategic importance attached to Africa by the United States provides the running thread between the different sections of the chapter.

From Clinton to George W. Bush

The Africa Policy Advisory Panel (a Congressionally mandated body) released policy recommendations in 2004 on ways in which American policies toward Africa could be reinforced. According to the Panel, "President Bush, expanding on the precedent set by President Clinton, [has] consciously chose[n] to make Africa a higher priority and to mainstream it in US foreign policy" (Africa Policy Advisory Panel, 2004: 3). The report noted how an increase in terrorist attacks against American interests in Africa had been obvious throughout the 1990s, climaxing in the simultaneous bombings of American embassies in Nairobi and Dar es Salaam in 1998.

Yet the Panel noted that it was only after 9/11 that policymakers "appreciate[d] fully" how the African continent fitted into American national interests in five crucial areas: HIV/AIDS, energy (primarily oil), terror, armed conflicts and developmental assistance (ibid.: 2). What is important to note here is that Washington *had* recognized the dangers associated with issues before 9/11, but it was the terrorist attacks on that day that stimulated not only an increased awareness and engagement by the United States with Africa, but also engendered a securitization of these perceived threats at every level of policy formulation.

The shock caused by 9/11 certainly acted as a stimulus to a renewal of American (and global) attention toward the continent, but it is important to remember the continuities. American foreign policies in Africa have continued to be generally consistent, certainly since the demise of the Soviet Union and the ending of the Cold War. As is well known, during the Cold War, Africa played host to a variety of proxy wars and could be characterized during that period as a chessboard for Superpower machinations. During this period, the maintenance of alliances with those elites deemed to be (or posturing themselves as) anti-communist trumped other policy considerations, such as the spreading of liberal democratic values, something that is claimed to be a central tenet of American foreign policy. The issue of human rights similarly went out the window when it came to combating Soviet influence on the continent. A somewhat stark realpolitik governed American engagement with Africa throughout the 1970s and 1980s.

However, at least initially, the end of the Cold War saw a relative reduction of American interest in Africa as the continent was deemed to have lost much of its strategic value, according to the policymakers' calculations. As one analyst put it, "when the Cold War ended, America's strategic interest in Africa ended" (Jack Spencer, a Heritage Foundation analyst, quoted in Kraxberger, 2005: 53). Disengagement was reflected by the fact that of the 21 American missions for foreign aid that were to be closed down in 1999, nine were in Africa (Martin and Schumann, 1998: 25). Previously, American bilateral aid to Africa went from a peak of US$ 2.4 billion in 1985 to US$1.2 billion in 1990, and this did not rise any higher throughout the 1990s (Reno, 2001: 200). In fact, the 1990s has been dubbed the "decade of disengagement" as American (and European) concentration focused itself on the new states emerging out of Central and Eastern Europe. This is not to say that there was a total abandonment; American administrations did remain engaged, particularly in matters pertaining to trade and development. Most graphically, the African Growth and Opportunity Act (AGOA) was introduced as law in the United States in May 2000.

AGOA offered "tangible incentives for African countries to continue their efforts to open their economies and build free markets," proving "reforming African countries with the most liberal access to the US market available to any country or region with which the United States does not have a Free Trade Agreement" (US Department of Commerce, 2007: 1). Due to the fact that, with the limited exclusion of Mauritius and South Africa, no African exporters of clothing were able to satisfy the original rules of origin provisions within AGOA, the rules of origin were modified (to last at first to September 2005 and then to September 2007) to permit least developed African countries to employ materials originally from least cost contractors worldwide. This provision had an important impact on textile manufacturing in Africa because as soon as AGOA came into effect, various textile manufacturers (mostly Asian) set themselves up in Africa as a means to evade the obstacles placed on them by the Multi-Fiber Agreement (MFA) of the World Trade Organization (WTO). The effect was that under AGOA, African exports of textiles and clothing to the United States boomed. In 2000 the value of SSA's apparel exports to the US was US$776 million; by 2004 it had reached US$1,782, an increase of 130 percent. This collapsed when the special measures were scrapped.

Terrorism and the Securitization of US-Africa Policies

The material circumstances that facilitated terrorist activity had been long in place in Africa prior to 9/11, yet even after the embassy bombings of 1998 it would be fair to say that Africa-originated threats to American national security were somewhat off the radar screen of policymakers. This is not to say that there was a lack of awareness of the problems, particularly in the Horn of Africa. Certainly the regime in Sudan had long been cast as a "rogue state" and one which actively supported terrorism and provided sanctuary to terrorist groups who utilized Khartoum as a base to destabilize the whole region. Osama Bin Laden's residency in Khartoum in the early 1990s is probably the most commented upon, but the attempted assassination of President Mubarek of Egypt in 1995 was equally controversial as the perpetrators were allegedly trained in Sudan and returned to Sudan once they had carried out the (unsuccessful) operation.

Furthermore, the 1991 collapse of Somalia's central government had produced an anarchical milieu that was conducive for a variety of radical and extremist groups and it became known that a variety of Islamist organizations developed operating bases in Somalia, but also Kenya, Ethiopia and Tanzania. Yet despite this knowledge, the 1990s saw a reduction in resources directed at managing the growing threat. The number of American personnel serving as diplomats in Africa was cut by 15 percent, intelligence personnel were cut by over 30 percent, military and security assistance was reduced, and around a dozen United States Agency for International Development (USAID) missions were shut down (House Committee on International Relations, 2001: 21). Commentators made the case that such reductions impacted negatively on the ability by Washington to envisage and analyze processes in Africa that might pose a threat to American interests and in fact "create[d] acute vulnerabilities that can be brutally exploited" (ibid.: 21).

In response, the Clinton administration pointed to policies that "crafted and funded innovative counter-terrorism, counter-crime, and counter-narcotics strategies" in Africa, including police training centers in South Africa and American activity in brokering and helping sponsor peace processes in the Congo, Ethiopia and Eritrea, Mozambique and Sierra Leone (Rice, 2000). What is interesting to note here is that even as Washington under Clinton cut back on the amount of resources it was dedicating to Africa, the necessity of maintaining policies that would promote stability in Africa and, by extension, counter conflictual situations and security threats to American interests remained constant.

Thus in this sense the environment post-9/11 saw an *intensification* of security concerns about Africa from Washington's perspective, rather than marking a new start. As J. Stephen Morrison, Director of the Africa Program for the Center for Strategic and International Studies, phrased it, "post-September 11, Africa matter[ed] to US interests in significant new ways, both good and bad. There [was] greater recognition in the United States that Africa's institutional weaknesses, autocratic governance and economic marginality pose[d] a serious threat to US security interests" (House Committee on International Relations, 2001: 20). The problem of what became known as "failed states" in Africa was central to this revitalization of interest, stimulating "new international, not just US, attention to the potential security threats posed by failed or collapsed states as epicenters of crime, disease, terrorism, and instability" (Mills, 2004: 159). In this way, Africa was seen as playing a key role in the ongoing "War on Terror"; Bush's secretary of state, Condoleezza Rice, famously asserted to African ministers in Washington for an African Growth and Opportunity Act Forum that "Africa's history and geography give it a pivotal role . . . Africa is critical to our war on terror" (quoted by House Committee in International Relations, 2001: 2). Similarly, Susan Rice informed the Committee on International Relations that "Africa is unfortunately the world's soft underbelly for global terrorism." Consequently, "we have to drain the swamps where the terrorists breed" (Rice, 2001).

In the post-9/11 period, therefore, American policies toward Africa became heavily securitized and a variety of new initiatives revolving around counterterrorism were developed. Security assistance programs in Africa were ramped up and a number of "antiterrorism-based 'lily pads'" established across Africa as a means of rapidly deploying military forces (Mills, 2004: 264). Djibouti was probably the most well known of these "lily pads." Washington also quickly secured the cooperation of various African regimes, with Memoranda of Understandings (MOUs) being signed with Gabon, Ghana, Namibia, Senegal, South Africa and Uganda focusing on the training of and provision of equipment to various African militaries.

As part of the wider policy to encourage military-to-military cooperation and training and as part of the "War on Terror," a Combined Joint Task Force-Horn of Africa (CJTF-HOA) was established in 2002, based in Djibouti. The CJTF-HOA's mission was to "deter, preempt, and disable terrorist threats emanating from Somalia, Kenya and Yemen." A year later, in 2003, Bush unveiled plans to spend US$100 million on various counterterrorism initiatives in the Horn of Africa (Lyman and Morrison, 2005: 77). An East Africa Counterterrorism Initiative (EACTI), incorporating Djibouti, Eritrea, Ethiopia, Kenya, Tanzania and Uganda was announced, as well as the Pan-Sahel Initiative, which included Chad, Mali, Mauritania and Niger. An Economic Support Fund Aid was also introduced as a means to help Washington's "strategic partners" on matters such as "cooperation on border control, freezing terrorist assets, implementation of the peace agreement in southern Sudan, and other activities" (Langton, 2006: 6). Thus "Bush . . . moved farther and faster than any recent administration in constructing a network of military and political alliances, with military-to-military linkages being expanded all across the continent" (Martin, 2004: 587). In short, within a relatively short period of time, the Bush administration had most of Africa covered in terms of military and security cooperation—way beyond those initial African states who had signed up to the "coalition of the willing" in the immediate aftermath of 9/11.

AFRICOM

In 2007, it was announced that a dedicated African military command, AFRICOM, was to be established, putting the continent on par, within the Pentagon's command structure, with the Pacific Rim (Pacific Command), Europe (European Command), Latin America (Southern Command), the Middle East (Central Command), and North America (Northern Command). AFRICOM stood up in October 2008, taking control of 172 missions, activities, programs and exercises, which were previously divided among various military Commands. Previously, because Africa had been subsumed under other regional commands, the continent had never been a main concern for the American military. As has been mentioned, American military activities in Africa have been recently centered on the CJTF-HOA, based in Djibouti and providing training and assistance programs for African militaries to begin to conduct peace support operations and humanitarian missions. AFRICOM changes this scenario.

Officially, the two main functions of AFRICOM are aiding in stabilization operations and helping build indigenous security forces. The Command was formed to bring together all Defense Department programs on the African continent under one umbrella, to include missions ranging from antiterrorism programs in the Horn of Africa to maritime security initiatives, as well as military-to-military training exercises in numerous countries.

Yet the attempt to bring American military efforts dealing with the continent under one unified command was viewed with considerable concern by African leaders as well as Western critics, who saw AFRICOM as an instrument of American corporate interests. For instance, one American critique asserted that

> AFRICOM is a dangerous continuation of US military expansion around the globe. Such foreign-policy priorities, as well as the use of weapons of war to combat terrorist threats on the African continent, will not achieve national security . . . The US militarization of Africa is . . . rationalized by George W. Bush's claims that AFRICOM "will enhance our efforts to bring peace and security to the people of Africa" and promote the "goals of development, health, education, democracy and economic growth". Yet the Bush Administration fails to mention that securing and controlling African wealth and natural resources is key to US trade interests, which face growing competition from China. Transnational corporations rely on Africa for petroleum, uranium and diamonds—to name some of the continent's bounty. (*The Nation* [New York], November 1, 2007)

African responses were equally critical: "It [was] disturbing to note that democracy, health, education, economic growth and development are being tied to military interests" commented one South African newspaper (*Business Day* [Johannesburg], February 14, 2007), while "surveys taken . . . in Africa of local leaders and journalists, among others, produced suspicions that US intentions with AFRICOM were to protect oil interests and 're-assert American power and hegemony globally'" (*Middle East Times* [Washington, DC], July 23, 2008).

The Pentagon had originally planned to base AFRICOM in Africa (Liberia and Botswana were both suggested as potential bases), but because the plans were met with almost universal hostility, the Command currently operates from Stuttgart, Germany, with two forward operational sites—one at Ascension Island, the other in Djibouti. AFRICOM has considerable work to do to overcome the popular view that it is a narrowly self-interested American instrument to secure access to oil resources and advance the "War on Terror" in Africa.

The Securitization of Africa's Energy

The overwhelming dependency of the United States' economy on oil is well known. In the 2006 State of the Union address, Bush famously asserted that "America [was] addicted to oil, which is often imported from unstable parts of the world." The inherent security threat this posed to American interests was intrinsic to the President's demand that the United States "replace more than 75 percent of our oil imports from the Middle East by 2025 . . . and make our dependence on Middle Eastern oil a thing of the past" (quoted in *New York Times* [New York], February 1, 2006). Apart from the potentiality of new energy technologies to help break this dependency, locating alternative sources of oil supplies other than those found in the Persian Gulf were central to Bush's message. Africa fits neatly into this energy-security nexus, indeed is "central in its efforts to reduce [American] dependency" on oil from the Middle East (Rothchild and Emmanuel, 2005: 79).

Early on in the post-9/11 environment, the assistant secretary of state for Africa Walter Kansteiner had asserted in mid-2002 that "African oil is of strategic national interest to us" and this reality would only "increase and become more important as we go forward" (quoted in Volman, 2003: 574). Later that year it was stated that "Africa, the neglected stepchild of American diplomacy, is rising in strategic importance to Washington policy makers, and one word sums up the reason—oil" (*Washington Post* [Washington, DC] September 19, 2002). Yet such pronouncements were not simply a counterreaction to the Arab-originated attacks on September 11, 2001; reducing a dependency on oil from the Middle East was viewed as vital to American national interests prior to the calamitous events of 9/11. For instance, in May 2001 the National Energy Policy Development Group, chaired by Vice-President Dick Cheney, characterized America's reliance on imported oil as a major national security issue, stating that the "Concentration of world oil production in any one region of the world" was a "challenge" and that the American economy's reliance on Middle Eastern oil fostered "a condition of increased dependency on foreign powers that do not always have America's interests at heart" (National Energy Policy Report quoted by Volman, 2003: 574). In this sense, 9/11 merely propeled and speeded up policy calculations that had been made *before* the attacks.

How and why Africa fitted into these above calculations was directly related to estimates that West Africa would supply 25 percent of imported oil to the United States by 2015, up from 14 percent in 2000 (Carmody, 2005: 100). As a result, "there is greater recognition that Africa matters to the United States as an important and growing source of non-Gulf oil" (House Committee on International Relations, 2001: 2). The growing abundance of oil supplies in the Gulf of Guinea fits with American policies to diversify oil supplies. Yet this provides a challenge to American policies given that West Africa was only in the initial stages of an "extended oil boom that will significantly enhance the global position of Nigeria and Angola and bring greater attention to emergent, unstable producers" such as Chad, Equatorial Guinea, and São Tomé and Príncipe (Africa Policy

Advisory Panel, 2004: 6). Trying to promote stability and governance in such states will not be easy, though may prove vital to American security interests.

As noted above, the Cheney Report issued its finalized findings in May 2001, fully four months *before* 9/11. It can therefore be asserted that although 9/11 intensified American efforts to diversify supplies and consequently place even stronger weight on sourcing African oil, it was not 9/11 specifically that generated a major change in American energy diplomacy. Rather, 9/11 and the clamor to further lessen dependence on oil from the Persian Gulf merely provided another—if particularly compelling—reason why Africa's energy fields should be accorded a greater priority in Washington's policy considerations and why American oil companies have been particularly encouraged to explore opportunities there.

Africa and HIV/AIDS

In 2003, the then secretary of state Colin Powell stated before the United Nations (UN) General Assembly that HIV/AIDS was "more devastating than any terrorist attack" and that as a result, Washington would "remain at the forefront" in the international campaign against its pernicious effects. That year, Bush actually made HIV/AIDS a focus of his tour of Africa, asserting that "this is the deadliest enemy Africa has ever faced, and you will not face this epidemic alone" (all quotes from Cook, 2006: 13). A continual theme of Bush's tour was of the threat and dangers HIV/AIDS posed to Africa. Such pronouncements came off the back of the 2002 National Security Strategy which had argued that "a special concerted effort" to counter HIV/AIDS and aiding its victims was imperative for American interests on "both moral and security grounds" (Africa Policy Advisory Panel, 2004: 2). While the HIV/AIDS issue was securitized as part of the Bush Administration's foreign policy agenda in Africa, it can be stated that under Bush, the campaign against HIV/AIDS gained particular prominence in American policies toward the continent.

This is not to say, of course, that the Bush administration was the first American government to discover AIDS was an issue, nor the first to see it in security terms. As early as 1987, Congress had set aside resources to counter HIV/AIDS globally; the House of Representatives had even noted the devastating potential that the pandemic may have in "undermining all development efforts" gained thus far in Africa (Cook, 2006: 12). Findings from the National Intelligence Council during the Clinton administration had equally characterized the pandemic as "not only a humanitarian crisis in Africa but also a security threat to the US," primarily because it "devastated populations, reduced economic growth and threatened governments" (cited by Rothchild and Emmanuel, 2005: 89). Indeed, under Clinton a US$100 million "Leadership and Investment in Fighting an Epidemic" (LIFE) initiative was launched in 1999, concentrating on 14 African countries (and India) where it was deemed that the epidemic was most severe, where the highest number of new infections were found and where the potential impact was the greatest. Other initiatives enabled Washington to claim that such spending had made Washington the largest bilateral donor of HIV/AIDS assistance in the world. In this sense, the Bush administration was building upon and expanded earlier efforts.

Soon after assuming office in January 2001, George W. Bush made a "founding pledge" of US$200 million toward the Global Fund to fight HIV/AIDS, Tuberculosis and Malaria and a year later put forward a proposal for a US$500 million "International Mother and Child HIV Prevention Initiative" to avoid the transmission of HIV from mother to child (Cook, 2006: 13). Later, in 2003, Bush launched PEPFAR or the "President's Emergency Plan for AIDS Relief," proposing US$15 billion in funding over a five-year time frame. PEPFAR included US$10 billion in new funding that was not previously allocated to ongoing projects (although the fact that two-thirds of the funds went to pro-abstinence campaigns and would not be given to any organizations that operated abortion clinics was criticized by some). In short, under Bush American bilateral expenditure on HIV/AIDS increased by over 600 percent: from US$139 million in 2000 to nearly US$900 million in 2005 (Cook, 2006: 16). Given the overall negative evaluations of Bush's presidency, it should be remembered that his administration oversaw the greatest spending on the fight against HIV/AIDS ever seen. Such a legacy prompted the BBC to ask "Has Bush been Africa's best friend?" In an overview of American policies toward Africa under Bush, the report noted that

> At the time [of PEPFAR's launch] just 50,000 Africans were on anti-retroviral drugs. By 2007, 1.3 million Africans were on medication, much of it paid for by the Bush administration . . . no-one denies that the funding has made anti-retrovirals widely available, saving hundreds of thousands of lives. (*BBC News*, January 16, 2009)

The Good Governance Agenda

As it has been noted above, American policies toward Africa during the Cold War were rationalized along strict realpolitik lines and there was little room for talk of democracy promotion or the need for "good governance." Indeed, the dynamics of the Cold War inspired a cynical approach to aid; in 1973, 22 percent of American bilateral aid was for political and strategic purposes, and 78 percent for development. By 1985, 67 percent was for political and strategic purposes and only 33 percent was for development (Spero and Hart, 2002: 204). Whether an African leader was on side was all that mattered, explaining continued US support for the likes of Mobutu Sese Seko, Samuel Doe, Daniel arap Moi, etc. even when it was palpably obvious that such autocrats were little more than criminals. As Raymond Copson noted, "the US typically justified its aid to Africa, whether economic or military, by stressing the strategic importance of the countries getting the aid" (Copson, 1994: 104).

The end of the Cold War and the subsequent ending of strategic competition in Africa (and elsewhere) with the Soviet Union made possible the (selective) application of conditionalities when supplying developmental assistance; recipients could no longer threaten to approach alternative sources if they deemed such conditions intrusive. Subsequently, a particular feature of Clinton's Africa policies was the promotion, via conditionalities, of neoliberal capitalism, liberal democratic governance and liberal conceptions of what constituted human rights. This enlargement of liberal democracy around the world, but particularly in Africa, became the Clinton administration's "ideological lodestar" (Alden, 2000: 357). All Western actors, not just the United States, seized on the opportunities afforded by the "End of History" to demand that liberal values be implemented in Africa in return for aid and assistance. Indeed, while on his first visit to Africa in 1998 and on his second trip in 2000, President Clinton focused first and foremost on advancing these norms in Africa. As Susan Rice noted in 2000, "the President's trip symbolized our ongoing commitment to strengthening democratic institutions throughout the African continent . . . Our commitment to supporting democracy in Africa has gone hand in hand with our support for human rights" (Rice, 2000).

Why this was so was found in the belief that conditions hostile to capitalist accumulation and foreign investment were prohibiting development and investment (not necessarily in that order). Certainly, Africa's return on investment had fallen from nearly 31 percent in the 1960s to just over 2 percent by the 1980s and during the immediate post–Cold War period, SSA's share of global investment went down to under 3 percent (compared to the 12 percent it had enjoyed in 1985) (Callaghy 1996: 8–9).

With the Soviet presence eliminated, Clinton inserted "good governance" conditionalities in all of his new trade initiatives for Africa and seized the opportunity to promote regime change (though it was not called this) during his presidency. For instance, the AGOA legislation (see above) was specifically established to "reward African states adopting certain market-oriented reforms" (Alden, 2000: 361). In response, the *Association of Concerned Africa Scholars* drew parallels between AGOA and the conditionalities associated with the discredited Structural Adjustment policies of the World Bank and IMF.

The driving force behind AGOA was American capitalist interests, specifically the Corporate Council on Africa (CCA), which was involved with AGOA at every level, from the AGOA Steering Committee to its involvement in past AGOA Forums, to the State Department's flagship AGOA grant—the AGOA Professional Development Programme. One critic, Congresswomen Maxine Walters, in fact argued that AGOA was "a 'Christmas tree' for multinational corporations [and] show[ed] little regard for the importance of leaving the ownership of Africa in the hands of Africans" (Waters, 1998).

Within such a context, it is unsurprising that when Bush assumed office, he followed the lead set by Clinton in such matters. Clearly seeing the utility the trade initiative had for American business interests, Bush extended AGOA past 2008. And following on from the principles established by Clinton, Bush also set up the Millennium Challenge Account (MCA) in 2002 which was an initiative to grant aid to those states that adopted "good governance" and liberal markets. Notably, Bush asserted during a visit to Africa in 2003 that the Account's aim was to grant aid to those states whose governments "rule justly [and] encourages entrepreneurship" (quoted in Mills, 2004: 160). Obviously, the sort of entrepreneurship that Bush had in mind coincided with market-friendly policies and was to be welcoming of American capital. Thus Bush's comments follow on from Clinton's own policies, spelt out in his administration's *A Comprehensive Trade and Development Policy for the Countries of Africa: Executive Summary* of 1997, which had asserted that "If obstacles that hinder investment are removed, benefits will accrue to both the US investors and the African nations" (United States Trade Representative on Africa, 1997: 3).

Post-9/11 thus merely saw intensification of such policies, as the lack of "good governance," associated with an absence of liberal democracy and, by inference, "open markets," was seen as part of the wider security threat to American interests. Thus even after the events of September 2001, there was no seismic change in Washington's policies toward Africa vis-à-vis trade and aid; conditionality and the advancement of neoliberal economic and political values remained, and in fact trace their lineage to the Clinton administration.

Conclusion

It is true that after 9/11 Africa "assumed a new strategic place in US foreign policy and in the definition of vital US national interests" (Africa Policy Advisory Panel, 2004: 2). Washington considerably ramped up its focus on an American military presence in Africa and mainstreamed counterterrorism as an integral part of its security relationship with cooperative African countries. But what was notable was that despite the securitization of much of the rhetoric surrounding American-African relations, policy principles and trends remained constant and in many cases can be seen as continuations of policies established by previous administrations. Indeed, "the new policy initiatives notwithstanding, hard evidence of a radically new American geopolitical code for Africa is limited" (Kraxberger, 2005: 61).

As we have seen, the need to diversify American imports of energy away from the volatile Middle East predated 9/11. Africa thus had been a focus of diversification efforts before September 2001 and the realization that dependence on Gulf oil was extremely problematic. Condoleezza Rice admitted that "nothing has really taken me aback more as secretary of state than the way that the politics of energy is—I will use the word 'warping'—diplomacy around the world" (*New York Times* [New York], April 5, 2006). Yet continuities are evident—notably in the way Rice publicly labeled Equatorial Guinea's notorious president, Teodoro Obiang Nguema, as a "good friend" of the United States (*Washington Post* [Washington, DC], April 18, 2006). We saw precisely the same rhetoric back in the 1970s and 1980s with the likes of Doe and Mobutu.

Likewise, in the promotion of neoliberal policies and the push for "good governance," Bush's government followed previous administrations, albeit post-9/11 the need for liberal democracy was securitized and the non-presence of democracies in Africa (and elsewhere) was cast within the ambit of a threat to American interests. In the context of the "War on Terror," American policy-making conceptualizations seem predicated on the belief that poverty, weak institutions and corruption lead to weak and unstable states, deemed fertile breeding grounds for terrorism. Africa's importance in America's strategic interests and Washington's engagement on the continent is thus demonstrated in initiatives such as AFRICOM and the EACTI, as well as the Trans-Sahara Counterterrorism Initiative (TSCTI). Other examples include the MCA. Even in the realm of disease, specifically HIV/AIDS, the Bush government framed the issue within a broader milieu of the pandemic posing security hazards to American interests. This though did massively increase American commitment to the fight against the pandemic, with a whole raft of new initiatives and programs being introduced by Bush.

What 9/11 arguably did do was to bring to a close the "decade of disengagement" that had characterized American policies toward Africa; American policies toward Africa became of greater significance as the continent was conceptualized within a securitization discourse that saw Africa as posing a possible threat to American interests. Yet, beyond such securitization, Washington's policies in Africa did not fundamentally alter. It was merely in the scope and intensity, rather than actual principles, that changed post-9/11. Having said that, the Bush legacy in Africa is stronger than Clinton's, despite the latter's much-vaunted reputation as someone who was sympathetic to Afro-American and African causes. Rwanda's genocide in 1994 happened under Clinton's watch as Washington looked the other way, and it was under Clinton that the "decade of disengagement" occurred.

Despite Bush's disastrous foreign policy initiatives in other areas, and despite Bush's infamous remarks in his first presidential campaign that Africa held no interest for him, one commentator has asserted that "Bush's Africa policy is the most distinguished foreign policy legacy of the administration . . . Although few expected such interest eight years ago, the president has clearly been deeply and personally committed to strengthening US-Africa relations" (Todd Moss, quoted in *BBC News*, January 16, 2009). Though these commitments are clearly linked to conceptualizations of threat that incorporate Africa into a broader security framework, closer engagement has, at least in the health realm, had a positive effect—for instance, Bush's malaria program has seen the disease halved in 15 African countries. Yet when looking at the broad sweep of recent American-African relations, continuities stand out rather than disjunctures.

Where the new administration will fit in to such patterns is unclear at the time of writing, although early indications are that the parameters set by Bush (and Clinton earlier) will continue. There will likely be no paradigm-changing initiatives under Barack Obama toward Africa. A continuation of security "partnerships" with cooperative African states as part of the broader counterterrorism agenda will almost certainly continue. The Bush legacy on aid and HIV/AIDS will equally likely continue, although the ongoing global financial crisis may well affect budget lines. However, the wild expectations within Africa that a half-African president of the United States would somehow prioritize the continent are likely to be disappointed—and for the same reasons why Donald Rumsfeld did not feel particularly sympathetic to his ancestral homeland in "old Europe" i.e. Germany. Obama is first and foremost—and exclusively—American and what are constructed as American "national interests" will always triumph in any policy considerations that he may undertake.

Indeed, an early indication of where Africa ranked in importance in the new Obama administration was Secretary of State Hillary Clinton's remarks at her confirmation: of the 5,000 words, two paragraphs—a little over 100 words—were devoted to Africa. As one African commentator remarked, "what concerned me even more was Clinton's assertion that the top US priority in Africa was 'security', which she described as 'combating al-Qaida's efforts to seek safe havens in failed states in the Horn of Africa'. In short, America isn't going to think about Africa much, but when it does, it will be to continue the Bush-era habit of worrying that there is an al-Qaida militant under every bed" (*Nation* [Nairobi], March 23, 2009). Whether this turns out to be true, only future analysis will decide, although it is likely that energy and security will be high on Washington's agenda. It *is* true that a very large proportion of the United States Ambassador to the United Nations' staff is made up of Africanists who are conflict and security experts. And it is true that Obama's first state visit as president was to a country that had just discovered oil (Ghana), but at the time of writing, the contours of any distinctive Obama set of Africa policies were not readily discernible.

CHAPTER TWO

Of Spin and Mirrors: Britain and New Labour's Policies toward Africa

The United Kingdom has had a long-standing relationship with Africa, primarily engendered by the colonial experience. Yet unlike other ex-colonial powers, for a relatively long period in the postcolonial era, Britain did not retain a particularly strong interest in the continent after decolonization. Instead, British policy toward postcolonial Africa had always been one of seeking to "turn its imperial legacies from liabilities into assets" (Williams, 2004: 41). In other words, Africa was seen as a problem rather than an opportunity for most British governments. Even under Conservative governments, whose members probably have the most favorable attitude toward the colonial endeavor and who retain romantic attachments to the Commonwealth, "Africa was not a core priority" for either Margaret Thatcher or John Major (even though Major himself had previously worked in Nigeria) (Khadiagala, 2000: 100). What interaction that did exist throughout the 1980s was based upon aid and/or trade, with a rearguard action aimed at thwarting sanctions against apartheid South Africa being perhaps the most notable political action on the part of Britain in Africa.

In recent times (i.e. post-1997), however, there has been a *relative* prioritization of Africa in official policy. Indeed, under Tony Blair and New Labour, Africa ostensibly became a major policy concern for the New Labour government and there was certainly a great deal of rhetoric about New Labour's "passionate" commitment to the continent. However, examining the realities (rather than the rhetoric) of policy and stripping away the spin and media presentations is crucial for anyone wishing to have a coherent picture of what contemporary British policy toward Africa is. Doing so reveals in fact that New Labour's Africa policies have largely continued on the same path as previous governments, maintaining a "calculating eye to the national interest and Britain's international reputation" (Abrahamsen and Williams, 2001: 249). In order to come to this conclusion, a contextualization of recent British policy toward Africa is required, beginning with developments under the Conservative governments of Margaret Thatcher and John Major (1979–97).

Conservative Policy toward Africa

In general, as we have noted, the trend among London policy-making circles has historically been to see Africa "as a source of trouble rather than an opportunity" (Clapham, 1996a: 88). Under the Conservative governments of Thatcher and Major there appeared to be very little substance to Britain's engagement with Africa, leading one commentator at the time to remark that Britain had a "dwindling set of interests and activities in Africa" (Styan, 1996: 64). What interests that existed were largely based on Commonwealth members in Africa—typically Nigeria, South Africa and, for a short period of time, Zimbabwe. But apart from these, Britain's Africa policies were minimal and marginalized. During the Thatcher era (1979–90), British foreign policy was devoted toward developing an intimate relationship with the United States under Ronald Reagan. With very few exceptions, London was reluctant to involve itself in African affairs.

Notably, Margaret Thatcher advanced the notion that the optimal method to deal with the continent was to emphasize "African solutions to African problems." Consequently, British diplomatic missions were either reduced in size across the continent, or even closed. British developmental assistance toward Africa similarly was reduced; in 1987 Africa received only US$325 million in aid from Britain, less than the 16 percent that was being supplied by Paris at the same time (Cumming, 2003).

John Major's government (1990–7) was little better in this regard, with a set of policies characteristically "reactionary" and based on "damage limitation" (Williams, 2004: 42). While the UK committed itself to "cancel two thirds of the official debts of fifteen of its poor African debtors," this was heavily based on conditionalities related to IMF stipulations (ibid.: 54). Even here, the exercise was largely symbolic and most of the states in SSA did not benefit from the initiative. At the same time, British aid to Africa continued to decrease. While a Human Rights policy unit was established within the Foreign and Commonwealth Office (FCO) and aid was suspended to regimes that held back from the ostensible democratization wave in Africa in the early 1990s (Sudan's aid suspension in 1991 and Malawi's in 1992 being two examples), British aid policies in Africa could not be described as activist in this period (Cumming, 2003: 65). Notably, aid policy was run by the Overseas Development Administration (ODA), a wing of the FCO. Officials within the ODA generally saw Africa as a continent reliant upon help. Yet being an auxiliary arm of the FCO meant that the ODA did not have the independent capability (or financial resources) to strike a different path than that being advanced by an FCO strongly promoting perceived "British interests." One of the first things the incoming New Labour government did on assuming power was to create the Department for International Development (DFID) as a separate entity to the FCO (see the text below).

Under Major, London refused to commit troops to the peacekeeping efforts of either UNOSOM (United Nations Operation in Somalia) I or II. And relating to one of the worst disasters to have affected postcolonial Africa, Britain showed remarkable indifference toward the 1994 genocide in Rwanda, largely because Rwanda was considered "outside the zone of [Britain's] interest" (Williams, 2004: 43). Later reflecting on his time as prime minister, Major asserted that "I should have done more" for Africa (*Guardian* [London], July 6, 2005). By then, of course, it was too late. Under the recent Conservative governments, therefore, British official policy can be said to have been marked by a lack of prioritization of Africa. It was arguably not that the Conservatives lacked interest in African problems, but rather that they did not possess the political will to invest in long-term strategies that might help alleviate them (Cumming, 2003: 70).

New Labour and Africa

One of the characterizing features of New Labour's administration (both Tony Blair's and Gordon Brown's) has been a strong focus on political spin, presentation and the control of the public representation of policy. Notably, early on in Blair's tenure, the normally sympathetic *Independent* newspaper described New Labour as "Spinderella: A People's Pantomime in Two Acts" (December 30, 1997). Certainly, under New Labour, "public statements [were] no longer fact-based, but operational. Realities and political narratives [were] constructed to serve a purpose, dismantled, and the show move[d] on" (Oborne, 2005: 6). Foreign policy was no exception and "never before ha[d] the public of a democratic state been subject to such a tirade of propaganda about a government's moral motives than Britain under New Labour" (Curtis, 2002). Indeed, the level of public declarations from London about its foreign policy led to commentators arguing that it was time for the British government to tone "down its foreign policy rhetoric in line with its actual practices" (Abrahamsen and Williams, 2001: 261).

Initially, ongoing developments and processes in Africa in the 1990s, such as conflict and widespread poverty, were seen as potential threats for British interests. Illegal immigration, transnational crime and terrorism were among the key cause of concern for policymakers (Porteous, 2005). Yet when it came to defining what the key interests of Britain were overseas and how policy should be constructed to realize these, "a problem of bewildering complexity for the policy makers" was opened up (Dickie, 2004: 2). British foreign policy has always sought to construct environments that are positive for investment by private British corporations and the promotion of "good governance" and liberal reform is integral to this broad aim. Yet although "the new consensus denies that there's a conflict between ending poverty and business as usual" (*Guardian* [London], July 5, 2005), evidence suggests otherwise. This immediately stimulated problems for a government that was so keen to posture its supposed differences from previous British administrations.

Certainly in the early stages of the Blair government it appeared that there *was* change in British policy toward Africa. This was most graphically illustrated by the British intervention in Sierra Leone in 1999 (see Kargbo, 2006). "The underlying motives behind the intervention were mixed . . . and complex," but included "the protection of UK citizens, averting humanitarian crisis, defending democracy, supporting President Kabbah and supporting UNAMSIL [United Nations Mission in Sierra Leone]" (Williams, 2005: 83). The intervention mission was successful in a variety of ways, evacuating British citizens, containing (and ultimately defeating) rebel forces, and reestablishing UN authority and the position of the legitimate Kabbah government. Furthermore, Britain remained in the country in a substantial program to help rebuild Sierra Leone.

Yet "while the Sierra Leone intervention . . . demonstrated the government's commitment to global responsibilities, it has also illustrated various contradictions in New Labour's international agenda, stemming from a reluctance to match rhetoric with action" (Ero, 2001: 57). There was an arguable correlation between the "Arms to Africa" affair and the intervention—prior to the intervention, London was found to be turning a blind eye to the sale of weapons to the Sierra Leonean government, despite a UN ban. Britain also "proved reluctant to speak out about Kabbah's own rather poor record on human rights and corruption," provoking questions about Britain's level of commitment to "good governance" (Williams, 2005: 85). However, such criticisms do not alter the fact that the mission in Sierra Leone was successful.

British policy toward Robert Mugabe's regime in Zimbabwe was however a failure. Few events in Africa in recent years excited British opinion on foreign affairs as the downward spiral of Zimbabwe under Mugabe's disastrous rule, yet London found itself hidebound in how it could act toward the Commonwealth country. In particular,

British policy was hugely frustrated by the persistent reluctance of African elites to criticize Mugabe's behavior. Apart from pushing for Harare's suspension from the Commonwealth and "smart" sanctions against leading Mugabe cronies, there was little London could do (see Taylor, 2005b; Taylor and Williams, 2002). Indeed, British foreign policy vis-à-vis Zimbabwe soon collapsed into shouting from the sidelines, something that played straight into Mugabe's hands. Hill (2001: 347) in fact has argued that "It was in Zimbabwe where the limits of British influence were most sharply exposed . . . ultimately Britain was shown up as having responsibility but not power."

Problematically for British foreign policy, the prime minister had a wholly naïve and idealistic view of Africa, one which envisioned a grateful continent, eager to lap up the largesse and vision of the British leader. "Saving" Africa became, for a time, the narrative that Blair projected, with his talk of the continent as a scar on the conscience of the world (which Blair would promptly heal). Yet when this did not go very far and Blair was confronted with the actual complexities of Africa, rather than a caricature, there are indications that he simply gave up. The Zimbabwe issue was a case in point: "a political researcher who works closely with MPs involved in Africa suggested: 'Blair found the whole subject so painful, that he wouldn't allow officials to brief him . . . If you've got a bit of an idealized view of Africa it [Zimbabwe] really buggers it up'" (quoted in Gallagher, 2009: 441).

New Labour, New Britain, New Foreign Policy?

The real problem for New Labour's Africa policies, however, arguably stems from the grandiosity of stated claims to be somehow different from *all* previous British administrations. This included a claimed progressive outlook on international politics grounded in "democracy, liberty, justice, mutual obligation and internationalism" (Dixon and Williams, 2001: 152). Such hubris naturally invited scrutiny. Claiming to be advancing a Third Way between socialism and capitalism, official policy had it that the Third Way was about promoting "good governance," human rights and "sensible" economic policies. Critics however asserted that New Labour's "overriding concern [has been] to maintain the existing neo-liberal global economic system" (Cumming, 2004: 124). Such realities question a further maxim of Blair's, notably that New Labour was somehow the "political wing of the British people."

Carrying on the "difference" theme, New Labour's first foreign minister, Robin Cook, (in)famously claimed that under his tenure, British foreign policy would be "ethical," with a claim that he would "focus British Foreign Policy more sharply on issues like political governance and human rights, and to tighten up on arms exports to regimes with poor records in these areas" (Porteous, 2005: 285). Both Blair and Cook informed the world that an "age of internationalism" had arrived, where we were "obliged to accept moral responsibility" for activities occurring beyond our borders and that "foreign policy is not divorced from domestic policy . . . our foreign policy must have an ethical dimension and must support the demands of other peoples for the democratic rights on which we insist for ourselves" (quoted in the *Guardian* [London], May 12, 1997).

Furthermore, New Labour's promotion of itself as representing a "New Britain" which was totally different from previous incarnations went to absurd lengths, to the point that British government ministers were posturing themselves as not actually

British. For instance, in November 1997 Clare Short, the then secretary of state for international development, sent a letter to the minister of agriculture of Zimbabwe, in which she asserted that London under New Labour had no special responsibilities in Zimbabwe as "We are a new government from diverse backgrounds, without links to former colonial interests. My own origins are Irish and, as you know, we were colonized, not colonizers" (*Mail and Guardian* [Johannesburg], December 22, 1997). As one commentator put it, "Short's amazing assertion—that because her family was of Irish stock there was no need to honor a commitment to Zimbabwe entered into by a previous British government—was an inimitable mixture of shamelessness and sanctimony (*Independent* [London], September 21, 2007).

Hoisted on their own petard, New Labour's Africa policies have been shown to fall far short of such claims; problematic given that it is "impossible to tackle poverty in Africa without also tackling other big issues: conflict, trade, arms sales, corruption, debt" (Porteous, 2005: 283). Yet reading New Labour documents on Africa, no thought is ever given as to which actors and processes (possibly, in part, British in origin) might be responsible for the "inequality, economic decline, state collapse [or] history" of postcolonial Africa (DFID, 2001: 6), never mind how and in what ways London may need to change a swathe of policies if it truly wishes to promote positive change on the continent. Blair was persistently committed to a "neo-liberal interpretation of global economics which aimed to protect and spread free markets in order to increase worldwide prosperity," despite being leader of an ostensibly socialist political party (Ware, 2006: 143). This is rarely if ever reflected upon in commentaries on UK policies toward Africa. Nor is the pernicious effect of London's reliance on private consultancy firms for policy advice, despite the fact that "The consultancy companies, which have grown out of the privatization of utilities in the UK, see their long term profitability depending on increasing their portfolio overseas and the support (both financial and political) of donors such as DFID and the World Bank is critical" i.e. they have institutional and personal interests, driven by profits and careerism, to encourage the ever increasing outlay of British taxpayers' money by DFID and to encourage privatization and liberalization (World Development Movement, 2005: 11). Part of this support for "free trade" has been a continued support for British arms manufacturers.

Britain, the Arms Trade and Africa

Britain has long played a central role in the international arms trade. This in itself arguably "completely undermines the [British] government's professed agenda of global development" (*Guardian* [London], February 3, 2002). Within a couple of years of assuming office, Blair visited South Africa to "lobby for a British chunk of a 4 billion pound arms deal that South Africa defense officials signed. In the same year, Clare Short's DFID department granted a miserly 4.7 million pound aid package to Pretoria" (*Guardian* [London], February 3, 2002).

Under New Labour and in spite of the ostensibly ethical dimension to its foreign policy, British arms exports to Africa continued. Export licenses were granted by the Department of Trade and Industry (DTI) to Eritrea, Ethiopia, Algeria, Sudan, Zambia, Uganda, Namibia and Somalia, four of which, ironically, were listed as priority countries for poverty reduction by DFID. Either there was an alarming lack of communication between different British government departments (a possibility) *or* British policy under New Labour was disingenuous and cynical. Tension between different departments, in part stimulated by Blair's propensity to a presidential style of government (in contravention of British traditions and practice) in fact meant that DFID allegedly sees the "FCO's promotion of UK commercial interests as being in conflict with its own developmental concerns" (Porteous, 2005: 286).

Despite claims to be "different," Britain remains among the top arms-selling nations, supplying billions of dollars worth of military equipment to South Africa, Nigeria and Kenya as well as other parts of Africa. Of note, the arms industry employs some 400,000 people in the United Kingdom, perhaps explaining why "national interests" have systematically trumped the rhetorical promises of the New Labour government, in spite of the politicians' claims to be qualitatively different from previous British administrations (Ware, 2006). Indeed, "British commercial interests, including arms sales, ha[ve] been promoted in Africa with little regard for human rights and governance" (Porteous, 2005: 284).

One commentator, at the time of the G-8 Summit in 2005 (hosted by Britain), argued that "It would seem obscene that at a time when one arm of government is focusing on debt relief, behind the scenes another arm is boosting this unacceptable [arms] trade" (*Guardian* [London], June 12, 2005). Arms export licences and ethics generally do not go together and this has been a persistent source of criticism of British connections with Africa under New Labour (and previous British governments, it should be noted). Indeed, "on the issue of arms and light weapons, the fit between New Labour's words and deeds is less impressive" (Abrahamsen and Williams, 2001: 252). While the British government has repeatedly asserted that "tackling the [arms trade] problem will require comprehensive action that not only addresses the issue of illegal transfers, but also ensures large scale destruction of surplus weapons" (DFID, 2001: 18), London has been slow in ratifying and implementing the Arms Trade Treaty (ATT). In fact, although London has "introduced a number of progressive policies on arms exports in the past ten years, its apparent reluctance to enforce its own guidelines, and its willingness on occasion to flout them, have undermined the potential improvements that these policies seemed to promise" (Saferworld, 2007: 3). When nearly half a million British jobs remain dependent on Britain staying as one of the world's top arms exporters, actual commitments to Africa (rather than rhetoric and spin) are quickly put aside.

Furthermore, New Labour is accountable for agreeing to the selling of inappropriate equipment to some of Africa's least developed countries. The developmental trajectories of nations are surely further undermined when those countries expend their budgets on weapons systems they cannot afford. Infamously, in 2001 Tanzania signed a contract for a "£28 million BAE military air-traffic control system which many, including the World Bank, said was both unnecessary and beyond Tanzania's means" (Porteous, 2005: 287).

Under New Labour, "specific licences for arms sales to Africa total more than £631m since 2000. But experts believe the true figure is closer to £1bn when the values of 'open' licenses are taken into account" (*Guardian* [London], June 12, 2005). Through such clear contradictions between an ethical foreign policy and an activist arms exporting regime, London is continuously placed in a "contradictory position; trying to keep the peace, while simultaneously supplying the warriors with weapons" (Abrahamsen and Williams, 2001: 253) The contradictions between rhetoric and reality are further revealed when looking at British trade policies toward Africa. In fact, "Trade, as before, comes first, second and third in importance even when it is a trade in arms; [meanwhile] human values, and coherence, come amongst the also-rans" (Allen, 1998: 405). British trade with Africa is something we turn to now.

British Trade and Africa

Under New Labour, British policy has sought to foster favorable "business climates" for British companies internationally. A government-supported arm, Business Action for Africa, is aimed at promoting British corporations across the continent. Yet despite the professed ethical claims to British policies, "on the issue of labor standards in international trade, the New Labour silence has been deafening" (Coates and Hay, 2001: 455). Britain's commercial lobbyists', active in and around Westminster, "primary concern is with winning arms contracts, securing export credits and maintaining stable trade relations with African countries" (Cumming, 2004: 114). New Labour has never "shown enthusiasm for regulatory measures that would make it harder for UK businesses to get involved in or facilitate the abusive exploitation of African resources," something in stark contrast to the spin (Porteous, 2005: 295).

Currently, an Export Credit Guarantee Department (ECGD) is in operation to insure British foreign trade. The Department remit is to help exporters of British goods and services to win contracts and to facilitate British companies investing overseas, by providing guarantees, insurance and reinsurance against loss. What this Department can mean in practice is that "arms companies pursue deals to countries which may well default on payments, and the debt itself is then owed to the exporting government" (Campaign Against Arms Trade, 2005). Where African countries have become indebted to the ECGD, debt has at times been cancelled through being written off "against the overseas development aid (ODA) budget" (*The Times* [London], April 6, 2008). Since "'most of the debt owed to the ECGD involves arms deals, in effect the ODA is being used to finance the arms, something it's not supposed to do" (ibid.).

Under New Labour, the unfair trading practices engendered by mass subsidization for European producers have also continued. While claiming to promote the development of agriculture in the developing world, "UK wheat exports are being sold at 30% less than the cost of production, whil[st] white sugar is being sold at 40% below production costs" (Actionaid, 2005: 7). As part of the spin, continental Europeans were routinely blamed by London for continuing the EU subsidies regime, though Britain was equally complicit. More importantly, in such circumstances, how "can African agricultural exporters hope to compete in the West when it is estimated that Western nations pay their farmers $350 billion per year in subsidies (nearly $1 billion per day)?" (Taylor, 2005c: 307). In fact, Britain has been at the "forefront of pushing this trade liberalization on Africa, and remains one of the most ardent proponents of the 'free trade' model" (Actionaid, 2005: 5). As one commentator noted on British trade policies toward Africa, London's stance reflected "an ever-widening gap between the noble rhetoric of Western politicians on the links between trade and development and the reality of what their governments were actually pushing for on behalf of domestic farming and manufacturing interests in world trade negotiations" (Porteous, 2008: 48). New Labour has been no exception.

British Aid Policy

Official rhetoric has it that DFID acts as the "moral aspect of the UK government, claiming a relationship of partnership between the UK and developing countries based on a common concern for poverty reduction and respect for human rights" (Marriage, 2006: 489). However, despite the creation of DFID by New Labour and the claim to have placed Africa centrally to British foreign policy, there has been a perpetual "tension between the liberal internationalism of the Third Way and traditional concerns for the national interest" (Abrahamsen and Williams, 2001: 249). Getting behind the spin has thus been a preoccupation of analysts of British policies toward Africa, aid being one such area of interest.

Under New Labour, it was claimed that British developmental assistance was to be explicitly untied from the promotion of British commercial interests (Porteous, 2005: 282). However, the notion of untied aid suggests that the rollout of aid is neither bilateral nor mandatory to be expended on specific areas, both of which DFID stipulates. While asserting that British "aid should no longer have the parallel aim of promoting UK business interests" (Abrahamsen and Williams, 2001: 255) by using "the concepts of human rights, humanitarian principles and a poverty focus, DFID developed a terminology that was seductive domestically, being ostensibly ethical, long term and positive sum" (Marriage, 2006: 488). In fact, Blair "introduced a policy of political conditionality whereby British aid has been linked to political reforms by African governments" (Cumming, 2004: 110). Rhetoric failed to hide the fact that creating environments that would be good for British business was a central concern.

Under New Labour, there has been a continual strategy of double counting budget streams and issuing misleading press statements when it comes to Britain's aid contributions and initiatives. For instance, when the issue of heavily indebted poor countries (HIPC) was addressed, "the UK proposal use[d] money from existing aid budgets, rather than providing genuinely new money to fund debt relief" (Actionaid, 2005: 11). While claiming to be "passionate" about poverty alleviation and development, British development assistance continually fell far short of the 0.7 percent target set by the UN. In fact, if "debt relief is excluded from aid calculations, UK aid actually fell between 2000/01 and 2002/03" as British aid figures "include debt relief, often on loans that were taken out for purposes unrelated to poverty reduction" (Actionaid, 2005: 8). Despite bold claims to have a qualitatively superior set of African policies than that existed under the Conservatives, aid devoted to Africa in 2005/2006 was only equivalent to that given in 1989 (Williams, 2004: 53).

In 2005, Britain hosted the G-8 Summit and a great deal of effort was expended by the Blair government on being seen to be focusing on the African continent. The then chancellor of the exchequer Gordon Brown early on declared that 2005 "will be a milestone in our campaign to meet the UN Millennium Development Goals to reduce poverty, illiteracy and disease across the world" (Brown, 2004: 127). Due to Britain's chairmanship of both the G-8 and the European Union in 2005, London seemed to believe that an opportunity to raise the continent's star in global politics (or rather, raise New Labour's star as being "passionate" about Africa) presented itself. However, the perpetual tension between Blair and Brown (something that was not to be resolved until Brown took over as prime minister in June 2007) was a feature of the G-8 meeting and needs remarking upon, as does the high profiles granted to myriad celebrities.

After Brown announced a £30 billion package of debt relief, "unnamed Blairites" were briefing the media against Brown and claiming that "that the Chancellor would not have been able to make his historical announcement had it not been for the Prime Minister's lobbying of Mr. Bush" (*Telegraph* [London], June 13, 2005). Remarkably, Blair and Brown "even set up rival websites for the British presidency of the G-8. Mr. Blair's include[d] recent speeches in Addis Ababa on climate change and Africa. Mr. Brown's G-7 website, accessed through the Treasury, focuse[d] on himself and his fellow finance ministers . . . like so much else it gives the impression of two hostile tribal leaders" (*Guardian* [London], January 8, 2005).

In fact, in January 2005, the British public were treated to the spectacle of Blair and Brown giving simultaneous speeches, with Blair in London and Brown in Edinburgh, speaking at exactly the same time and on exactly the same topic: tackling Africa's poverty. As *The Times* [(London], January 7, 2005) put it:

> The appearance of two leading politicians apparently attempting to outbid each other for ownership of disaster relief and aid to the Third World is little short of obscene. Africa might well need market-driven solutions to many of its problems, but political competition of this form is not the appropriate formula. It was a shameful display.

Such feuding carried on despite the rock star Bono's informed advice that Blair and Brown had to "to get their act together." "As the Lennon and McCartney of politics, he told the prime minister and chancellor at [2004's] Labour party conference, they had to work together as a team for the good of Africa" (*Guardian* [London], January 8, 2005). As Cooper (2008: 27) noted, Blair was "celebrity-obsessed, a condition that stood out as a marked feature of New Labour politics." Thus the presence of Bono, Bob Geldof et al. at the time of Gleneagles was another feature of Britain's tenure as head of the G-8. Consequently, "the nexus between celebrities, public diplomacy and spin [proved] close to Blair's heart" (ibid.: 62). Such "Bonoization" of British foreign policy invited ridicule— and despair from within the FCO's policy-making circles. As one commentator caustically put it at the height of Blair's attempted use of celebrities to sell Britain's Africa policy:

> Look, there's Angelina Jolie! Angelina, how is the world faring on the health and human rights fronts? Oh my gosh! It's Bono! Bono, what needs to be done about African poverty? Hey, Richard Gere and Sharon Stone, how can we tackle the AIDS crisis? (*New York Times* [New York], January 30, 2005)

Given the attractiveness of gesture politics and the headlines that these would generate (particularly if endorsed by Bono et al.), the proposals advanced by London at the time of the G-8 summit were unsurprising and essentially centered around the doubling of the G-8's development aid. Specifically, £26 billion was to be collectively added for that purpose each financial year. The plan also included getting wealthy countries to meet the United Nation's Development Goals of spending 0.7 percent of their gross national income on overseas aid. Brown set out detailed plans to use the IMF's gold to write off debt owed to the institution and to request from World Bank shareholders that they take over the debts owed by up to 70 of the poorest states to them (Abrahamsen and Williams, 2002: 316). Brown also advocated that an International Finance Facility (IFF) be set up to generate US$50 billion annually between now and 2015. The IFF was to be instituted upon long-term donor commitments from the G-7. Essentially, the British proposed that the IFF would involve G-7 members stating and committing multi-year aid budgets to the Facility and then the IFF using these pledges to borrow capital now to be used for aid and debt relief now.

Yet the spin around the IFF at the time of the Summit that it would create "additional" aid money was totally false. The IFF would merely bring forward future aid promises in a supposedly binding manner to ensure donors keep their pledges. Problematically, of course, the IFF could actually eat into future aid budgets. The World Development Movement (WDM) in fact estimated that "according to the Treaty's own calculations, the IFF was likely to raise . . . an extra nineteen billion dollars per year . . . rather than the fifty billion target" (Lee, 2009: 177). Remarkably, "WDM asserted that there would be (at 2006 prices) $316.6 billion less available for aid during [the] period, meaning that 'the IFF will result in an overall net loss of some US$108 billion less than there otherwise have been available in total aid between 2006 and 2032'" (ibid.). New Labour's media managers failed to mention such realities.

Of course, a one-sided focus on aid carries within it inherent dangers, something which New Labour has been circumspect in admitting, preferring the snappy headlines to long-term policy pursuance. A common hazard is that aid recipients waste resources. For instance, in 2007 Britain announced a Development Partnership Arrangement (DPA) with Uganda that entailed more than US$14 million to Uganda over a ten-year period. Yet when Uganda hosted the Commonwealth Heads of Government Meeting (CHOGM) in December 2007, US$150 million was spent on hotel renovations, tree planting and the provision of cellular phones for attending elites. In fact, in spite of the notoriety of Uganda's corruption levels, the country has long been a high priority for British aid by New Labour. The actual effectiveness of focusing solely on aid and the problems that this engenders, primarily "because of the perverse incentives and soft options it pro-vides for both gives and receivers" (Mistry, 2005: 677) is something which DFID and the New Labour government in general have studiously avoided.

In fact, it is clear that DFID (despite the plethora of well-paid development "experts" employed as consultants—DFID's budget for consultants for the period 2008–13 is around £1 billion) has failed to comprehend the *political* dynamics behind Africa's poverty (see Fyson, 2009). In its landmark 2000 White Paper (DFID, 2000), the most explicit acknowledgments by DFID of the "problem of corruption" were stated thus:

> Weak and ineffective states, with problems of corruption, inadequate infrastruc-ture and cumbersome bureaucratic procedures, are not an attractive destination for [private capital] flows. (ibid.: 23)

More effective government and greater benefits from markets require tougher action—by developing and developed countries—to deal with corruption. The evidence suggests that investment levels are lower in countries with high levels of corruption, "due to the uncertainty created, the cost of bribes, and time-consuming bureaucracy . . . It is poor people who suffer most from corruption" (ibid.: 25).

These meek comments were essentially side-thoughts, tacked on incidentally. One must infer that DFID failed to adequately get to grips with the most pressing determinant of African underdevelopment: pervasive, insidious neo-patrimonial norms that extend throughout all layers of the African state. DFID is naïve therefore to treat patrimonial norms as simply minor "corruption problems" to be healed (like everything else) with the simple bandage of "more effective government" and liberalization, perhaps aided by the ointment of "democratization." DFID *is* right to recognize that "uncertainty and the cost of bribes" deters investment. Yet it is a gross underestimation of the political dynamics of African underdevelopment to reduce the neo-patrimonial state to a slight impediment "deterring private capital flows." DFID's resulting technocratic and superficial prescriptions, "requiring tougher action on corruption" by those who are themselves corrupt, seems intuitively fairly likely to fail. A real and deep focus on the *politics* involved, rather than "governance" symptoms, is needed. As Matthew Lockwood put it:

> The donor community has played down the significance of clientelist politics as anything more than "incidental", focusing instead on the symptoms of weak capacity and corruption. This leads to a technical approach, with capacity building programmes and anti-corruption reforms that promote greater administrative "hygiene" and technical expertise. This ignores the real nature of the hybrid neo-patrimonial system. (Lockwood, 2005: 91)

On the basis of its superficial analysis of corruption in African politics, DFID's practices in the field under New Labour left much to be desired. They either failed to tackle corruption, or even directly fostered it.

For example, in Kenya, where corruption and graft is rife, DFID actively undermined efforts to try and reign in sleaze. The British High Commissioner for Kenya between 2001 and 2005, Edward Clay, made it a priority of his tenure to tackle the rampant corruption of the Kenyan government. Though one might think this would help make British aid efforts more effective, promote development more efficiently and save British taxpayers' money, DFID was not interested. In fact, DFID "had little appetite for the antics of [the] high commissioner . . . 'They found it an embarrassing obstacle, because it got in the way of their plans to spend more', says Clay" (Wrong, 2009: 210). "Sir Edward Clay . . . spoke out courageously against corruption, his DFID counterparts did their best to undermine him" (*Economist*, February 26, 2009). The fact that a British wing of government felt emboldened enough to actively undermine the senior British representative in Kenya speaks volumes.

Lest this be thought of as interdepartmental wrangling, the Kenyan whistleblower on corruption, John Githongo, was similarly treated after exposing the Kenyan government's rampant corruption and theft of aid money: "[D]uring a lunch at a London hotel with Simon Brand, head of Nairobi's DFID office, and Dave Fish, DFID's director for Africa . . . the message was: 'This is Africa, it's always been corrupt' . . . [Brand and Fish] were very provocative and sneering, talking through gritted teeth. They kept referring to [Githongo's] 'allegations', basically saying: 'You've upset our program'" (Wrong, 2009: 267). "Kenya's donors . . . had understood the scandal's contours even before [Githongo] had, and had determined to carry on lending regardless" (ibid.: 266–7).

In such circumstances, institutional self-interest and spin came together. Instead of focusing on the real issues about African development and/or the efficacy of aid, the politicians went for the headlines. New Labour under both Blair and Gordon Brown hence focused on issues more obviously recognized by the media, rather than the "boring" structural issues such as the roots of inequality in Africa, social justice, the fungibility of aid, etc. While this is understandable for a media-conscious regime, it does not greatly assist in identifying Africa's real problems.

Consequently, DFID paid little attention to corruption issues and deeper clientelist politics, choosing to brush them under the carpet in the face of pressure to spend and "to come up with 'good news' stories [and] quick wins" for their political masters at home (Porteous, 2005: 292). "Like the 'Hear No Evil' monkey, hands clapped firmly over their ears, humming furiously to drown out the voices," DFID had "no interest" in graft and the theft of British taxpayers' money (Wrong, 2009: 267). A simplistic desire to increase aid became central to New Labour's Africa strategy. While this may have appealed to the liberal guilt of Blair's Western audience and "the compassion entrepreneurs in the huge aid and humanitarian industry" (Abdul-Raheem, 2005: 2), the benefits that Africa can hope to gain are questionable. The sociology of bureaucracies and the tenacity within the aid industry to expand their own budgets for both institutional and personal professional reasons can never be discounted here.

London: A Center for Money Laundering

Corruption and capital flight, with its attendant detrimental effect on Africa's development, can be said to be integral to British-African relations. London is not only the world capital of finance but is also in the top league of money laundering. Unimaginable sums of money "including loans from Western donors" which have been "looted from state coffers by national leaders such as Nigeria's Abacha and Zaïre's Mobutu" are safely nestled in the City of London "where banking officials [fail] to ask the most basic questions about where the money came from" (Porteous, 2005: 284). "It is . . . difficult to assess with any precision the extent to which money laundering takes place in London. According to Home Office estimates, dirty money represents about 2% of the UK's Gross Domestic Product, which is £18 billion. This figure must be supplemented by the laundering through London of the proceeds of criminal activity occurring outside the UK" i.e. Africa (Transparency International, 2003: 24).

In fact, "the City of London has been a major beneficiary of stolen money and other assets looted from Africa" (Abdul-Raheem, 2005: 2). In 2001, the UK banking regulator, the Financial Services Authority (FSA), found that 23 banks in London, including British banks and London branches of foreign banks, had handled US$1.3 billion of the US$3–5 billion looted from Nigeria by the late dictator Sani Abacha (Global Witness, 2009: 21). Billions of dollars leave Africa illegally, much of it via banks under British control. Yet British policies toward Africa treat the continent as if it is utterly poverty-stricken and is wholly dependent upon foreign aid, which now must be massively increased, while Africa's debt—which has been in part contributed to by such levels of flight—must be wiped clean.

Questions need to be asked as to why London is not *primarily* aimed at encouraging local investment and discouraging capital flight, rather than focusing on aid. In September 2004, it was announced that there were over 100,000 African millionaires on the continent, worth around US$600 billion in total (*African Business* [London], September 2004: 8). No shortage of capital or resources there, yet current British policy seems to ignore such things and instead want huge amounts of aid to plug the supposed resource gap that hinders the attainment of the Millennium Development

Goals (MDGs). At the time of the 2005 G-8 Summit, one commentator indeed noted that "the much publicized G-8 deals will deliver about $1bn in debt cancellation and $25bn in aid flows mostly to sub-Saharan Africa. But this is dwarfed by the $50bn the region loses in capital flight. Disturbingly, this capital flight out of Africa is on the rise so any rise in aid threatens to be eroded by money flowing out" (Kapoor, 2005: 2).

It could be persuasively argued that for coherence to be attained in British policies toward Africa, there needs to be far greater commitment to tracking down and returning illicit capital flight from Africa, now stashed in banks throughout the United Kingdom or in territories under the control and/or influence of London (35 of the 72 tax havens are British territories, dependencies or ex-colonies i.e. Commonwealth members). "Tax evasion and tax avoidance for both companies and rich individuals in developing countries is . . . widespread with tax havens playing a very major role in facilitating capital flight and money laundering which depletes the governments and countries of scarce resources needed for development. It has been estimated that developing countries collectively lose as much as $500 billion of money every year to dirty money flows" (ibid.: 6). Interestingly, Western governments were quite capable of tracing Al-Qaeda funding and getting the banking industry to freeze such accounts. Can the same amount of energy be spent by London in advancing Africa's cause? "Disingenuous hand-wringing substitutes for action on both sides of the Atlantic. Addressing the dirty-money problem suffers from a lack of will, not a lack of solutions" (Baker, 1999: 30). In fact, Britain was extremely slow in ratifying the United Nations Convention against Corruption (the Convention has been open for signature since December 2003).

Plugging the leaks and returning the loot is far more coherent than making pronouncements about increasing aid because, apparently, there are no resources in Africa to finance development. As Transparency International put it, commenting on British policy, "One cannot be 'tough on crime and the causes of crime' [a famous Blair aphorism] while starving the fight against money laundering of resources and adopting a 'light regulatory touch' in the enforcement of AML [anti-money laundering] regulations" (2003: 7).

Conclusion

"The nature of Britain's relationship with Africa appears still to revolve around extracting profits and preventing 'their' problems ending up 'over here'" (Williams, 2004: 58). Britain's foreign policy toward Africa has consistently found "itself caught between rhetoric and performance" (Coates and Hay, 2001: 466), particularly in the areas of trade, aid and arms policies. Britain has "play[ed] a direct role in many of Africa's conflicts, both through its colonial legacy and through its more recent commercial and political activities in the region" (Actionaid, 2005: 19). However, "dramatic changes in Britain's policy towards Africa require substantial changes to be introduced at home. The British government must take some difficult decisions on issues like its domestic arms industry" (Williams, 2004: 58).

A major issue when disentangling British policies toward Africa is getting behind the political spin that has been so closely associated with New Labour's tenure. An example of this would be British efforts at promoting inter-African collaboration. In 2001, the New Partnership for Africa's Development (NEPAD) was created in order to address and work toward solutions for Africa's developmental impasse. Initially, Blair and New Labour supported NEPAD, at least rhetorically. Yet just four years into NEPAD's existence, Blair instigated the "Commission for Africa" in order "to define the challenges facing Africa, and to provide a clear recommendations on how to support the changes needed to reduce poverty" (Commission for Africa, 2005). This initiative was a clear replication of NEPAD, though "the report for the Commission of Africa was an entirely UK-driven and -controlled initiative" (Porteous, 2008: 61). While the political rhetoric emanating from London was that Blair's government was supportive of African initiatives and regional cooperation, the Commission demonstrated the belief that Africa was unable to work together without Western supervision. As one analysis noted:

> Playing to the industrialized world's guilt complex, the Make Poverty History campaign, Africa Commission and Gleneagles summit all shared one characteristic: the emphasis was on Western, rather than African, action. Top-down, statist, these initiatives were all about donor obligations, pledges and behavior. What they definitely weren't about—despite token references to "good governance" and a supposed pact between North and South—was highlighting the shortcomings of African governments set to benefit from future Western largesse. (Wrong, 2009: 206)

Such initiatives also demonstrated the hubris of Blair in his attempt to rescue a political reputation ruined by the Iraq invasion and the attendant perfidy forever associated with the Bush-Blair axis. Needless to say, the Commission for Africa a.k.a. the "Blair Commission" "was not particularly well received, either in African political circles or by the other donors" and has sunk without a trace (ibid.).

It is true that after the 2005 G-8 Summit, the British seemed to have extracted apparently new commitments. But when one gets behind the spin there were a whole host of difficulties with what was "achieved" at Gleneagles. First, the G-8 initially appeared to have agreed to increase aid by US$48 billion a year by 2010, along with 100 percent of the multilateral debts of the most indebted countries. But later on it emerged that the aid "increase" included money put aside for debt relief. In fact, Russia's increase in aid is made up entirely of debt write offs while one-third of France's aid budget is money for debt relief. In short, the debt deal is not in addition to the aid increase, as Tony Blair asserted, but part of it. And the "100 percent debt write off" applied to only 18 countries, saving only around US$1 billion a year in payments. The deal also involved only those debts to the IMF, World Bank and the African Development Bank.

To compound the problems around New Labour's "passionate" commitment to Africa was the actual goings-on in Whitehall. Under the government, the FCO was systematically sidelined in favor of DFID and political advisers and/or spin-doctors. The lack of expertise on the continent's politics became startling:

> If we want to help Africa effectively, we must try to understand it. That is what the Foreign Office is for but . . . Mr. Brown does not think you need to understand people in order to save them. His cuts in Whitehall have substantially reduced the number of political analysts at the Foreign Office. There are now no desk officers for individual African countries based in London, fewer who know at first hand the difference between Ghana and Gambia or Mali and Malawi. Thanks to Mr. Brown our ability to understand Africa, and therefore to help it, is actually diminishing. (*Observer* [London], January 9, 2005)

Indeed, material I gained under the Freedom of Information Act revealed something quite different from the supposed new emphasis on Africa within Whitehall. While Blair was publicly energetic on the question of Africa, cuts and static budgets within the FCO belied a very different story to Blair's claimed different focus on the continent, as did actual British behavior in Africa. At the time of the "Year of Africa" (2005), the overall budget for the FCO's two Africa Directorates had remained roughly constant and Blair's government had actually cut their staffing levels. Since January 2004 alone, the number of desk officers within the two Africa Directorates had been cut by six, which equaled a staff cut of over 25 percent. It is the Africa Directorate that pays most of the in-country costs of British diplomatic posts in Africa. Such cuts came on top of the fact that Britain was then in the process of actually closing down three British High Commissions/Embassies in Africa: Maseru (Lesotho), Mbabane (Swaziland) and Antananarivo (Madagascar). This was in addition to the British Embassy in Mali that was closed in 2003.

In contrast Britain opened two new embassies, both for strategic reasons, in Conakry (Guinea) and Asmara (Eritrea). The UK had initially opened a permanent mission in Conakry in 2000 in response to developments in Sierra Leone, where Britain was (and is) heavily involved. The Conakry mission was upgraded to an Embassy in September 2003. The Asmara Embassy was opened in March 2002 and is linked to increased concern over terrorist activity in the Horn of Africa. What is interesting is that at the same time that Blair was publicizing his aid commitments to the continent, Britain's diplomatic missions in Africa were told to focus on trade and were to be run on a hub and spoke system, managed regionally. In fact, despite the supposed commitment to Africa as a central piece of British foreign policy, the government put in place plans to cut more than £100 million from the budget of the FCO.

Defenders of New Labour sought to assert that DFID now handled Africa under New Labour, but as Richard Dowden pointed out:

Africa has been handed over to the Department for International Development. The signal that sends to Africa is that Britain treats Africa as a mere recipient of aid, not to be respected as an equal. DFID has huge resources and a guaranteed yearly increase in budget. It also wields the British vote at the two most powerful organizations in the developing world: the IMF and the World Bank. But it also means that British missions in Africa are no longer led by people whose prime job is to watch, analyze and interpret. Britain is now represented by officials primarily concerned with pushing aid into these countries: experts in development, health, education, but with little or no understanding of the history and politics of the country. (*Independent*, [London] July 2, 2005)

It should be noted that New Labour's policies on Africa, particularly when they were mediated through DFID, were influenced by the incessant demands by the aid industry to spend more and more on aid. Issues of governance were shouted down by such actors—note Bob Geldof's dismissive comments that sceptics should "get off the corruption thing" (*Daily Telegraph* [London], June 10, 2005).

"By the turn of the century, Western policy in the developing world was increasingly being set not in ministerial offices but by the NGOs—organizations like Oxfam, Save the Children, Christian Aid" (Wrong, 2009: 205). The problem in this cosy relationship between the likes of Oxfam and Christian Aid and DFID or British policy toward Africa, more generally, is that it is in the institutional and personal interest of the aid industry to ensure continuous giving, regardless of the effectiveness of such assistance:

> Mistakes make no impression on the development aid industry. That is due in part to a lack of suitable quality control procedures. Effective analysis . . . does not give any reliable information about a project's efficiency. This is because the ministry monitors itself. Or it lets its procedures be regulated by "independent assessment researchers", who of course want to get hired again later and therefore allow themselves to make, at best, timid criticism. The main duty of aid workers is to make themselves redundant. Understandably they take their time doing this. (*Der Spiegel* [English edition], July 4, 2005)

According to the Gershon Efficiency Review, a review of efficiency in the British public sector conducted in 2004–5, £422 million of efficiency gains were identified within DFID that the ministry should make. The James Review of Taxpayer Money (2004–5) went further and highlighted *nearly one billion British pounds* (£809 million or US$1.3 billion) within DFID that should be redirected or saved. Of note, the emasculated and weakened FCO had the lowest inefficiencies of any government department. Either way, both reviews highlighted incredible amounts of taxpayers' money that DFID was wasting. Given this milieu, it was no wonder that much of Britain's much-vaunted plans for Africa were misplaced and seemed more headline grabbing than well thought through.

Britain could help through more open trade, addressing illicit capital flight and targeting development assistance in a more coherent and stricter fashion. But these are long-term measures that require political commitments that must last beyond immediate headline-grabbing time frames. It also requires instituting a far more *political* relationship with the aid recipients. Whether New Labour's consultants embedded within the lucrative aid industry and DFID will (or could) recognize this and move beyond the spin and disbursal of more and more cash was a defining issue in Anglo-African relations at the turn of the century.

CHAPTER THREE

Effronterie Magnifique: Between *La Rupture* and *Realpolitik* in Franco-African Relations

It might be argued that France, alone of all ex-colonialists, has actively retained strong political, economic and social ties with Africa. Certainly, the word *la Françafrique* has no equivalent with regard to Britain or Portugal's connections with the continent (Chafer, 2002a). Initially, *la Françafrique* was a positive expression, crafted by President Félix Houphouët-Boigny of Côte d'Ivoire, denoting France's historically close ties with Africa. However, the term in contemporary usage has primarily negative and neocolonial connotations, being reused by the noted French critic of Paris' relations with African autocrats, François-Xavier Verschave, in his book, *La Françafrique, le plus long scandale de la République* (Verschave, 1998).

Indeed, Paris has historically tolerated very high levels of corruption and misman-agement among its client states on the continent, while crafting highly personalized relations with sitting presidents (Manning, 1998). Critics see this as a core element of *la Françafrique*, something redolent of the colonial officer-chief relationships that marked much of the French colonial experience. Arguably, French elites never equated decoloni-zation with retreat nor fully accepted the idea of African independence (Chafer, 2002b). As one analyst noted, "De Gaulle may not have regarded [the] transition to 'international sovereignty' (as he preferred to call it) as fundamentally important; *real* independence in the modern world could be enjoyed only by *ensembles organists,* and he relied upon enlightened self-interest and the pressure of circumstances to keep most African leaders in step" (Hargreaves, 1982: 439). This attitude sprang from the broad French philoso-phy toward colonization, which saw French expansion into the continent as a mission to "civilize" Africa and the Africans—alongside, of course, material exploitation. Furthermore, in foreign policy terms, "Africa was not a matter of foreign policy: it was a part of greater France" (*BBC News*, September 26, 2007) and part of Paris' wish to maintain its international status as a global player and project *la grandeur de la France*.

Intriguingly, after independence thousands of French officials, advisers and teachers ran African government policy behind closed doors, with the result that even today there are more French citizens in postcolonial Africa than there were at independence. This was in stark contrast to the Portuguese (and to a lesser extent, British) experience, which saw a mass evacuation of nationals once the metropolitan flag was lowered. The origins of this reality can be found in the substance of official French attitudes toward the colo-nial venture and the nature of the French state, with its propensity for presidentialism. Indeed, rigid presidential control over African policy has long been utilized to develop strong personal links with many African leaders.

Yet as the 1980s progressed, perceived French national interests redefined Paris' priorities away from its long-established obsession with *la grandeur française*, particularly as this exercise became not only increasingly expensive in financial terms, but also in reputational costs for France. Problems such as economic mismanagement, the debt crisis, chronic political instability and continual conflict and humanitarian crises made French involvement costly (Chafer, 2002a: 354). As the 1990s unfolded, the reputational costs became starkly apparent with the debacle around Rwanda in 1994 and the revelations surrounding various political scandals involving Franco-African ties. Consequently, there has been somewhat of a rethink regarding relations between France and Africa and a move away from some of the more nakedly disreputable activities associated with *la Françafrique* (Cumming, 2000). This has now been included in President Nicolas Sarkozy's wider calls for a "rupture" in French politics and economics, "the shock treatment . . . needed to bring recalcitrant France—wedded to its vast welfare state, creaking with arthritic social hierarchies and laboring under delusions of global grandeur—kicking and screaming into the 21st century" (*Observer* [London], December 23, 2007). *La Françafrique* is ostensibly included in this break from the past. How far this is likely to go vis-à-vis Franco-African relations and whether there is in fact a rupture, rather than a limited rethinking, is the subject of this chapter.

The Background

The discourse of *la mission civilatrice* was a deeply held conviction, both at home among bourgeois circles in France and in French interactions with the colonized, even while camouflaging tangible material French interests (see Chafer and Sackur, 2002). It has been difficult for many elites to move beyond the mindset associated with this discourse, arguably more so than with any other ex-colonial power. In general terms, three key characteristics of French colonial rule may be delineated, all of which in some way were informed by the civilizing discourse (Cumming, 2006).

Foreign policy as an expansion of domestic policy would be the first aspect. Here, continuing domestic policy abroad concerned the creation of a political system based on direct rule but one which promoted the creation of a class of Francophone elites (*évolués*) who might gain access to (limited) positions of power. In doing so, Paris consciously crafted a unique relationship between itself and a cadre of privileged Francophile African notables (Manning, 1998). These "emerging politicians have proved to be elitist, non-radical . . . occasionally anti-colonialist, and almost always pro-French" (Reed, 1987: 289). Note that "in 1965 all heads of state in French-speaking African countries had been members of the French Parliament between 1946 and 1958. Three of them had been members of the French government—M. Senghor in 1955, M. Modibo Keita in 1956 and 1957, and M. Houphouët-Boigny from 1956 to 1958" (Pepy, 1970: 158). This policy of sustaining a slavishly Francophile elite in Africa has historically generally served French interests well, even up until contemporary times. For such African elites, the non-presence of France in Africa has been virtually inconceivable—as Omar Bongo of Gabon once put it, "Africa without France is like a car without a driver. But France without Africa is like a car without petrol" (quoted in *BBC News*, June 13, 2009).

Secondly, France's colonial adventure was a means by which the perceived superiority of French culture and its language as well as the republican values (explicitly universal in nature) of the French Revolution could be distributed. Here, the idea that the French language was the language of liberation and indeed of the progressive Enlightenment project was quintessentially bound up in much of the discourse associated with the civilizing mission: "*La France, c'est la langue française*" as Fernand Braudel once put it. The notion of France's *rayonnement* in the world—the projection of French identity and its ostensible values abroad—is central here (Chafer, 2002a: 345).

Finally, the idea of a Greater French Republic, transnational and ostensibly nonracial in nature, provided a foundation for French colonialism (Cumming, 2005). Here, an assimilationist policy incorporated colonial elites, both culturally and politically, into a notion of a wider France that surpassed the mere boundaries of metropolitan constraints. Citizenship was here deployed as one facet of a greater transnational Francophone community. This sprang from, in the words of one French analyst:

> [T]he philosophical theories of the eighteenth century and the creation of the "*Bon sauvage*" immortalised by Rousseau. As a matter of fact, these doctrines are the expression of very deep feelings, which were born very long ago in the bosom of the French conscience. They show themselves in a very lively curiosity regarding the people and events of other countries, and in a naive and spontaneous sympathy for the stranger whom one wishes to welcome and instruct and save from error by persuading him to adopt our civilization, the highest and the best of all civilizations. (Labouret, 1940: 22)

The civilizing discourse held considerable purchase in the public imagination throughout the nineteenth century, arguably up until France's calamitous defeat in the Franco-Prussian War of 1870–1. Thereafter, the naked materialism of French imperial ventures became ever more apparent and the civilizing discourse proved to be a rather small fig leaf to cover Paris' economic and political ambitions. Exposed as being weak and corrupt, the French elite classes within Paris rapidly realized that colonial territories were a possible quick route to (re)gaining France's status as a great power: colonization "would mark the re-entry of France into international politics" post-1871 (Chipman, 1989: 49).

Such a realization shaped French colonial policy throughout the twentieth century as Paris' colonial possessions, particularly those in Africa, were deemed vital for French aggrandizement and even, its self-image. This was particularly so after the Second World War, which saw France's speedy surrender to the Germans, the humiliation of the *l'occupation allemande* and the (arguably worse) humiliation of having to be rescued by the Anglo-Saxons. Africa provided a possibility for Paris' elites to psychologically rehabilitate themselves—as Gaston Monnerville (the first black man to hold a senior position in the French government) noted back in 1945, "without the empire, France would only be a liberated country today. Thanks to its empire, France is a victorious country" (quoted in Ela Ela, 2000: 87).

Yet the disjuncture between the self-proclaimed grand ideals of "civilization" with the colonial reality was ever more stark, particularly as anticolonial sentiment began to develop in the 1940s and 1950s. Certainly, French law and education were on offer, but in practice were largely unobtainable to most colonial subjects. Meanwhile, the promise of a transnational French community via actual citizenship was predicated on outright collusion and loyalty to Paris. The status of becoming an *évolué* necessarily involved a rejection and betrayal of one's own indigenity, something which became less and less palatable to some Francophone African leaders as African independence moved inexorably forward in the 1950s and 1960s.

One means to manage this problem and continue the intimacy deemed as a characteristic feature of Franco-African ties was to reconstitute relations through the fostering of compliant local elites who were prepared to maintain intimacy with France in exchange for French aid and military backing. Thus as it became clear that Africa was heading toward a postcolonial future, in 1958 President Charles de Gaulle offered a choice to Paris' territories: the (in)famous *Oui ou Non* ultimatum. Yes to the continuation of the status quo of French custodianship of international affairs, or total independence. Only Guinea, under Sékou Touré, rejected de Gaulle's referendum option of "partnership." "We would rather have poverty in freedom than riches in slavery," Touré told de Gaulle prior to the vote, provoking the French leader to storm off in a rage (forgetting his kepi in the process). Guineans then voted overwhelmingly in a referendum to go it alone and for a total break with France. Guinea's stance inured the wrath of Paris, and de Gaulle ordered all French nationals to leave Guinea with all their technical files, surveys and logistic documents. French expertise and assistance rapidly disappeared— even telephone cords were ripped out of the walls. The lesson had been taught (see Schmidt, 2007: 170–2).

The rest of France's colonial empire in Africa thereafter subscribed to the "partnership" being offered, signing up to various *accords de coopération*. Hence the situation continued generally to Paris' advantage: the agreements signed between Paris and its African clients reified existing ties with France and fostered a strong form of dependency, while granting French interests privileged access to markets and raw materials in Africa. Any African leader who sustained this relationship could expect French support. For instance, early on in the postcolonial period, the strongly pro-French president of Gabon Leon M'ba was overthrown in 1964 in an army coup, which aimed to restore parliamentary democracy (M'ba had sought to entrench himself with French-style presidential powers). "Although this popularly supported military intervention had been quickly and bloodlessly successful, it was immediately reversed, without even an official Gabonese request for assistance, by French troops flown in from Dakar and Brazzaville. Once back in power, M'ba was more repressive than ever. Months of student and labor demonstrations followed, though to no avail, and Gabon has been 'tranquil' ever since" (Reed, 1987: 283). Again, the lesson had been taught. In fact, between 1962 and 1995, there were 19 military interventions in Africa by Paris "to protect French nationals," i.e. quell coup attempts against pro-French governments (Chafer, 2002a: 345–6).

In turn, those who sought to question or overturn French-sanctioned arrangements in Africa were ruthlessly dealt with: Félix-Roland Moumié, a Cameroonian Marxist leader, was assassinated in Geneva in 1960 by French secret services, while Outel Bono, Chadian nationalist and opponent of the staunchly pro-French government in N'djamena, was assassinated in Paris in 1973 with the complicity of French agents. French vengeance against Guinea has already been noted. One commentator linked much of this initial milieu to de Gaulle's character and the legacy it left in French political circles:

[De Gaulle was] the incarnation of the father image—severe, demanding obedience, and dependable. His "children" knew that if they obeyed the rules, they would be compensated; and if they revolted, punishment was to be expected. The caricature of the obedient son was, of course, Jean-Bedel Bokassa, who openly referred to de Gaulle as his father and cried at the General's funeral. The rebel member of the family was Sekou Touré of Guinea; he was to be punished. (Golan, 1981: 6)

Those who stayed within the family often seemed to have a genuine affection for de Gaulle. Famously, when de Gaulle died, Central Africa's Jean-Bedel Bokassa lamented that "I lost my natural father when I was a child and now it's the turn of my true father, General de Gaulle . . . All Central Africans today feel like orphans" (cited in Titley, 2002: 67). Later, at the graveside of de Gaulle, "Bokassa was in a state of obvious emotional distress, and his distraught weeping was a source of widespread embarrassment. 'I lost my Papa', he was heard to sob repeatedly. Madame de Gaulle was particularly exasperated by his performance" (ibid.). Tellingly, it is utterly inconceivable that any African leader would respond so hysterically to the death of *any* British prime minister.

Presidentialism and Policy

The privileged position of the president within the French political system has histori-cally engendered a highly personalized tone in French links with Africa. Under constitu-tional provisions, foreign policy falls under the president's domain, and African policy, in particular, has traditionally come under the exclusive control of the presidency: "Africa policy has always been considered the *domaine reservé* of French presidents" (Medard, 2008: 316) and the president has exercised this prerogative with the assistance of a special bureau known as the *Cellule Africaine de l'Elysée*. Notably, only the President has "the power to dispatch regular . . . troops overseas without reference to parliament or min-isters" (McNulty, 1997: 6), something which has particular resonance vis-à-vis France's African policies where military interventions in support of loyal regimes were a distinc-tive hallmark throughout much of the postcolonial era (Utley, 2002).

In fact, the French political system has helped facilitate the sort of relations that we witness in *la Françafrique* as "the French political system, which was transplanted to its African colonies, is a centralized system . . . When exported to French Africa, this system has meant that in many states a small, tight group holds all the strings of power. It has also meant that one well-placed adviser can have a powerful influence on developments" (Golan, 1981: 7). For decades this one person was Jacques Foccart, who was chief adviser for Africa policy during the rule of de Gaulle (1958–69) and Georges Pompidou (1969–74) and held special advisory roles under François Mitterand between 1986 and 1988 and Jacques Chirac between 1995 and 1997 (Foccart died in 1997). Arguably, Foccart was the epitome of the "special" way France did business in Africa. As Medard (2008: 316) explains:

> [The] patron-client system was institutionalized through a highly differentiated for-mal structure, articulated through an informal and covert substructure of networks (*réseaux*). *Françafrique's* formal structure was based on a certain number of supports: the presidency; the Ministry of Co-operation; technical assistance and cooperation agreements (both civilians and military); the CFA (*Communauté Financière Africaine*) franc monetary zone; and later, the Franco-Africa Summit.

As noted above, French personnel in Africa actually *increased* postindependence. "During the first decade of independence, the immediate entourage of most Francophone leaders included many Frenchmen in key positions—chief of cabinet, private secretary, bodyguards. In some countries this is still a reality" (Golan, 1981: 6). Furthermore, with the creation of the Ministry of Cooperation in 1961, planned to oversee Paris' policies in Africa post-decolonization, the presidency found a way to evade—if not marginalize— the Foreign Ministry at the Quai d'Orsay and "continue its peculiar form of personalized diplomacy with African autocrats" (Adebajo, 1997: 148).

It was only really with the end of the Cold War that this cozy arrangement came under threat and French policy toward Africa was particularly scrutinized by French opinion. Indeed, once the Cold War ended, the guarantees that Paris had afforded its clients began to look rather dubious and it became ever more apparent to many on the continent that "France's Africa policy generally failed to advance the conditions of African peoples" (Utley, 2005: 27). According to Medard (2008: 317), the "system of Franco-African relations, as set up by de Gaulle and Foccart, survived under succeeding French presidents and political majorities, from the political right and the left, without fundamental changes, until 1994, when this relationship went through a deep crisis which brought about some transformation."

Civil society organizations in both Africa and France began to critique French policy in Africa, receiving major boosts from Paris' support for the genocidal regime in Rwanda in 1994 and by France's staunch support for Zaïre's Mobutu up until the very end of his calamitous regime. French support for Mobutu discredited Paris. Indeed, "events in Zaïre have produced a triple failure for France: tactically because Mr. Kabila was backed by the United States and Anglophone African countries, morally because France had given the impression of supporting the discredited Mobutu to the end, and geo-politically because Zaïre was an essential element in the French presence on the continent" (Gregory 2000: 441).

That developments in Rwanda and Zaïre between 1994 and 1997 were seen by many French politicians and diplomats as evidence of an "Anglo-Saxon conspiracy" against France, part of an ostensible plot to develop a sphere of influence extending from Ethiopia and Eritrea via Uganda, Rwanda and Zaïre to Congo-Brazzaville and Cameroon, indicated just how archaic the attitudes of Paris elites were with regard to Africa (Huliaras, 1998). That the "Fashoda syndrome" (a knee-jerk tendency to assert French influence in Africa where British influence is seen on the rise) could result in Paris siding with the *genocidaires* was clearly deeply problematical.[1]

French civil society activists demonstrated against what they saw as the sizeable gap between France's rhetoric about its universal republican values and the considerable reality of a naked pursuit of perceived French national interest. Domestic outrage added to the pressure on Paris, with the Elf corruption scandal being most notable. The scandal in France revealed that "annual cash transfers totaling about £10 million [$5 million] were made to Omar Bongo, Gabon's then president, while other huge sums were paid to leaders in Angola, Cameroon, and Congo-Brazzaville. The multimillion dollar payments were partly aimed at guaranteeing that it was Elf and not US or British firms that pumped the oil but also [at] ensur[ing] the African leaders' continued allegiance to France" (*Guardian* [London], November 13, 2003).

Exposed, Paris became diplomatically and militarily isolated and, arguably more importantly, exhausted at the political and economic cost of repeated interventions to save the necks of some pretty disreputable allies on the continent. In addition, new economic rivals such as the Americans and Chinese gradually expanded into Africa, with both American and Chinese companies even exploring links with Angola and Gabon, key oil-rich states generally held to be within French spheres of influence. As a result, France simply could no longer uphold its supremacy within Francophone Africa as an unquestioned feature of continental politics (Golan, 1981).

Partial Reform

The above conditions stimulated a *partial* reform in French ties to Africa. A new generation of leaders in Paris in the 1990s saw clearly that France's African policies needed a reformation and were repelled by some of the relationships that had long marked out Franco-African ties. One consequence of this attempt to partially reform ties was that the Ministry of Cooperation (a nest of old guard Africa hands in Paris) was incorporated into the Ministry of Foreign Affairs in 1998. "This was of great symbolic value. It meant that Francophone Africans had lost their privileged ministry" (Medard, 2008: 318). Revealingly, Jacques Chirac had previously blocked his prime minister Alain Juppé when the latter had sought to integrate the Ministry of Cooperation into the Ministry of Foreign Affairs. A compromise was arrived at whereby the ministry was not simply absorbed into the Quai d'Orsay but retained a position in the Cabinet through the Minister for Cooperation and through *La Francophonie* (Kroslak, 2004).

From this emerged a relatively new Africa policy that avoids bilateral structures in favor of multilateral military cooperation, both with international forces and African regional organizations. The symbolic generational change crystallized by the assumption to power of Nicolas Sarkozy in 2007, someone who by no means is a member of the old political class and who has no attachment to the notion of *la Françafrique* is also seen as important in this regard (Touati, 2007). After all, "the new generation of [French] politicians haven't the same contacts and will approach Africa with less emotion and more economic considerations" (*Daily Telegraph* [London], February 19, 2007).

Indeed, while still interior minister, Sarkozy had "called for a more transparent relationship between France and Africa instead of the 'unofficial networks' which used to exist" (*BBC News*, May 19, 2006). Addressing an audience in Benin, Sarkozy asserted that "We have to build a new relationship, cleaner, free of complexes, balanced, clear of the dregs of the past and of obsolescent ideas that remain on both sides of the Mediterranean" (ibid.). Sarkozy's secretary of state for cooperation Jean-Marie Bockel later announced that "*La Françafrique* is moribund. I want to sign its death certificate" (quoted in Shaxson, 2008: 2). Yet the age-old patterns of personal relationships, deeply rooted via informal linkages remain, maintaining at least a vestige of the neocolonialism that has so long marked out French relations with the continent. In fact, it is precisely these networks of client states between Paris and many of Africa's leaders that is the most enduring political aspect of France's colonial legacy in Africa and that has permitted France to hold on to the myth that it is a world power (Chafer, 2002b).

The Enduring Ties

France's political elites have in recent times sought to publicly distance themselves from the sort of notorious relationships that are so resonant with the concept of *la Françafrique*. "*Adieu Afrique*" was the term deployed in the late 1990s to depict the ongoing institutional reforms at the Cooperation Ministry, as it was reduced and French troop levels in Africa were cut by 40 percent. However, actually dissolving the personalized ties and recrafting them into something more respectable has been problematic and in fact much of the substance of the relationships has endured, irrespective of which political party is in office. As one commentator has asserted, the reality is that the logic of *la Françafrique* continues to function even when French officials claim it has been abandoned (Touati, 2007).

One way in which this has continued despite the promise of reform is through the long-established semi-formalized institutions, which act as a structure for intense clientelistic relations that maintain the neocolonial relationships. French semiformal institutions facilitate a mechanism for patron-client associations that sits side by side with the formalized expressions of state power, such as the military (Charbonneau, 2006). Throughout the postcolonial era, actors with intimate ties with Africa circumvented official diplomatic channels and operated directly out of the president's office, answerable only to him. Tellingly, prior to the Ministry of Cooperation being downgraded, the Ministry's budget was subject neither to parliamentary scrutiny nor public debate—it was merely approved by the National Assembly. In constructing these semiformal links, sympathetic African elites were nurtured and protected and in turn guaranteed French capitalist interests, clearing the way for French corporations to have priority access to energy and primary materials. Such behind-the-scenes practices served French interests well, successfully replacing the formalized (but rigid) colonial institutions of domination with something far more flexible, but equally capable of enabling Paris to maintain its control over Francophone Africa.

What is of great interest is that such informal and semiformal institutions have proven to be incredibly quick to recover and flexible when under attack, precisely because they are not governed by any accountability that other arms of the state must operate under. Consequently, the reduction of the Cooperation Ministry changed but never fundamentally destabilized the personalized nature of Franco-African relationships. Indeed, President Chirac maintained his own set of personalized ties with Africa relatively unscathed, even after promising reform and even after a wave of scandalized French public opinion demanded reform. According to one analysis, "the most enthusiastic proponents of *Françafrique* were François Mitterrand and Jacques Chirac. Both paid lip service to human rights in Africa and withdrew troops that had become too expensive to maintain. But talk of normalization and clean government was just that" (Astier, 2007: 9).

Initiatives to reform French policy toward Africa very early on were derailed and tepid. At the Franco-African summit in La Baule in 1990, President Francois Mitterrand had grandly declared that "French aid will be lukewarm towards authoritarian regimes and more enthusiastic for those initiating a democratic transition" (Martin, 1995: 14). Given Paris' historic ties with some of the worst regimes in Africa, this initially appeared to be revolutionary—a stance dubbed "Paristroika" by one analyst (Adebajo, 1997: 148). But, in fact, under Mitterand (and later Chirac) French support for liberal democracy was indifferent—Chirac in fact considered democracy to be a "luxury" that Africans could ill-afford and declared himself in favor of one-party regimes in Africa (Cumming, 1996: 457). After all, "French leaders do not see why they should run the risk of losing a friendly strongman in exchange for an unfriendly democrat" (Medard, 2008: 325).

Notably, Bernard Debra, minister of cooperation, also asserted that "democratization in Africa leads to instability and institutional weakness. We must therefore encourage, assist, and help stabilize those regimes and leaders who are progressing on the path to democratization *at their own pace*" (quoted in Martin, 1995: 17–18, emphasis added). Reflecting on his speech regarding Paris' supposed new policies linking aid and democracy, Mitterrand in fact cynically exclaimed that his speech at La Baule changed nothing with regard to Franco-African ties (Bayart, 1998: 264).

Yet with the emergence of a new generation of political leaders in France, a process of adaptation instead of the promised meaningful change in Franco-African ties has become apparent. During the presidential elections of 1997 it was noteworthy that "neither Ségolène Royal nor Nicolas Sarkozy . . . [had] the same affection or regard for Africa" (*Daily Telegraph* [London], February 19, 2007). Ségolène Royal (herself born in Senegal), felt compelled to say that "*En privilégiant systématiquement les amitiés personnelles au détriment de l'intérêt général, la pratique présidentielle a terni l'image de notre pays, qui se trouve associé dans l'esprit des Africaines et des Africains aux régimes les plus contestables du continent*" (By favoring personal friendships to the detriment of the general interest, the presidential practice has tarnished the image of our country, which is associated in African minds with the most questionable regimes on the continent) (*Témoignages chrétiens* [Paris], February 15, 2007).

Such a milieu has led to some confusion for the remains of *la Françafrique* complicate—and often block—new policy principles. Consequently, it might be said that currently, "France is caught in a middle ground between the vestiges of neo-colonial paternalism and new ideas for recasting its military role and 'Europeanizing' aspects of is relations with the continent" (*Financial Times* [London], December 2, 2005). "Africa experts say France is suffering from a 'lack of direction' on the continent [and] 'There is a crisis of confidence in France about what to do about Africa,' said Tom Cargill, manager of the Africa Project at Chatham House in London" (*Daily Telegraph* [London], February 19, 2007).

The long-established links have however in fact made sure that *la Françafrique* has continued to exist. Indeed, though President Sarkozy operates within a milieu where Paris' foreign policy has had to adapt to transformations in Africa, his stance on the continent is not especially original. Sarkozy has in fact asserted that the old discredited personal networks are not fully comprehended by the new African and French generations and that "France does not have the intentions or the influence it is credited with," as if Paris is some sort of innocent bystander wrongfully accused of crimes it has not committed (*Business Day* [Johannesburg], February 29, 2008). Instead, it is clear that Sarkozy has not sought any radical change in Paris' foreign relations with Africa; only incremental change has been adopted, something that was in any case a development that can be traced back to the 1990s. Two elements of this are the growing Europeanization of France's external ties and the hardening of positions vis-à-vis African immigration into the French mainland.

The Europeanization of French Foreign Policy

Beginning in the 1990s, French policymakers moved toward a multilateralization of its Africa policy, recognizing the increasing costs. Subsequently, Paris has endeavored to distribute the risks involved in intervention, as well as the expenditure, and this will likely have important ramifications for future French actions in Africa. Indeed, as part of this move, Sarkozy has sought to advance the development of the European Union's military capacity as a major plank of his broader foreign policy. This new commitment to multilateral military intervention under Sarkozy can be seen by the fact that in contemporary times, French intervention operates under the sponsorship of the European Union (EU) or UN, as exemplified by French involvement in Chad and the Democratic Republic of the Congo (DRC). This development is a sign of France's relative decline as a military and economic power (witness the structural problems associated with the French economy). Paris has thus moved toward a role that hopes to maintain some influence while cutting actual French expenses. Indeed, "involving Europe in Africa has the advantage, for France, of sharing the aid burden while maintaining French influence" (Medard, 2008: 320). It is also a means to relegitimize French military activity in Africa after the Rwandan debacle of 1994 (see Charbonneau, 2006).

While Paris has sought after endeavors where it might retain some authority and influence (the EU being a prime example), the overall move toward a multilateralization and Europeanization of its policies in Africa will possibly limit future French maneuverability on the continent. One example might be witnessed in the fact that the introduction of the European Monetary Union has obliged budget cuts, limiting the total amount of aid France can dispense to the African continent. Another example was the emergence of an EU Common Foreign and Security Policy which in 2002 meant that France felt obliged to support an EU-wide suspension of aid to Togo's autocratic regime—a regime that had hitherto enjoyed French protection for decades.

In the context of traditional Anglo-French rivalry on the continent (a rivalry that stimulates more excitement in Paris than it ever does in London), France has also attempted to develop stronger relations with Britain as a means to advance cooperation on African affairs and to draw Britain into a greater willingness to commit to a strengthening of the EU's ability to project itself abroad. The decision in March 2009 by Sarkozy for France to rejoin the North Atlantic Treaty Organization (NATO) as a full member reflects the desire by Paris that fellow European members should reexamine the way that they can develop the EU's collective capability to act. This stance stands in contrast to Jacques Chirac's policies that promoted a particularly strong divergence from the United States in foreign policy, ostensibly in the furtherance of a multipolar world but in reality as a means to continue the Gaullist myth of France as a global player of import.

It might be argued that Sarkozy the pragmatist has recognized this reality. For instance, the first full defense review for 14 years has taken place under Sarkozy and the principle underpinning this review was that policy had to be henceforth made according to needs and *not* habits, though—for now—"ties of history [may] keep French soldiers in Africa" (*Economist* [London], January 17, 2008). A decision to renegotiate France's various defense agreements with former African colonies has been described as the "strongest signal yet" that Sarkozy will change Paris' posture toward the continent (*Financial Times* [London], February 28, 2008). In addition, Sarkozy has asserted that all the defense agreements will be made publicly available—a dagger at the heart of the secretive and corrupt nature of *la Françafrique*.

As mentioned above, France is now moving toward a multilateral approach toward African problems within the framework of the EU. This is not to say that old habits die hard: the direct intervention in Côte d'Ivoire in 2002 was certainly reminiscent of the old days. And while 300 French troops remain stationed in the Central African Republic (CAR) officially to "stabilize the region" and help resolve the Darfur conflict, Paris' support for its client in the form of President François Bozizé is a key factor in explaining the French military presence (Hansen, 2008). Indeed, as one report noted:

> The French government says it is in the CAR because it signed a military agreement back in the 1970s to protect the country from external aggression. The rebellions in the north are, they say, supported by Sudan—so this counts . . . But I couldn't find anyone in the CAR—not a single person, not even the most pro-French—who thought Sudan had anything to do with the rebels. The motives for this war are . . . drenched in dollars and euros and uranium. The overarching goal is to take African resources and funnel them towards French corporations . . . The CAR itself is a base from which the French can access resources all over Africa. That is why it is so important. They use it to keep the oil flowing to French companies in Chad, the resources flowing from Congo, and so on. And of course, the country itself has valuable resources. CAR has a lot of uranium, which the French badly need because they are so dependent on nuclear power. At the moment they get their uranium from Niger, but the CAR is their back-up plan . . . also a lot of this money has been funneled, through corruption, straight back into the French political process. Say somebody needs a road built here in the CAR. The French government will insist on a French company—and the French company back home donates a lot to the "right" French political party. (*Independent* [London], October 5, 2007)

That Paris has been successful in portraying its role in the CAR as somehow connected to Darfur—and then linking this to the EU's own policy goals vis-à-vis Sudan reflects a wily approach very much fitting with the old traditions of *la Françafrique.*

It appears that French military policy toward Africa remains in a state of flux with contending trends pulling in different directions. This might be summarized as an emerging European and multilateral identity in contestation with the resilience of *la Françafrique.* The unresolved nature of this struggle was illustrated in 2007 with the deployment of 3,000 EU troops to Chad and CAR. The military force was half French and came on top of extant French troops in the region supporting the government of Chad. So, is the European Union Force (EUFOR) really a mission to protect Darfurian refugees, as well as people displaced by the rebel insurgency in Chad and northern CAR, or is it a projection of de facto French influence utilizing the cover (and budget) of the EU?

Such questioning became intense when, days before the first EUFOR units were set to deploy, Chadian rebels crossed over from bases in Sudan and besieged the presidential palace in N'Djamena. Sarkozy calculated that the EU mission in Chad depended on French troops keeping President Déby in office (Hansen, 2008). Thus the assault was eventually defeated with French medical, logistical and surveillance support. Because French troops had not engaged Chadian rebels directly, Sarkozy highlighted French "restraint" and argued that it represented an unprecedented change in French policy. The EUFOR contingent was compelled to postpone its deployment, but more importantly, by highlighting Paris' involvement in Chad's internal politics, the question of the mission's impartiality became a focus of criticism "and reinforced the perception among critics that EUFOR Chad amounts to a French operation camouflaged in EU colors" (quoted in Grunstein, 2008).

One member of the European Parliament dubbed EUFOR and others that preceded it as "French operations with an EU label," while Jean-Dominique Merchet, military affairs reporter for the French newspaper *Libération*, described EUFOR as "a French operation with European elements, desired by the French, in a French sphere of influence" (ibid.). In response, and echoing Sarkozy's own apparent position, Yves Boyer, deputy director of the *Fondation de Recherche Stratégique*, asserted that "With French unilateral intervention having become politically untenable, it's only natural that the EU help fill that role" (ibid.). Though Sarkozy asserts that Chad is not the "Gaullist action of old" because France had won approval from the United Nations Security Council (UNSC), it does illustrate that long-standing relations are hard to completely break (*Economist*, February 7, 2008).

Though it is clear that Sarkozy recognizes that the days of unilateral military interventions by France are largely over—as one French defense official noted, "there are things one can't do, quite simply"—(ibid.)—Paris does remain committed to playing a leading military role in Africa, albeit one whose political and financial costs are offset by multilateral cooperation. Consequently, Paris will maintain one military base for each strategic region in Africa (Dakar for West Africa, Libreville for Central Africa, Djibouti for East Africa and Réunion for Southern Africa). Ultimately, Sarkozy has stated that France no longer has any compelling reason to keep armed forces based in Africa and that Africa must soon take responsibility for African security issues (*BBC News*, February 28, 2008). That the reason why France maintains French forces in Africa may not actually have much to do with African security issues per se is something that is usually left unsaid (N'Diaye, 2009).

Immigration and Africa

Illegal immigration into France from the developing world, particularly Africa, has become a pressing domestic issue for any French policymakers. Unassimilated Muslim youth from the Maghreb combined with waves of sub-Saharan migrants have made immigration a major political topic. During the presidential elections, Sarkozy ran in part as an anti-immigrant candidate, stating that France was "exasperated by uncontrolled immigration" (*BBC News*, April 2, 2007). Indeed, Sarkozy believes that the "youth of Africa" are a big problem for France and Europe as a whole, as "no European country will be able to stand up to [the immigration] challenge if Africans continue to believe that their economic salvation lies in Europe" (Sarkozy, 2007: 196).

As soon as Sarkozy assumed office, he announced that his government was preparing a major reform of France's immigration policy, linking future cooperation from Paris with African capitals with the issue of Africa's brain drain and the notion of "co-development" whereby immigrants should be active in promoting the development of their own countries of origin. That African migrants do not necessarily share this vision, but rather simply wish to move to France for a better life, i.e. escape and discard their own countries of origin, may be a problem for Sarkozy.

In October 2008, the EU, under French influence and largely with France's input, adopted a new immigration pact (the European Pact on Immigration and Asylum) that sought to tailor EU policies to meet labor needs within the Union while clamping down on illegal immigrants. French Immigration Minister Brice Hortefeux sought cooperation from African states, arguing that "A policy on migration cannot be defined without or against Africa, but rather with Africa" (*AFP* [Paris] November 25, 2008). As part of the pact, cooperative programs against illegal immigration and development programs to create work opportunities for Africans in Africa were central. Getting the immigration pact voted through was a priority for the French EU presidency, which ended on January 1, 2009.

Under Sarkozy, Paris has already signed accords with Gabon, Senegal and other African countries, which allows for the repatriation of illegal migrants. While there remain limits to the effectiveness of such policies, what are important are the ramifications for Franco-African ties. The "special relationship" between Africa and the French "motherland" is clearly under strain as mass immigration has stimulated a backlash against the very notion of a seamless *la Françafrique*. How this will in future affect African feelings toward France and how this may complicate French interests in Africa is something that observers will be analyzing. Certainly, the days of a cozy relationship where Africans could flit back and forth to Paris—and identified themselves as *Français noirs*—seems to be over.

French Economic Interaction with Africa

Under Sarkozy, there has been an expressed desire to alter the corrupt relationships that have often characterized Franco-African commercial ties. Yet powerful French capitalist interest will resist such a move. It is true that some French actors have abandoned the old informal networks in Africa, deeming the potential risks as just too high to rationalize the investment. In fact, some French companies are no longer that interested in African markets—over the past 15 years French investment in Africa has fallen and the formerly omnipresent French neocolonial capitalist networks have been increasingly displaced (Touati, 2007). China for one has replaced a great deal of former French commercial interests. The wave of liberalization and privatization that the WTO has demanded has made many African economies no longer the captive markets they once were to French business interests; competition is now displacing a great deal of French commercial concerns. In contrast to the past, in contemporary times, few French corporations have a specific African strategy.

This is remarkable, given that Paris is the architect of perhaps the strongest practical links between Africa and Europe: the *Communauté Financière Africaine* (CFA franc), the currency of Francophone Africa. Numerous Francophone African countries relied upon a stable, convertible currency linked to and backed by the French treasury from 1948 to 1994. When it was launched in 1948, the CFA franc was worth 50 to the French franc; it remained unchanged until the 1994 devaluation by 50 percent, to 100 to the franc.

According to one commentary, the devaluation "represent[ed] a shift in French Africa policy away from its former colonies and toward a more pragmatic, commercial approach" (*Independent* [London], January 12, 1994). Previously, African countries using the CFA could obtain foreign exchange easily while the high fixed exchange rate meant that French imports were relatively cheap—something which was widely appreciated by Paris' clients in various African capitals anxious to gain luxury goods, but disadvantageous for any country hoping to engage in the export of commodities. Furthermore, "French business clearly benefited from the CFA and discouraged competition in Africa from businessmen from other countries . . . [while] the chief advantage to the French government, or at least the presidency, has been political. With 14 African countries clinging to its skirts, France could claim to be a world power with an influence far beyond Europe" (ibid.).

Pressure for devaluation of the CFA came from the IMF and the World Bank, eased by the emergence of the new generation of French political leaders not so enamored of French taxpayers subsidizing corrupt autocrats. With the IFIs pushing for structural adjustment policies, a government in France unwilling to bestow unlimited largesse on its allies in Africa and the implications of the scrapping of the French franc to be replaced by the euro, something had to give.

In fact, only oil and telecommunications underpin most French business interests in Africa—and both are highly susceptible to competition, particularly in a liberalized business environment. However, this competition has in part stimulated a diversification of French business interests beyond the old Francophone markets—again something that may weaken la Françafrique. For instance, France Telecom aims to double its African subscribers by 2010, and has been involved in contract bids in Ghana. On the majority of Sarkozy's overseas visits, French business leaders have accompanied him and French commercial diplomacy has been a focus of Sarkozy's administration. This has seen results, with a US$2 billion deal being signed in 2008 by the French industrial group Alstom for a coal-fired power plant in South Africa. South Africa, in fact, has been one focus of Sarkozy's commercial diplomacy—its lack of Francophone credentials notwithstanding. Indeed, the economic outreach to Anglophone territories (as well as Lusophone) is part of a policy to diversify beyond what are often deeply underdeveloped and corrupt Francophone states—which obviously have limits in their usefulness to French commercial interests. In response to the accusation that his administration was neglecting the commercial potential of the continent, Sarkozy indeed pointed to Paris' emerging links with South Africa and rhetorically asked, "who will dare talk about France disengaging from Africa?" (Business Day [Johannesburg], February 28, 2008).

The Response from Francophone Africa

When Sarkozy assumed office as president in May 2007, his reputation as a no-nonsense interior minister, one who had described rioting immigrants (most of them Africans) as voyous (thugs) and racaille (scum) went before him. It might be said that Sarkozy did not initially help matters vis-à-vis his image in Africa. In late July 2007, soon after assuming presidential office, Sarkozy delivered a speech in Senegal in which he referred to "African peasants" and asserted that colonialism was not the cause of all of Africa's problems, nor that Paris had ever exploited Africa. Sarkozy went further and in decidedly nonpolitically correct language asserted:

> The tragedy of Africa is that the African has never really entered into history . . . They have never really launched themselves into the future . . . The African peasant, who for thousands of years has lived according to the seasons, whose life ideal was to be in harmony with nature, only knew the eternal renewal of time . . . In this imaginary world, where everything starts over and over again, there is room neither for human endeavor, nor for the idea of progress . . . The problem of Africa . . . is to be found here.

Africa's challenge is to enter to a greater extent into history . . . It is to realize that the golden age that Africa is forever recalling will not return, because it has never existed. (*The Times* [London], July 27, 2007)

Many African intellectuals greeted the speech with anger and Alpha Oumar Konare, head of the African Union Commission, stated that "This speech was not the kind of [rupture] we were hoping for . . . It reminded us of another age, especially his comments about peasants" (*Business Day* [Johannesburg], July 31, 2007). Although Sarkozy repeatedly asserted in his speech that colonialism had been a "mistake," most African commentaries reacted negatively to the French leader's rhetoric, characterizing it, as Achille Mbembe put it, a "profoundly demeaning representation of the continent by an arrogant former colonial power that has . . . actively stood against the African project of emancipation" (quoted in *Mail and Guardian* [Johannesburg], August 27, 2007).

What was interesting about Sarkozy's 2007 speech was that he had apparently ignored the advice of French experts on Africa and went ahead with comments that he must have known would be poorly received. But equally so, the continuities that Sarkozy's visit to Africa demonstrated must not be obscured by his "straight-talking." For instance, while on the one hand Sarkozy asserted that "One cannot blame everything on colonization—the corruption, the dictators, the genocide; that is not colonization" (*Business Day* [Johannesburg], July 31, 2007), this was said in Libreville, Gabon. This was the same Libreville that was controlled by a corrupt dictator Omar Bongo between 1967 and 2009. It is interesting to note that on the day of Sarkozy's presidential victory in May 2007, Sarkozy spoke to just one foreign leader: Bongo, who remarked on the conversation:

Sarkozy, I know him well. I've already said that he's a boy whom I like a lot. After his victory, he called me to say: Omar, thank you. I congratulated him for having listened to me. In return, he thanked me for certain parts of my advice. (quoted in Shaxson, 2008)

Sarkozy's very visit to Gabon during his first trip to Africa as French president, arguably represented continuity, given that President Omar Bongo was very much of the old school and a "symbol of *Françafrique*" (*BBC News*, September 26, 2007) while his country was dubbed "a neo-colonial enclave of enduring French interest" (Reed, 1987). His death in mid-2009 *may* open up some changes in Franco-Gabonese ties, but one should probably not bet on it. It is interesting here to note that at Bongo's funeral in Libreville on June 16, 2009, not only did Sarkozy attend in person, but so did Bernard Kouchner, the foreign minister, and ex-president Jacques Chirac.

Bongo was in fact the second head of state received at the Elysée Palace shortly after the election of Sarkozy. During his visit to Libreville, Sarkozy was quoted as saying that "*La rupture, cela ne veut pas dire qu'on doit se fâcher avec des amis historiques de la France comme le Sénégal et le Gabon*" (The "rupture" does not mean that we should be angry with historic friends of France, such as Senegal and Gabon) (quoted in Boisbouvier, 2007). This phrase rather neatly fixed the limits of any reformation in Franco-African ties. Thus while African responses to Sarkozy have been mostly negative, the mixed messages that Sarkozy sends to the old guard of African leaders destabilizes any analysis that argues that Sarkozy is seriously interested in dislocating Franco-African ties.

True, Francophone Africa's elites are used to smooth rhetoric and honeyed clichés about Franco-African solidarity and brotherhood and Sarkozy's blunter style obviously injures these sensitivities—the Gabonese government expressed its anger by asserting that "since his arrival as head of France, we hear shots that are contemptuous of Africans [as if they are] vulgar beggars seeking alms without end from France" (quoted in *Reuters* [Libreville], January 18, 2008). But despite such spats, there is little evidence that France under Sarkozy is about to abandon Africa—its elites just do not want Africans to continue to live under the delusion that Europe is their salvation, particularly now that alternative sources of cheap labour can be found in Eastern Europe.

Conclusion

Sarkozy's abandonment of the rhetoric of assimilation is perhaps the most noteworthy aspect of his approach to Africa. Lacking any historical or biographical ties to the continent, Sarkozy is not as emotionally attached to Africa as previous French leaders. The most "Anglo-Saxon" president France has ever known, the pursuit of pure national interest is what motivates Sarkozy, not mythical notions of trans-Mediterranean brotherhood. It seems apparent that the very concept of *la Françafrique* when it pertains to a form of gross dependency on France by African elites is now unattractive. But conversely, when it facilitates the benefits that may be accrued from parts of Africa being within the French sphere of influence, or the continuation of the exploitation of the continent's raw materials, then close ties between Paris and African capitals is desirable.

Traditionally, French leaders have indulged in the Gaullist fantasy that France is a Great Power, and Africa has been an integral element to pursuing this—a "shortcut to international prestige" (Utley, 2005: 26). After all, Africa was the only continent where France could still "change the course of history with a few hundred men," as Giscard d'Estaing's foreign minister Louis de Guiringaud said in 1977 (quoted in Adebajo and O'Hanlon, 1997). Similarly, Jacques Godfrain, ex-head of France's special Ministry of Cooperation with Africa was quoted as stating that France was "a little country, with a small amount of strength [but] we can move a planet because we have relations of friendship and intimacy with 15 or 20 African countries," while François Mitterrand once famously declared that "Without Africa, France will have no history in the 21st century" (both quoted in *Newsweek* [New York], March 30, 1998). Thus extremely close relations—invariably personal in nature—have characterized Franco-African ties at the elite level. This has taken place within the wider context of a major decline in France's global standing, yet "failure notwithstanding, France has been able to hold on to some shreds of empire, especially in Africa, chiefly by learning to play the sly imperial game of indirect rule under its modernized name: independence" (Armah, 1986: 884).

Sarkozy, however, lacks sentimentality and is also evidently more interested in reincorporating France into international affairs as a partner within the transatlantic milieu, rather than as the awkward problem child of Europe. So a relative move away from the mutual dependency between Africa and France—"the family character of relationships between France and French-speaking African states" as one French commentator once put it (Pepy, 1970: 161)—is possible.

However, Sarkozy is also very much focused on perceived French national interests and so will be unlikely to give up the French presence on the continent, with its attendant lucrative investments for French capitalists. This suggests a prolongation of policy based on *realpolitik*, rather than any "rupture" and indicates a degree of continuity. After all, as one analyst remarked over ten years ago, "although camouflaged under the mantle of cooperation, France's Africa policy is, in fact, primarily motivated by a narrow conception of its national interests, and blatantly disregards African concerns and interests" (Martin, 1995: 3). Back in the 1970s, President Valéry Giscard d'Estaing openly admitted vis-à-vis Franco-African ties that "I am dealing with African affairs, namely with France's interest in Africa" (Martin 1995: 6). Thus Sarkozy's pursuit of elite French interests, although perhaps marked with less hypocrisy than the heady days of *la Françafrique*, is a continuation of a long-established trajectory.

Indeed, as new actors emerge in Africa, such as China and India, the increased competition for resources and influence may well spur Sarkozy to pursue engagement with Africa—albeit of a different nature than that typified by the discredited concept of *la Françafrique*. In fact, Gabon's government has warned France that "Africa will undoubtedly find partners more respectful of the dignity of its peoples and the sovereignty of its states" (quoted in *Reuters* [Libreville], January 18, 2008), a thinly veiled reference to China, who many Francophone African countries are increasingly choosing as a preferred partner, to the detriment of France. Such realities introduce new complications for French calculations vis-à-vis Paris' African policies.

The institutional nature of the French state no doubt complicates Sarkozy's ability to show more respect to the *dignité* of Francophone Africa's Big Men. For instance, in May 2009 a French magistrate opened a preliminary investigation into alleged embezzlement by Omar Bongo of Gabon, Denis Sassou-Nguesso of Republic of Congo and Teodoro Obiang Nguema of Equatorial Guinea, following lawsuits brought by the French branch of Transparency International. The Paris prosecutors' office, which answers to the Ministry of Justice, opposed the opening of the case, even though a 2007 French police investigation had found the leaders of the three countries and their relatives somehow owned homes in exclusive areas of Paris and on the French Riviera along with luxury cars, including Bugattis, Ferraris and Maseratis (*BBC News*, May 6, 2009). Bongo and his family alone were found to own 33 properties in Paris and Nice worth an estimated US$190 million. Bongo's bank accounts were subsequently frozen in France following bribery allegations. Of course, Beijing does not pull such judicial stunts—something that many African elites no doubt carefully ruminate upon.

While Sarkozy is scornful of much of the processes that *la Françafrique* generates (unwanted African immigration, corruption and dependency), the history of Franco-African ties does lay the foundations for a continuation of policies that maintain the French presence in Africa at a qualitatively higher level than all other former European colonial nations. Thus despite the rhetoric of a "rupture," it was noteworthy that Jean-Marie Bockel was reported to have complained to *Le Monde* newspaper that "This 'rupture' is taking its time to arrive. There are still too many private interests; too many intermediaries without clear utility; too many parallel networks to allow a clean, uncomplicated partnership of equals" (quoted in Shaxson, 2008: 2). One astute French commentator noted that skepticism about any rupture is realistic and necessary in light of the "unanimous (and suspicious) insistence of French politicians and journalists in telling us that *Françafrique* is over" (Medard, 2008: 322). Ultimately, France needs Africa for its elites' own self-image as important people from an important country, just as much as Africa may (or may not) need France.

Notes

1. In 1898 an Egyptian military post in Anglo-Egyptian Sudan was occupied by a French force from the Congo. This gave rise to a great deal of tension between Britain and France and eventually led to the French forces being forced to withdraw in humiliating circumstances.

CHAPTER FOUR

Back to the Future? The Rising Chinese Relationship with Africa

The expansion of Chinese political and corporate interests into Africa is arguably the most important development for the continent since the end of the Cold War. Official trade figures alone bear testimony to the exponential speed by which the Chinese presence in Africa has grown in recent times. China is now Africa's second largest bilateral trading partner, behind the United States but ahead of both France and the United Kingdom, despite the historic and long-standing relations of France and the United Kingdom with the continent. Published trade figures are indicative of this massive surge in Chinese economic interest in Africa. In 1996, the value of China's trade with Africa was US$4 billion; by 2008, this had grown to US$106.7 billion. Much of this expansion is driven by a desire to obtain sources of raw materials and energy for China's ongoing economic growth and for new export markets for Chinese producers and traders compelled to seek new markets by domestic dynamics within China's economy. Official trade between Africa and China began to noticeably accelerate around 2000—between 2001 and 2006, Africa's exports to China rose at an annual rate of over 40 percent (Wang Jianye, 2007: 5). Politically, Beijing is stepping up its engagement with the continent and in general has been welcomed by most Africans. That the current Chairman of the Commission of the African Union, Jean Ping, is half-Chinese is, anecdotally, emblematic of the burgeoning Sino-African ties.

China's Africa Policies

Domestically, the post-Mao Chinese state has been arguably based on "an unwritten social contract between the party and the people where the people do not compete with the party for political power as long as the party looks after their economic fortunes" (Breslin, 2005: 749). Externally, "foreign policy that sustains an international environment supportive of economic growth and stability in China serves these objectives" (Sutter, 2008: 2). The developing world has long been a particular area where Beijing's foreign political policy has been pursued actively, using the development of "common interests" with the South to raise the global stature of the People's Republic of China and increase Beijing's bargaining leverage with the United States. Economically, Africa has emerged as a relatively important factor in Chinese calculations at multiple levels, whether state, provincial, municipal or individual. Within such calculations, the need to project China's "peaceful development" (*heping fazhan*) provides a broad framework, albeit often constrained and/or frustrated by the actions of China's growing diversity of actors.

Chinese engagement with Africa is long-standing (see Duyvendak, 1949; Hutchison, 1975; Snow, 1988; Han Nianlong, 1990; Taylor, 2006a). Politically, Africa has been diplomatically important for China since the late 1950s when Chinese diplomacy began to emerge from the fall out of the Korean War and the shadow of the Soviet Union. During the early period of Sino-African interaction, China's role was ideologically motivated and included support for national liberation movements as well as direct state-to-state aid, most noticeably with Tanzania (Yu, 1970; 1975). Indeed, by the mid-1970s, China had a greater amount of aid projects in Africa than the United States.

Yet as the Socialist Modernization program picked up under Deng Xiaoping from the late 1970s onwards, there was a concomitant scaling-down of Chinese interest in the continent (see Taylor, 1997). This can in part be explained by the fact that "Africa's failure to develop its economies efficiently and open up to the international market militated against Chinese policy aims, and the increasing extraneous role the continent played in global (read Superpower) geopolitics resulted in a halt to closer Chinese involvement. Essentially, Beijing not only viewed Africa as largely immaterial in its quest for modernization, but also saw that the rationale behind its support for anti-Soviet elements in the continent was no longer valid" (Taylor, 1998: 443–4). In contrast to the past, Chinese ties with Africa were based on the cool realities of trade and profit a.k.a. "socialism with Chinese characteristics" (*Jianshe you Zhongguo tesede shehuizhuyi*).

However, an event and two processes—one within Africa and the other within China—came together to stimulate the current close involvement of Chinese actors in Africa. First, the events of June 4, 1989 in and around Tiananmen Square meant that Beijing underwent a major reevaluation of its foreign policy toward the developing world. While Tiananmen Square resulted in an (albeit temporary) crisis in China's relations with the West, Africa's reaction was far more muted, if not openly supportive: "it was . . . our African friends who stood by us and extended a helping hand in the difficult times following the political turmoil in Beijing, when Western countries imposed sanctions on China" (Qian Qichen, 2005: 200). Indeed, Angola's foreign minister, for example, expressed "support for the resolute actions to quell the counter-revolutionary rebellion" (*Xinhua* [Beijing], August 7, 1989), while Namibia's Sam Nujoma sent a telegram of congratulations to the Chinese army (*Xinhua* [Beijing], June 21, 1989). As one commentator noted, "the events of June 1989 . . . did not affect the PRC's relations with the Third World as it did with the Western world . . . what changed [was] the PRC's attitude towards the Third World countries, which . . . turned from one of benign neglect to one of renewed emphasis" (Gu Weiqun, 1995: 125).

As a result, the developing world was ostensibly elevated in Chinese thinking to become a cornerstone of Beijing's foreign policy. Post-1989 the 1970s rhetoric of China being an "all-weather friend" (*quan tianhou pengyou*) of Africa was dusted off and deployed with vigor and this has remained the case today (Taylor, 2004b). This posture is a reaffirmation of the Five Principles of Peaceful Co-existence, formulated in 1954 and setting out the guidelines for Beijing's foreign policy and its relations with other countries. These Five Principles are mutual respect for each other's territorial integrity, nonaggression, noninterference in each other's internal affairs, equality and mutual benefit, and peaceful coexistence. Thus Chinese policymakers have returned to their roots in reasserting what is in fact an old theme in Beijing's foreign policy.

The two macro-processes were first, as Africa's economic reform programs gained momentum in the 1990s, Beijing began to believe that the macroeconomic situation in Africa was taking a favorable turn with resultant opportunities for Chinese commerce. This analysis was based on the belief that African countries have adopted a set of active measures to push forward the pace of privatization, opening up international trade and reform based on bilateral and multilateral trade agreements. Beijing has sought to take advantage of these developments in Africa and has officially encouraged joint ventures and economic cooperation at multiple levels. This couples with the belief held by many Chinese manufacturers and entrepreneurs that the types of goods (household appliances, garments and other domestic products) which Chinese producers produce and sell have immense potential in Africa, where the economy is not yet as developed as in Western nations and where the consumers are perceived to be more receptive to the type of inexpensive products that Chinese manufacturers typically produce. That the domestic markets of many African countries are relatively small and that there is relatively little competition means that market share can be large almost from day one of operations. Additionally, Africa is perceived by both the Chinese government *and* by Chinese companies to be rich in natural resources, particularly in crude oil, nonferrous metals and fisheries.

The above then links up with the second macro-process, namely that China's rapidly developing economy in itself propels Sino-African trade. China's growth in recent years has been extraordinary and needs no rehearsing here. However, what is often overlooked in discussions of Sino-African ties is that the significance of China to Africa has to be appreciated in terms of Beijing's own development trajectory. China's real economic growth—on average just under 9 percent annually for the last 30 years—has been grounded in an export growth averaging over 17 percent. This commerce is based on Chinese factories processing and assembling parts and materials that originate from outside of China. China's leadership is dependent on this high-speed growth continuing as, with the effective abandonment of Marxist ideology, the only de facto thing that legitimates continuing Communist Party rule is economic growth. However, mounting saturation of China's existing export markets as well as a rapid increase in the price of imported raw materials into China (due to mainly Chinese demand which caused the increasing prices) makes Africa more and more important to China's economy. Indeed, as the growth in the worth of Chinese exports decelerates, Beijing has to maintain the growth of its economy through adding more Chinese "content" to its exports (*Business Day* [Johannesburg], February 22, 2007). Getting hold of sources of raw materials is integral to this strategy and where Africa fits squarely into Chinese foreign policy *and* domestic necessities. Indeed, it might be avowed that the importance of Africa to China's own development cannot be overstated.

Fight the Power

Although maintaining good links with Washington is fundamental to Chinese foreign policy, the developing world is becoming more and more important in Chinese policy calculations. Beijing has often expressed concern about the rise of an unchallenged hegemon, maintaining the opinion that in the current international system it is imperative that China and the developing world support each other and work together to prevent the overdomination by this one power. Asserting that respect for each other's affairs and noninterference should be the basis of any new international order is fundamental to this stance, as is a policy of accommodating and hedging with Washington when deemed appropriate (Foot, 2006).

With regard to Sino-African relations, this feeds into the long-held stance by Beijing that it is the leader of the developing world (formerly, the "Third World"). Typically, when in South Africa in early 2007, Hu Jintao remarked that while "Africa is the continent with the largest number of developing countries," "China is the biggest developing country" (*Xinhua* [Beijing], February 8, 2007). This is a familiar theme in Sino-African diplomacy, as is the refrain that "As it is known to all, Western powers, not China, colonized Africa and looted resources there in the history" [*sic*] (*China Daily*, April 26, 2006). Similarly, as former Chinese Foreign Minister Qian Qichen put it, "as developing regions that . . . once suffered the oppression and exploitation of imperialism and colonialism, China and the African countries . . . easily understand each other's pursuit of independence and freedom and . . . have a natural feeling of intimacy"(Qian Qichen, 2005: 200). Such sentiments are utilized to argue that "there is no . . . interest conflicts [*sic*] between China and African countries" (*China Daily*, April 26, 2006). Of course, whether there are in fact "interest conflicts" [*sic*] has animated a growing number of analysts of Sino-African relations.

Paradoxically, as China's leadership increasingly integrate Beijing into the global economy and starts to tentatively play by essentially Western rules, as exemplified by Beijing's membership of the WTO, they have sought to strengthen political ties with various African countries, arguably as, in part, a defensive mechanism, to be deployed against these very same impulses if and when they threaten influential domestic interests. This irony reflects the overall tension in China's diplomatic policy of pursuing both engagement and a certain distant coolness vis-à-vis the global order (Breslin, 2007; Lanteigne, 2008). This, and the notion that China seeks to "restore" its "rightful place" in world politics (Mosher, 2000; Scott, 2007) by being seen as some sort of leader of the developing world, while casting itself as a "responsible power" (*fuzeren de daguo*), is seen by many to be important rationales influencing policy. Certainly, such coalition building can be seen to help explain the recent diplomatic developments in Chinese links to Africa, so graphically exemplified by the Sino-Africa Forums, held in 2000, 2003 and 2006.[1]

Forum on China-Africa Cooperation (FOCAC)

The first Forum met in October 2000 in Beijing and was attended by nearly 80 ministers from 44 African countries. The second ministerial conference was held in Addis Ababa, Ethiopia, in December 2003 and passed the *Addis Ababa Action Plan (2004–2006)*. The FOCAC Summit and the third Ministerial Conference were held in Beijing from November 2006.

The initial meeting essentially had three main objectives. First, the Forum was part of Beijing's overall strategy in its foreign policy to at least rhetorically declare its aim of overhauling the global order and advance a traditional hostility to "hegemony" (Blum, 2003). This domination, dressed up as "globalization" (*qianqiuhua*), is at times seen as detrimental to the autonomy and sovereignty of China and needs careful management (Breslin, 2006). By extension, this applies to the developing world. As the then Chinese Premier Zhu Rongji said at the first Forum, Sino-African ties help "build up our capacity against possible risks, which will put us in a better position to participate in economic globalization and safeguard our economic interests and economic security." They also "improve the standing of the developing countries in the North-South dialogue so as to facilitate the establishment of a fair and rational new international political and economic order" (Embassy of the People's Republic of China in the Republic of Zimbabwe, 2000a).

Such a position is based on the belief that, according to the then minister of foreign trade and economic cooperation Shi Guangsheng, "when the new international economic order has not been established and countries differ considerably in economic development, the benefits of economic globalization are not enjoyed in a balanced way." Consequently, "developed countries are benefiting most from economic globalization; but the large number of developing countries are facing more risks and challenges, and some countries are even endangered by marginalization." As a result, the global community should "give more considerations to the will and demands of developing countries so as to promote the establishment of a fair and rational new international economic order." This can be advanced by developing countries building "a sense of self-protection" (Embassy of the People's Republic of China in the Republic of Zimbabwe, 2000a).

Crucially, China's leadership is intensely suspicious of the West's promotion of human rights and regards such calls as a Trojan horse through which the West might undermine Beijing. Importantly, the perceived Western strategy of "peaceful evolution"· (*heping yanbian*) being exercized on Beijing's political security has been cast—not unreasonably—as being analogous to regime change (Ong, 2007). Chinese policy in this regard has then been to consistently cast talk of liberal democracy and liberal conceptions of human rights (and, occasionally, the environment) as a tool of neo-imperialism being practiced toward both China and the developing world. This falls on many receptive ears in Africa at the elite level and China's policymakers are not unaware of this. This posture has been fairly long-standing and Beijing has long managed to piggyback on the developing world's power of numbers to evade international condemnation.

As part of this, FOCAC serves as a means by which Beijing can advance a position of moral relativism regarding human rights to a mostly sympathetic audience, consolidating its standing within African elite circles. The assertion in the *People's Daily* (October 12, 2000) at the time of the first FOCAC that China and Africa "should . . . enhance their co-operation and consultation in multilateral . . . organizations in order to safeguard the interests of both" is a reflection of this concern. Hence the Beijing Declaration of the FOCAC, released at the end of the meeting, asserted that "countries, that vary from one another in social system, stages of development, historical and cultural background and values, have the right to choose their own approaches and models in promoting and protecting human rights in their own countries" (Embassy of the People's Republic of China in the Republic of Zimbabwe, 2000b). Going further, the Declaration made the claim that "the politicization of human rights and the imposition of human rights conditionalities" themselves "constitute a violation of human rights" and that conditionalities for development assistance which are based on good governance and respect for human rights "should be vigorously opposed." All music to the ears of many African leaders sat in the hall in Beijing no doubt, and all arguably crafted as a means to promote an "alternative" global order.

The outcomes of FOCAC reflect the increased priority China's leadership places on Africa. The summit in late 2006 approved a three-year action plan to forge a "new type of strategic partnership," pledging that China will double aid to Africa by 2009 (to about US$1 billion); set up a US$5 billion China-Africa development fund to encourage Chinese companies to invest in Africa; provide US$3 billion in preferential loans and US$2 billion in preferential buyer's credits to African countries; cancel all debt stemming from Chinese interest-free government loans that matured by the end of 2005 for the 31 highly indebted and least developed countries (LDCs) in Africa that have relations with China (an amount estimated at around US$1.4 billion); further open China's markets to exports from African LDCs by increasing from 190 to 440 the number of products receiving zero-tariff treatment; train 15,000 African professionals, double the number of Chinese government scholarships given annually to Africans (to 4,000) and send 100 senior agricultural experts and 300 youth volunteers; build 30 hospitals, 30 malaria treatment centers and 100 rural schools (*Africa Renewal*, January 19, 2007). Bilateral loans are presumably separate from such an announcement. Whether all of the above materializes will be avidly watched by observers.

Equally, the capacity of the state to execute policies such as encouraging Chinese companies to invest in Africa or even opening up China's markets if and when this might undermine local economic and political interests within China (delaying transport once products reach China, warehousing them interminably, even "losing" them, are all curious possibilities) is a moot point. Having said that, symbolic diplomacy and rhetorical flourishes combined with some actual headline-grabbing initiatives are, like all other countries' foreign policies, integral to Chinese engagement with Africa. But what is important in recognizing the impact of FOCAC is the growing economic imperatives underpinning Sino-African linkages.

Economic Relations

As suggested, the legitimacy of the Communist Party of China (CPC) and its political system is today based upon the CPC's ability to sustain economic growth. Intimately linked to this, Beijing is faced with a long-term decline in domestic oil production (Taylor, 2006b). China's policymakers are actively encouraging national companies to aggressively pursue oil and other natural resources in Africa. China is currently the world's second largest oil importer and the second largest consumer of African resources. The abundance of natural resources in Africa has thus led Chinese corporations to seek long-term deals with African governments in order to ensure continued access to all varieties of raw materials and energy in Africa. As China's national oil companies are largely excluded from the majority of Middle Eastern oilfields and as Beijing wishes to limit vulnerability to the international oil market, there is a policy to encourage investment in Africa, courting states that the West have overlooked. Consequently, this approach toward securing access to African resources is what Zweig and Bi Jianhai have dubbed a resource-based foreign policy, which by its very nature has "little room for morality" (2005: 31). The potential fallouts in terms of China's reputation on the continent that stem from such a milieu has at times damaged China's overall reputation and promoted a growing maturity in policy calculations.

The interest in ensuring its resource security and economic growth through involvement in Africa is by no means restricted to oil, and encompasses all natural resources. From investment in copper in Zambia, platinum interests in Zimbabwe to supporting fishing ventures in Gabon and Namibia, Chinese corporations have vigorously courted and pursued the political and business elite in Africa to guarantee continued access, often lubricated with sweetener deals. One of the benefits of Chinese interest in African resources is that it has dramatically increased demand and has revitalized industries such as Zambia's copper industry. However, the influx of capital into weak and authoritarian governments also has potential for long-term consequences in Africa as leaders may be tempted to neglect necessary reforms, bolstered by newly perceived economic security from Chinese receipts. Yet this is not a problem that can be specifically associated with Chinese engagement with Africa and is in fact intimately linked to the nature of the state in much of Africa. Indeed, in this regard there is a real danger that "China" is being constructed (particularly within Beltway circles in Washington, DC, but also in some African capitals) as some sort of scapegoat for failures that have very little to do with Beijing.

Indeed, on the one hand one must note that with the exception of oil exports to China, Sino-African trade is generally lopsided in favor of Chinese exporters who are penetrating African markets with cheap household products. Such imports into Africa have been criticized as doing little to encourage indigenous African manufacturing. Yet on the other hand, it is the failure of African economies to industrialize and develop postindependence that means that they produce very few processed goods and are a natural target for Chinese exporters.

However, Chinese trade figures with Africa need to be treated with caution. The part played by Hong Kong as a transit point for Chinese imports and exports makes bilateral figures very dubious when estimating the levels of Chinese trade. A huge proportion of Chinese exports are routed through Hong Kong. This is important in calculating bilateral trade figures because whether an export is counted as a Chinese reexport or not obviously has an enormous bearing on trade statistics. In addition, foreign invested firms account for just over half of all Chinese trade, i.e. much of Chinese trade is not actually "Chinese" at all, and if domestic Chinese producers who produce under contract for export using foreign components are included, the figure goes upwards. In actual fact, the majority of Chinese exports are produced by foreign-funded enterprises, often joint ventures but increasingly wholly foreign owned. In addition, "as Chinese producers can claim a 15 per cent VAT rebate for exports, there is an incentive for producers to overstate the value of exports, or even to totally fabricate exports and sell them at home instead" (Breslin, 2007: 107). Any visitor to an African market these days will observe huge amounts of Chinese-made products on sale—that is not in dispute. The specific (and colossal) figures regarding Sino-African trade, provided by Beijing, however do need to be taken under caution.

Complicating this milieu is the fact that much of the products manufactured in China but which are sold in African markets are not actually brought into the continent by Chinese but by African traders. There are now quite elaborate trading networks linking China and Africa and much of this is centered in the southern province of Guandong where a relatively large population of African entrepreneurs now live and make deals. Indeed, in Guangzhou city there is an estimated 20,000 Nigerians alone living and working in the city (*This Day* [Lagos], September 13, 2007). Other African traders have long been established in Hong Kong, primarily based at Chungking Mansions in Tsim Sha Tsui, while Yiwu in Zhejiang Province is now a growing center for export trading to Africa and elsewhere. In fact, Yiwu is perhaps *the* key place where products from China are sold in wholesale quantities to traders from across Africa. African entrepreneurs generally buy in bulk, utilizing Chinese-owned cargo companies, and products are shipped direct to the continent.

The point of the above is crucial: Chinese traders are *not* "flooding" the African market with cheap Chinese goods. Rather, African actors are actively facilitating the penetration of Africa by Chinese-made products. Figures do not exist on what proportion of goods sold in Africa's markets were brought in by Chinese entrepreneurs or by African traders, but information I gleaned in various interviews across Africa and from observations in a variety of African marketplaces suggests that a large percentage was sourced and shipped by Africans. This is somewhat ironic given that condemnation by many African trade unions and civil society organizations of the "Asian tsunami" in cheap products lays the blame squarely on "the Chinese." If the trade pattern between Africa and China is becoming "colonial" in character, it is with the active connivance of many Africans themselves. And as the activities of African entrepreneurs in Hong Kong, Yiwu, Guangzhou, etc. demonstrate, "processes of globalization generate both localized and internationalized networks of relationships that need to be considered alongside the bilateral to gain a full understanding of how best to theorize contemporary Chinese international relations" (Breslin, 2007: 25).

A Chinese Model?

Politically as well as economically, China's presence in Africa has been based on the premise of providing an alternate development model for African states and leaders. According to Naidu and Davies (2006: 80), China is seen as "A refreshing alternative to the traditional engagement models of the West . . . African government see China's engagement as a point of departure from Western neo-colonialism and political conditions." Yet the absolute emphasis China places on respect for state sovereignty and noninterference as an article of faith for the Chinese leadership, as well as a willingness to deal with states ostracized by the West may appear promising to some African leaders, but it profoundly challenges the claimed Western vision of a flourishing Africa governed by democracies that respect human rights and the rule of law and embrace free markets. A common bond in their desire to overcome and shake off the legacy of colonialism has further united Chinese and African political interests, evinced in a portrayal of the former colonial powers as a common enemy.

In countering the Western promotion of neoliberal reforms in Africa, China has argued that this imposition of Western ideology on African states is a form of neo-imperialism. Moreover, China's state-directed model of development provides an appealing alternative to leaders when neoliberal economic reforms have not, for a variety of reasons, delivered their promised economic revival. A strong state also, of course, serves as a shield for authoritarian leaders to maintain tight control over economic policy and continue their patronage networks.

Through political and business summits such as the various Sino-African forums, as well as state visits by high-ranking Chinese political officials, Beijing symbolically accords Africa equal diplomatic status with the dominant powers. For instance, as an emblematic gesture, it has become a tradition that the first overseas visit that China's foreign minister undertakes each year is to Africa. Equally, African elites are deeply appreciative of being given the red carpet treatment whenever they turn up in Beijing. A research trip I took to Beijing in September 2007 coincided with the visit of Chad's president and it was quite revealing the way the visit was covered (top billing on Chinese television and in the newspapers) and how the Chadian flag was prominently displayed around Tiananmen Square.

In contrast, when an African leader visits London or Washington, unless they are from South Africa or Egypt or one of the few states deemed important, they are barely afforded a few minutes and even then they are more likely to be belabored for their numerous chronic failures in governance, than they are to be toasted as "dear friends" and, importantly, credible statesmen. China's leadership realizes this and thus expends energy on massaging the egos of Africa's leaders. And this pays off. Beijing has been successful in gaining African support at institutions such as the UN, where the vote of the African bloc has allowed China to block resolutions on domestic human rights abuses. African support also, of course, helped Beijing in its campaign to host the 2008 Olympics.

Symbolic diplomacy, defined as the promotion of national representation abroad, has become an increasingly important component of Chinese foreign policy in Africa and elsewhere (see Kurlantzick, 2007). As a developing nation Beijing's policymakers are very much aware of the importance of prestige projects in asserting the power of state leaders and as such has been involved in large-scale projects of this nature, such as building national stadiums, all over Africa. This approach has proven beneficial to both the ruling elites in Africa, who view these as projections of regime legitimacy and power (and suitably impress the local populations) and to Beijing, as it demonstrates China's rising prominence and presence. Through these kinds of projects, combined with aid packages and the notion that China may be a "model" for Africa, Beijing is very much asserting itself as an equal of Western powers as well as appealing to the African elite classes. Indeed, Dirlik (2006) notes that the "Beijing Consensus" draws its meaning and appeal not from some coherent set of economic or political ideas à la Ramo (2004), but from its intimation of an alternative pole, which those opposed to Washington and, by extension, "the West" can draw inspiration from. As Breslin (2007: 2) notes, "China's alternative path is partly attractive because of the apparent success of the experience of economic reform. Other developing states might also lean towards the Chinese way not just because China's leaders don't attach democratizing and liberalizing conditions to bilateral relations, but also because China is coming to provide alternative sources of economic opportunities (with non-democratizing strings attached)."

However, Africa's intellectuals must approach with caution the notion that China offers up an alternative model of development. Firstl conceptions of Chinese "soft power" built on "the appeal of China as an economic model" (Kurlantzick 2006: 5) overstate the ability of China to project and promote an alternative economic type (Yan Xuetong, 2006). It is true that economically liberalizing while preserving an authoritarian political system might be appealing to some African autocrats, but this surely has its limits, not least to the Chinese themselves in promoting such a message, given that supporting authoritarian elites in Harare and Khartoum has already stimulated anti-Chinese feelings among African civil society leaders. Furthermore, China's sustained growth has taken place not only with no reference to democracy or transparency, but has also generally shunned policy reforms promoted from outside. This must seem attractive for those African leaders who have no real legitimacy or who are tired of having to fend off criticisms from the IFIs and the wider donor community.

Yet, China's extraordinary economic growth has come about, certainly initially, within the broader context of a capable state and in a region that is itself economically dynamic. Rapid economic growth without democratization as per the East Asian model often required a strong developmental state. Analysis of China within this vein generally confirms such a proposition (Ming Xia, 2000) though with certain caveats (Breslin, 1996). Contrast this milieu with Africa. Granted even the relative declining reach of the Chinese state as liberalization progresses (Wang Hongying, 2003), the type of comparative internal strength and concomitant stability that Beijing is able to enact is beyond the ambition of most—if not all—current African leaders.

Furthermore, the irony is that those who applaud alternatives to Western dominated IFIs often—sometimes perhaps without realizing so—end up in a position where they not only support the authoritarian status quo in some African states, but also the emerging leadership of China. Opposition to neoliberalism—something that has considerable appeal—can result in the promotion not of social democracy, nor even Keynesian liberalism, but of illiberal authoritarianism. And, as Zha Daojiong notes (2005), within China itself there is a debate as to whether or not the Latin American malaise of social polarization, international dependency and economic stagnation is China's future fate unless appropriate policies are implemented. These debates often question the capitalist direction of Beijing's current course, again destabilizing the notion of a "model" (see Wang Chaohua, 2003; Wang Hongying, 2003). Even if we disagree with Gordon Chang's forecast (2002), such analyses of the so-called China miracle (Wu Yanrui, 2003), which offer up less sanguine interpretations, seem to have been missed by those advocating the Chinese model. Ironically, it is quite noticeable these days how touchy many African intellectuals are to any criticism of China and/or the suggestion that China is possibly *not* the savior of Africa, often defending Beijing's record on human rights within the African context.

Human Rights

Perhaps the aspect of Chinese engagement with Africa that is most controversial is the issue of human rights. It is certainly true that China's relations with some of the more egregious regimes in Africa cannot be seen as typical of Sino-African relations as a whole. But, conversely, it is precisely because of the negative attention that Beijing's ties with such regimes has generated, as well as the very real and destructive nature of such administrations that justifies a discussion of China's stance on human rights in its Sino-African relations. Equally, the notion that it is not China's business or duty to promote good governance and/or broad human rights (something that official Chinese statements have inferred) and that China's noninterference principle is valid in all cases and at all times contrasts with the growing norms of international accountability.

Obviously, the notion of human rights is an essentially contested concept and the Chinese state and outside critics invariably speak past one another when engaging on this issue. Beijing's discourse on rights is long-standing and has characteristic concerns that need to be taken seriously by anyone who seeks to engage with the Chinese state. It is also important to note that struggles about human rights have long been a way that power plays between countries that adhere to different political or economic models can be acted out. In this way, the persistent demand from Western capitals to universalize "international human rights," which when boiled down to its essence is arguably about universalizing specifically Western capitalist values, can be flagged by Beijing and its African allies as reflecting neocolonial impulses (Breslin and Taylor, 2008). In addition,

China's leadership may be seeking ways to rationalize their policies on human rights in a way that universalizes China's post-Mao developmental trajectories (Sullivan, 1999: 24). This is arguably a feature of the so-called Beijing Consensus mentioned previously, as well as also a product of anti-hegemonism, the Five Principles and statist development thinking.

But as Weatherley (1999) notes, some of the most serious violations of human rights in Africa that China is arguably held complicit with, due to its active support for the offending regimes, cannot be justified even in terms of the Chinese discourse on human rights. This is particularly so when the Chinese position on human rights intimately links social development and welfare to the concept. This is a perfectly respectable position to take, but Beijing's own coherence on the issue is arguably undermined by its diplomacy in practice if and when Chinese policy supports regimes that are antidevelopmental. It is evident that some states that enjoy close Chinese support, such as Sudan and Zimbabwe, not only crush the civil and political rights of their citizens but also threatens the economic and social rights of the population. Burma could also be seen an example of China trying and failing to maintain the sharp separation between trade and human rights.

Given that the economic and social rights of people are held by Beijing to be central in its discourse on human rights, this is surely problematic. Beijing deploys a particular stance on state sovereignty, i.e. that sovereignty is the ultimate guarantor of human rights and that it is therefore the choice of each sovereign state to institute its own understandings of the rights of its people. This is all very well and of course state sovereignty is the cornerstone of the international system, without which anarchy might reign. Yet the reification of states and the amalgamation of sovereignty and rights into a single principle of noninterference arguably loses much of its meaning in an African milieu dominated by quasi-states, neopatrimonial regimes, even warlordism.

As Li Xing (1996: 40) notes, the difficulty facing China's rulers is that on the one hand they have sought national independence from Western political influence and on the other hand have sought to "catch up" with the West and modernize the economy through ever-deeper integration with the capitalist world market. This contradiction is often played out around human rights issues and in fact, taking the analysis further, it might be argued that infringing some human rights in China itself (poor labor conditions, for instance) is a *pre-condition* for Beijing's reintegration into the global political economy, something which is actively encouraged by the West and its profit-seeking corporations. Indeed, it is a fact that "human rights abuses under the banner of 'preserving order' are aimed at maintaining the position of the ruling elements [in China]. But it is also undeniable that the state sees the necessity to maintain long-term stability and predictability of the system in order to attract much-needed foreign investment and technology" (Li Xing, 1996: 34). In this light, critiquing China's human rights stance when it is played out in Africa, while selectively overlooking the abuses that underpin much of the consumer boom in the developed world, driven in part by cheap Chinese imports, lacks coherence, as does ignoring continued Western support for assorted dictators and corrupt regimes across Africa.

However, such analysis does not help the average Zimbabwean or Sudanese laboring under autocratic and oppressive governments and casting a weary eye at Chinese support for her oppressor. We can pontificate about hypocrisy and selectivity, but Zimbabwe is still collapsing and women are still being raped in Darfur. Here, Beijing's thinking on noninterference and its hands-off attitude vis-à-vis human rights and governance needs to modify if it is to avoid being cast by critics as a unique friend of despots. There is actually some evidence that a rethink is occurring and Chinese thinking on human rights and sovereignty "is less a static concept than an idea in flux" (Gill and Reilly, 2000: 42). Indeed, "Beijing's recent handling of the situation in Sudan shows that it is learning the limitations of non-interference, however much that principle remains part of its official rhetoric. The concept may have been useful when China was relatively weak and trying to protect itself from foreign interference. But China has found non-interference increasingly unhelpful as it learns the perils of tacitly entrusting its business interests to repressive governments" (Kleine-Ahlbrandt and Small, 2008: 47).

It is true that at the moment there appears to be some divergence between Western and Chinese policy aims regarding governance and that this then at times suggests a convergence between Beijing and certain types of African leaders. But this can only ever be temporary in nature if China wishes to have a long-running and stable relationship with Africa. China is like all other actors in SSA—it needs stability and security in order for its investments to flourish and for its connections with the continent to be coherent. As Obiorah (2007: 40) notes, "After an initial phase of snapping up resource extraction concessions, it is almost conceivable that China will be compelled by instability and conflict in Africa to realize that its long term economic interests are best served by promoting peace in Africa and that this is most likely to come about by encouraging representative government in Africa rather than supporting dictators." This has started to happen:

> China's changing calculation of its economic and political interests has partly driven this shift. With its increased investments in pariah countries over the past decade, China has had to devise a more sophisticated approach to protecting its assets and its citizens abroad. It no longer sees providing uncritical and unconditional support to unpopular, and in some cases fragile, regimes as the most effective strategy. (Kleine-Ahlbrandt and Small, 2008: 38–9)

Thus, while in the current period there sometimes appears to be divergence, there can ultimately only be growing convergence with Western policy aims—maybe not with regard to democracy, but certainly with regard to governance and security and by implication, a greater connection to the downside of supporting African regimes that undermine development and China's own notions of human rights.

Furthermore, China's integration into the global economy and the concomitant responsibilities that have come with this greater incorporation necessitate structural and systemic reforms on Beijing, particularly through increasing membership of multilateral bodies. In the long term these could conceivably have an impression on Beijing in the development of a regime that incorporates increased respect for the rule of law and a better safeguarding for universal human rights. For instance, Beijing's key commitments pertaining to its membership of the WTO comprises responsibilities to advance the transparency, consistency and standardization of China's legal system. And it is more than obvious that over the past 20 years or so, Beijing has signed up to and ratified a growing number of international instruments pertaining to human rights and labor as it embeds itself in various multilateral regimes (Lanteigne, 2005). Recognizing that different interpretations of human rights may exist, but working to ensure that the sorts of abuses seen in Sudan or Zimbabwe are not repeated is in the interests of both Beijing *and* the West if stability and long-term relationships with Africa's economies are desired. On evidence, it appears that the Chinese leadership is beginning to realize this.

Conclusion

Chinese foreign policy in SSA has been based on several key aims. Beijing has focused on ensuring its regime security through access to crucial resources. By portraying itself as an advocate for the developing world and emphasizing the rhetoric of South-South cooperation, China has arguably sought to offer itself up an alternative model to Western dominance. However, to achieve its policy goals, Beijing has equally been prepared to defend autocratic regimes, some of which commit gross human rights abuses, such as Sudan. As a repressive government in its own right, the Chinese leadership has little sympathy with civil society in Africa if and when it challenges perceived Chinese interests, and too often Beijing has sided with authoritarian regimes. In this way, China's interactions with the continent fit the pattern of most external actors' intercourse with Africa: beneficial to the ruling elite but to the long-term disadvantage of Africa's peoples.

However, it must be emphasized that China's policies toward Africa are evolving and maturing and Beijing is going through a steep learning curve. Recent developments suggest that China is starting to realize that like all other actors in Africa, Beijing needs stability and security in order for Chinese investments to flourish and for its connections with the continent to be coherent. The history and development of Sino-African relations thus far suggest certain patterns, but the relationship is fluid and ever-changing. Indeed, it has to be said that in relative terms, the exponential increase in Chinese trade with Africa from the start of this century means that we are in the very early stages of a solidified Sino-African relationship, even though formal ties between Beijing and Africa go back to decades. Thus far the repercussions of this sustained and in-depth political and economic involvement by the Chinese for broad-based development in SSA has yet to be ascertained.

What can be stated is that Sino-African relations are processes not of colonization but of globalization and the reintegration of China into the global economy—a project that has enjoyed the hitherto enthusiastic support of Western capitalism. At present the picture appears mixed—there are instances where the Chinese role in Africa is clearly positive and appreciated. Equally, there are issues where Beijing is, at present at least, playing an equivocal role which arguably threatens to unravel some of the progress made in Africa in recent times on issues of good governance and accountability. Beijing's current role in Africa is, like all other external actors, diverse and its effect in the continent varies widely depending on local economic and political circumstance. A balanced appraisal on the various themes of China's engagement in SSA is thus needed. The diversity of both China and Africa, as well as the nature of the individual African states where Chinese interests operate is central if we are to have an accurate picture of what is going on.

Where there is coherence in Sino-African relations, a key intention is to encourage Chinese corporations to "go global" (*zouchuqu*), which encourages Chinese corporations to invest overseas and play a role in international capital markets (see Hong Eunsuk and Sun Laixiang, 2006) and aid in the policy of ensuring regime security through access to crucial resources. A Chinese Ministry of Commerce statement has in fact averred that Africa is "one of the most important regions for carrying out our 'go outward' strategy" (quoted in Gu Xuewu, 2005: 8). The resulting hike in commodity prices has been potentially good for much of Africa's economies, although the income from this phenomenon is obviously uneven and dependent upon a country's resource attributes. Certainly, in terms of receipts for such commodities, benefits are skewed to only certain economies. South Africa provides iron ore and platinum while the DRC and Zambia supplies copper and cobalt. Timber is sourced from Gabon, Cameroon, Congo-Brazzaville and Liberia, while various west and central African nations supply raw cotton to Chinese textile factories. It is, however, oil that remains China's biggest commercial interest in Africa—between 1996 and 2005, nearly 71 percent of the total composition of SSA's exports to China were mineral fuels (Mwega, 2007: 4). Given the nature of the oil industry globally—but particularly in Africa—this has attracted criticism.

Until relatively recently there was an arguable complacency within Beijing about its policies in Africa. The attitude seemed to be that third-party criticism (or even internal African condemnation) was motivated by "China bashing" and could be safely disregarded. However, a flurry of extremely negative articles in the international media about Sino-African ties, as well as incidents on the ground in Africa, has stimulated a rethink in Beijing. Although Beijing bristles at being singled out for criticism for its policies in Africa, it can be argued that since China is a rising power and arguably a great one, it has to accept the fact that it can no longer hide behind the idea of being a developing state—the fact that once a state becomes a great power (or at least is perceived by many to be) its policies will be placed much more directly under the microscope, especially by other great powers jockeying for influence. The US and the Soviet Union had to learn this during the last century and China is facing this fact today, albeit reluctantly. In fact, it is now acknowledged within Beijing that there is a desperate need to promote the positive side of Chinese diplomacy in SSA, and this facet of China's links with African states is receiving more and more attention. It will be interesting to see how Beijing accommodates to Africa's intricacies as Chinese involvement in SSA broadens and deepens.

Notes

1. This chapter was written prior to the fourth FOCAC meeting, planned for Cairo, Egypt, in November 2009.

CHAPTER FIVE

Hands across the Water: Indian Engagement in Africa

The growing presence of Indian corporations and a concomitant rise in New Delhi's political connections with the African continent reflects—as do Sino-African ties—a further diversification of Africa's international relations away from "traditional" North-South state-to-state linkages. Although, Indo-African relations can be traced to ancient times (Beri, 2003) and Africa is host to long-established communities of Indian origin, in the contemporary period a new set of dynamics are emerging that will undoubtedly expand relations into the new century.

Various commentators have noted the diverse motives for a variety of Indian actors to establish themselves in Africa. From the Indian state's perspective, energy security has been seen as paramount (Bava, 2007: 3), as has the ambition to be taken seriously as an important global player (Mohan, 2006; Sahni, 2007: 21–3). This feeds off of the celebratory rhetoric around India's supposed emergence as a (if not *the*) next Superpower (see Nayar and Paul, 2003). While the jury is very much still out over whether such pronouncements can be serious, there is no doubt that New Delhi's politicians harbor ambitions to take up a permanent seat in the UN Security Council as part of the "India Rising" discourse (Jobelius, 2007: 4). Equally, as India's economy continues to grow, Indian business interests have ambitions of themselves to expand their commercial empires; Africa in this sense provides opportunities for new investment sites and new export markets (Agrawal, 2007: 7). Consequently, "economic activity between Africa and Asia is booming like never before" (Broadman, 2008: 97).

Given that India's economy is currently one of the fastest growing in the world, this is arguably unsurprising; analysts predict a potential growth rate of an average of 8.4 percent until 2020 (Poddar and Yi, 2007: 9). By 2042, it has been averred that India will have overtaken the United States as the world's second largest economy, second only to China's (Ganguly and Pardesi, 2007: 10). While some of these analyses perhaps stem from an emerging (and arguably premature) Indian triumphalism, the modalities of Indo-African relations do need to be contextualized within the milieu of a burgeoning—and increasingly confident—India (see Goldstein et al., 2005).

History

As mentioned above, contact between India and Africa is long established and Indian trade with the eastern African seaboard is ancient. Colonization led to the incorporation of the Indian subcontinent and large swathes of Africa into the British Empire, which then facilitated the establishment of substantial Indian diasporas in Africa and elsewhere. Crucially, in light of much current Indian rhetoric about its relations with Africa, the struggle for Indian independence inspired African nationalism and is a powerful legacy that continues to have redolence today—even if only at state level. However, while Gandhi may have "laid the moral foundations for Indo-African relations, it was Jawaharlal Nehru who gave the relationship its political structure," with a strong element of South-South solidarity infusing India's early postcolonial foreign policies (Pham, 2007: 342). Central to Nehru's ambitions in this regard was the "gradual creation of friendly, cooperative, and mutually constructive relationships between India and the various countries of Africa" (Park, 1965: 350). However, because of the constraints of the Cold War and Superpower chicanery (and, equally, India's relative material poverty), such aspirations were largely confined to the realm of rhetoric.

Indeed, it has not been until the post–Cold War period and India's exponential economic growth that Indo-African relations have moved substantially forward. This has been accompanied by a downplaying of supposed common ideologies and a greater "pragmatism and a sober realization of new challenges facing both India and Africa as they get ready to take their place under the global sun" (Singh, 2006). And as previously mentioned, this is largely driven by a hard-nosed Indian agenda motivated by both economic (natural resources, market opportunities, etc.) and political (strategic partnerships, Indian global ambitions, etc.) considerations. This in turn contradicts Mahatma Gandhi's own prediction that "the commerce between India and Africa will be of ideas and services, not manufactured goods against raw materials after the fashion of Western exploiters" (quoted in Naidu, 2007: 1).

The role of Indian diasporas, a historical legacy of India's membership of the British Empire, also needs to be touched on as this constitutes a radical difference between India and most other international actors involved in Africa, with the possible exception of Britain (and in that context confined largely to southern Africa). There is at present a great interest within India in what are termed People of Indian Origin (PIO) in Africa. After a period of relative disengagement with PIO up to the late 1990s (often cast as traitors and/or failures who abandoned Mother India), India's growing presence in Africa and elsewhere has led to a transformation of its PIO policies. India now wishes to engage more vigorously with its diasporic communities and has proposed reforms such as a PIO identity card and the possibility of dual citizenship. This is all part of New Delhi hoping to utilize the PIO as an exploitable resource in support of Indian interests.

PIO in Africa are relatively assimilated; according to one study, "in a 2006 survey of 450 business owners in Africa, almost half the respondents who were ethnically Indian had taken on African nationalities (with most of the other half retaining their Indian nationality), compared with only four percent of firm owners who were ethnically Chinese (the other 96% had retained their Chinese nationality)" (Broadman, 2008: 99). Currently, PIO are seen by New Delhi as having the potential ability to facilitate cooperation and communication between Africa and India, as well as serve as economic agents for Indian commercial interests. This last point needs to be carefully managed by New Delhi as historic resentment against economically powerful ethnic Indians has long been a feature of a number of African countries—and is something which will not be helped by any notion that such actors are somehow advancing India's agenda in any form.

Political Ties

Officially, Indian foreign policy roots itself in Nehru's inclinations for multilateralism and South-South solidarity (Agrawal, 2007: 7). According to some commentators, this has stimulated India's long-held interest in UN peacekeeping (Chiriyankandath, 2004: 200). Indian peacekeepers have now been occupied with over 40 UN peacekeeping missions (Jobelius, 2007: 8), much of these in Africa. Arguably, such a commitment demonstrates New Delhi's willingness to support the UN system in practical terms, particularly vis-à-vis notions of peace and security in a way that stands in contrast to much Western practice (Bava, 2007). New Delhi *has* operated at times to open up a certain amount of political space within multilateral institutions where developing countries might cooperate for greater leverage (ibid.) and as part of this strategy has underwritten the financial costs necessary for such cooperation (Hurrell and Narlikar, 2006: 7).

As part of its general commitment to multilateralism, India has long emphasized both a cooperative new world order and the mutuality of Southern interests in combating global inequality. This rhetoric plays out well across Africa and has at times enabled New Delhi to (temporarily) project itself as the spokesperson of the global South (Narayan, 2005: 2), a role that India often, even if only implicitly, competes for with China (Ford, 2006). In emphasizing the claimed mutual interests behind Indo-African ties, the Indian government has in fact asserted that "India's contemporary Africa policy is aligned to a confluence of interests around justice in the global order leveled at increasing the leverage and influence of their [its] respective global positions and promoting a new international order" (quoted in Naidu, 2007: 2).

Having said that, India's diplomatic strategy cannot be said to be grounded in an idealism predicated purely on South-South solidarity. Contemporary India's foreign policy is more pragmatic than previous incarnations, such as during the Bandung era and although New Delhi continues an interest in nonalignment and notions of Southern solidarity, the focus these days is very much on the importance of national interests, particularly economic in nature. This is linked to a wider move within India away from socialist-inclined economic policies to those more in line with neoliberalism. In this way, India might be said to be following in the economic (and hence political) footsteps of China, particularly so with regard to developing ties with Africa. Indeed, "since 1991 . . . India has begun to liberalize its economy in a belated effort to achieve the growth and investment seen in China" (Alden and Viera, 2005: 1088).

According to one analysis, there is evidence that "India is also reportedly uncomfortable with the growing Chinese presence on the African rim of the Indian Ocean. The security of Indian Ocean sea-lanes is an area of major concern for India, which has traditionally seen the Indian Ocean as its strategic backyard. According to a recent report released by Chatham House, this is another issue that drives India's desire to strengthen its presence in Africa" (Haté, 2008: 2). Certainly, a surging economy within India requires new markets and new sites for Indian investment opportunities. Competition with Chinese companies for these productive investment locations almost surely stimulates much recent Indian energies. Either way, Africa fits as an important part of Indian businesse's own economic strategies.

Of note, during the 1990s, India was shutting diplomatic missions in Africa as an economic measure; today it has nearly 30 embassies and high commissions across the continent and the Indian Ministry of External Affairs is increasing its diplomatic initiatives by establishing three joint secretariats to manage the three regional divisions that encompass the continent. And India has copied China in developing its own India-Africa summit.

The first India-Africa summit in New Delhi occurred in April 2008 and signaled a serious and calculated push from the Indian government to strengthen and deepen its ties with important African nations. Fourteen African countries attended the summit, including Algeria, the DRC, Egypt, Ethiopia, Ghana, Libya, Nigeria, South Africa and Uganda. At the policy level, trade policy has been a crucial and important element (see the text below). As part of its commitment to both multilateralism and South-South solidarity, India coordinated closely with leading African countries on the Doha Round of negotiations at the WTO, especially with regard to agriculture. India has also been keen to develop strong ties with South Africa, and has been active in establishing a trilateral grouping alongside Brazil (India-Brazil-South Africa Dialogue Forum, IBSA). According to one analysis, "The formation of the IBSA (India-Brazil-South Africa) alliance in June 2003 created a new dynamic in international relations, drawing together the three most powerful economies of the southern hemisphere in a regional axis for the first time" (Lai, 2006: 4).

The India-Brazil-South Africa Dialogue Forum

The Forum was set up in Brazil in June 2003 and formally launched by Presidents Thabo Mbeki, Lula da Silva and Prime Minister Atal Bihari Vajpayee during the UN General Assembly in September 2003. The leaders of the three states intentionally promoted themselves as advocates for an emerging developing world—Lula da Silva spoke of an influential free trade area to rival the North American Free Trade Agreement (NAFTA) and the EU. Indeed, he commented that "A trilateral agreement between India, Brazil and South Africa [would] give us the political will at the WTO (World Trade Organization) to get the flexibility we need for our goods that are often taxed by the developed nations" (*Star* [Johannesburg], January 29, 2004). Until his electoral defeat in May 2004, Prime Minister Vajpayee, at his core an Indian nationalist, oversaw a resurgent economy and sought to project New Delhi's reach in an attempt to resurrect India as a global player as it was back in the days of Nehru. As mentioned earlier, the current government in New Delhi continues this theme amid much hyperbole (among mainly Indian academics) about the alleged imminent future status of India as a Superpower (e.g. Mathew, Ganesh and Dayasindhu, 2008; Nanda, 2008; Sanyal, 2008).

The IBSA Forum is based on what is known as the Brasilia Declaration, released in June 2003. The Declaration is a comprehensive document intended to bring about change within the global political economy. It has both political and economic ingredients. Politically, reform of the UN, in particular the Security Council, is of special note, with the Declaration stressing the necessity of expanding the Security Council in both permanent and non-permanent member categories, with the involvement of developing countries in both categories. India and Brazil support each other's membership bids and the IBSA Forum has committed itself to combining energies in order to obtain reform, as well as enhancing the effectiveness of the UN system.

While the IBSA acknowledges the expansion of economic growth, employment, and social development, and the accompanying rise in standards of living in several developing countries, with freer movements of trade, capital, and technology being seen as the source of such growth

> [t]he Foreign Ministers of Brazil, India and South Africa expressed their concern that large parts of the world have not benefited from globalization [and they] agreed that globalization must become a positive force for change for all peoples, and must benefit the largest number of countries. In this context, they affirmed their commitment to pursuing policies, programs and initiatives in different international forums, to make the diverse processes of globalization inclusive, integrative, humane, and equitable. (IBSA, 2003)

The IBSA promotes a now recognizable position, condemning protectionist policies in the G-8 and emphasizing the essential requirement to move ahead with the Doha Development Program, as well as reversing Northern protectionist policies and trade-distorting practices. The Brasilia Declaration reiterated the three countries' expectation that trade negotiations within the WTO would achieve increased political momentum so that deadlocks on issues of fundamental interest to developing countries, stalled at Doha, would be broken before the Cancún summit (this obviously failed).

In addition, the Declaration reaffirmed the import of a predictable, rule-based, and transparent multilateral trading system as a way through which "the South" (unproblematized) could take full advantage of development potentialities via trade and supposed competitive advantages. As the Brazilian negotiator Brazilian Luiz Felipe Seixas asserted,

> [The WTO] is an irreplaceable organization. We need it. We need it badly. We need a strong WTO and from the perspective of developing countries, this is really an irreplaceable forum—with all its shortcomings, with all its problems—this is where [the G-20] can make a difference. We can get some predictability. We can get some rules and we can get some enforceable rules in an area where in the past we had none. (*South Bulletin*, 2003)

Concomitant with this, the IBSA seeks cooperation toward making the international financial architecture more receptive to development in the South and toward increasing its efficiency in averting and tackling national and regional financial crises. This is seen as a key objective of the notion of global governance and critical if "globalization" is to be equitable on a global scale. Making neoliberalism work for all is thus a central point for the IBSA, something that now fits in with broader Indian elite ambitions to emerge as global economic players. It must be said, however, that this stance approaches globalization as a wholly unproblematized concept, devoid of any real structural interrogations of the global political economy and viable alternatives to "the free market."

The first meeting of the Trilateral Commission of the IBSA Dialogue Forum (to give IBSA its full name) met in New Delhi from 4 to 5 March, 2004, i.e. after Cancún. Observing the group and the meeting, the Brazilian foreign minister Celso Amorim asserted that the IBSA was "a group to spread goodwill and the message of peace [and that] we are not against anyone," while India's Yashwant Sinha emphasized "the need to redefine the content of globalization, to make it more pertinent to the needs and aspirations of the developing world." This was, however, as far as it went. The IBSA was, according to the ministers, "not just historic but irreversible," and the project would from then on work to get the three states to collaborate more closely at multilateral forums such as the United Nations and the WTO "with the aim of advancing an alternative perspective on world affairs" (*Bridges Weekly Trade News Digest*, March 10, 2004). The outcome of the meeting was the New Delhi Plan of Action. The Plan of Action covers such subjects as trade and transportation, infrastructure, science and technology, information society, health, energy, and education. In other words, after Cancún the IBSA has developed beyond simply calling for a reform of the global trading system into a nascent alliance between three important states in the global South.

At the second IBSA summit (in Pretoria, October 2007), an array of cooperation agreements were signed. Mbeki, da Silva and the Indian prime minister Manmohan Singh agreed to advance collaboration (*Inter Press Service* [Johannesburg], October 20, 2007). However, progress with regard to crucial matters key to commerce between the three regional powers was noticeably absent: "business representatives . . . expected the signing of 'breakthrough agreements' on free trade, connectivity and intellectual property. Instead, the seven memorandums of understanding signed by the three countries' leaders yesterday were on public administration and government, cultural co-operation, co-operation on social issues, health and medicine, customs and taxes administration, higher education and human resources" (*Business Day* [Johannesburg], October 18, 2007). Although there was a rhetorical commitment to double intra-IBSA trade to US$15 billion by 2010, steps forward vis-à-vis the issue of tariffs was lacking. While IBSA will remain important for some aspects of Indian foreign policy, ties with the wider continent will almost certainly take precedence as Indian presence in SSA deepens.

Indian Aid to Africa

India has emerged in recent years from being an aid recipient to an important aid donor. However, as there is no central agency managing disbursals of Indian development assistance, it is difficult to ascertain exactly how much India gives. In 2006 it was suggested that New Delhi's development assistance programs were at an annual level of over US$350 million (Khanna and Mohan, 2006), while in 2009 "according to the various existing sources India's annual financial volume for development cooperation is currently estimated as being in between half a billion and one billion US$" (German Development Institute, 2009: 2). In terms of geographical distribution most of New Delhi's assistance goes to India's neighboring countries, followed by African states.

Of note, India was the first Asian country (in 2005) to become a full member of the Africa Capacity Building Foundation (ACBF) after guaranteeing US$1 million to the ACBF to build capacity for sustainable development and poverty alleviation in Africa. As part of its aid profile, India has also cancelled the debts owed to New Delhi by countries under the HIPC initiative and also rationalized commercial debts. The total debt written off by New Delhi is, however, only about US$37 million, so it is largely symbolic. But nations such as Ghana, Mozambique, Tanzania, Uganda and Zambia have benefited. India is also a major donor to the World Food Program and has donated food to Namibia, Chad and Lesotho.

Indian emphasis vis-à-vis aid has gradually shifted from political aid (i.e. aid via the UN, the Organisation of African Unity (OAU) and the Non-Aligned Movement

(NAM) to support African anticolonial struggles) to development aid (McCormick, 2008). Partly, New Delhi has deployed developmental assistance as a means to attempt to counter Chinese activities, but also to help facilitate the opening up of new market opportunities and also to reinforce India's position within multilateral institutions as a means of enhancing Indian international prestige and presence (Jobelius, 2007: 4). As one report put it, "India's reform towards economic liberalization, privatization and globalization [meant that] the country's foreign policy became also increasingly influenced by geo-economic considerations" (German Development Institute, 2009: 1).

The state-owned Export Import Bank of India (also known as Exim Bank of India) has been a major agent of Indian aid and financial support to Africa. For instance, the bank has lent money to the Common Market for Eastern and Southern Africa (COMESA) to be used to acquire capital goods from India (Beri, 2003), and the bank has also financed Ethiopian sugar production, agricultural development in Botswana, and rural electrification and water provision in Ghana (Chaturvedi and Mohanty, 2007: 65). Such schemes actually make up around 30 percent of total Indian aid to SSA (Agrawal, 2007: 7). Exim Bank generally extends Lines of Credit to governments, parastatal organizations, commercial banks, financial institutions and to regional development banks to facilitate the export of eligible commercial products on deferred payment terms utilizing concessional interest rates of circa 4 percent (German Development Institute, 2009: 2). The Exim Bank also has a Focus Africa Program, through which the financing of exports to the Economic Community of West African States (ECOWAS) states was facilitated (Beri, 2005: 387).

Interestingly, the Exim Bank is also involved in a US$1 billion joint venture with the EU to develop a Pan-African E-Network, which will make available medical and educational information (Agrawal, 2007: 8). The initiative aims to bridge the digital divide and India's input will be in the realm of supporting tele-education, tele-medicine, e-commerce, e-governance, resource-mapping and meteorological services. The Pan-African E-Network and any attendant technology are to be handed over to the AU after five years of Indian management (Naidu, 2007: 6). This fits with an overall pattern whereby about 60 percent of Indian aid is applied toward technical assistance (Agrawal, 2007: 7). In a similar fashion, the Hindustan Machine Tools' construction of an Entrepreneurial Training and Demonstration Centre in Dakar costing US$4.49 million was ceded to the control of the Senegalese government in June 2000 (Beri, 2003). Since 1994, New Delhi has also supported the growth of small-scale industry projects in eight countries and committed about 10 percent of its aid to a variety of feasibility studies across Africa.

Unlike the West and China, India funds projects directly rather than supplying cash grants (Agrawal, 2007), a nontransferable method of aid that is arguably open neither to abuse nor capitalist conditionalities (Jobelius, 2007: 3). However, unlike Chinese aid, Indian assistance does not offer up to predatory African regimes an option to avoid governance reform (ibid.: 5). Indeed, emanating from the world's largest democracy, aid from New Delhi arguably reinforces "Western" notions of good governance and accountability (Vines and Sidiropoulos, 2008).

As part of India's development assistance, military participation in a wide variety of UN peacekeeping operations in Africa characterizes Indian policy toward Africa. Noteworthy contingents of Indian military personnel have been deployed as part of UN operations in Burundi, the Ivory Coast and Sudan, while the Indian contribution of 3,500 troops to the UN mission in the DRC and 1,400 troops to Ethiopia and Eritrea constituted the largest national contribution of military human resources. India is consistently in the top three largest troop contributors to the UN. Military assistance also takes the form of training, and since the 1960s Indian military academies have trained thousands of African officers (although such training is considered second best compared to what Western states provide at their academies). India has also sent training teams to various African countries such as Botswana, Zambia and Lesotho, where their cost effectiveness compared to Western trainers is a major plus. The Indian defense sector has also supplied patrol boats to Mauritius and Guinea-Bissau and light helicopters to Namibia.

Of course, Indian aid to Africa is not an expression of altruism. India, like all other countries, actively leverages its development assistance to promote specific political objectives. Indian aid not only helps to facilitate an increase in Indian economic activity across Africa, but also serves to project India as a major power and gain a support constituency as a means of "increasing the leverage and influence of [India's] global position . . . and promoting a new international order" (Naidu, 2007: 2). New Delhi views Africa as the source of potentially vital support (and important voting power) in international institutions. As part of this, Indian diplomacy seeks to encourage the belief that India is a long-time supporter of Third World interests. Here, Indian policymakers are looking to posture (with some success) New Delhi as the largest, wealthiest, and most diverse non-Western democracy (Bava, 2007: 2). Consequently, some analysts have argued that Africans perceive Indian behavior as less confrontational than China's and more genuine in their actions than what is often interpreted as Western "neo-imperialism" (Naidu, 2007).

Certainly, New Delhi has taken a leadership role at WTO negotiations on behalf of (particular) developing countries' positions and the Indian commitment to South-South cooperation has rhetorically continued, despite the ongoing economic liberalization project. Emblematically, in 2006, the Indian commerce and industry minister walked out of WTO negotiations which had failed to deliver on the reduction of Western farming subsidies and import taxes. Subsequently, India was hailed as embodying the voice of the voiceless and the minister's actions served to reify the belief held in many quarters across SSA that African and Indian strategic economic interests are closely aligned. The actions also arguably elevated India's global status as a non-Western power that does not allow itself to be kicked round, something that sells well in Africa.

The Indian Economic Presence in Africa

India-Africa trade has grown rapidly in the last five years, from US$3.39 billion per year in 2000 to US$30 billion per year in 2007 (Haté, 2008: 1). Some Indian commentators have sought to argue that India offers a more "equal" trading partner for Africa than the West (e.g. Sharma, 2007: 7). However, the balance of trade between India and SSA is in India's favor and shows no sign of changing (Chaturvedi and Mohanty, 2007: 55). In 2005, Indian exports to Africa were over US$6 billion while Indian imports from Africa were c. US$4 billion (Naidu, 2007: 4). The total amount of Indo-African trade is relatively small compared to many other of Africa's trading partners, but it is the rate of growth in trade that is important to remember when considering such figures.

One aspect of Indian engagement with Africa that holds promise is the promotion of regional trade agreements by New Delhi (Antkiewicz and Whalley, 2006). For instance, India has conducted a Joint Study Group on a Preferential Trade Agreement (PTA) with the Southern African Customs Union (SACU), incorporating Botswana, Lesotho,

Namibia, South Africa and Swaziland. According to one analysis, such moves may reflect a wider process whereby the emergence of powerful Southern economies opens up new opportunities for Africa, as such regional agreements may allow African economies to interact with each other and with external actors in ways that bypass the conditionalities imposed upon the continent by the Western-led IFIs and the dangers of bilateralism (Chaturvedi and Mohanty, 2007: 54). Accordingly, such activity possibly also signifies the nascent formalization of the global South's growing resistance to the North's agenda setting (Hurrell and Narlikar, 2006: 1–3, 8). In this analysis, India's penchant for multilateral trade agreements may serve to profit some African economies by precluding economically predatory—if not destructive—behavior arguably intrinsic to the WTO's unified methodology (Narayan, 2005: 7).

Tellingly, the guest list at the April 2008 Indo-Africa Forum consisted of the chair of the AU, the heads of the initiating states involved in NEPAD and the chairs of the eight African regional groups. This may be seen as evidence confirming New Delhi's continued preference for regional rather than bilateral agreements (Vines and Sidiropoulos, 2008: 7).

In addition to state-led engagement with Africa, Indian private companies are increasingly moving into Africa. The mid-1990s saw the initiation of a number of industry organizations such as the Associated Chambers of Commerce and Industry of India (ASSOCHAM), the Federation of Indian Export Organizations (FIEO) and the Federation of Indian Chambers of Commerce and Industry (FICCI). These have helped change the character of Indian economic interaction with Africa as such organizations have encouraged the involvement of non-state actors who, by definition, are outside New Delhi's control. Such actors are increasingly important; between 2005 and 2007 such companies invested nearly US$400 million in Africa.

Indian investment in infrastructure projects and enterprise has increased dramatically in recent years and New Delhi has "urged African nations to encourage Indian industry to grow its footprint in the continent" (*Financial Express*, March 21, 2007). Indeed, it might be averred that Indian ventures in SSA adds value to Africa's economies through their substantial investments in critical (yet underfunded) infrastructure projects. For instance, Rites and Ircon (state-owned engineering companies) are now active in Africa's rail and road development sector. Rites has refurbished and leased locomotives in Sudan and Tanzania, supplied technical assistance to rail authorities in Kenya and Mozambique and consulted on the design and construction of roads in Uganda and Ethiopia. Ircon has constructed 600 km of railway system in Mozambique, received a US$31 million contract from the Ethiopian government to build 120 km of roads and has been active in rail sectors in Angola, Nigeria, Sudan and Zambia (Naidu, 2007).

Meanwhile, private Indian companies are investing in African power projects. For instance, Kamani Engineering Corporation is involved in a 132 kV power project in Ethiopia worth US$40 million as well as a US$11 million project to build transmission lines between Namibia and Zambia. The corporation is also active in Algeria, Ghana, Kenya, Libya, Nigeria, Tunisia and Zambia. The Overseas Infrastructure Alliance currently has contracts worth US$65 million with Addis Ababa to supply electrical equipment (Naidu, 2008: 125).

A prime example of private Indian economic activity in Africa is the Tata Group, operating across SSA in a diverse array of economic sectors (Vines and Sidiropoulos, 2007). The Tata Group (with others) *has* helped to diversify African exports (Broadman, 2007: 12). For example, Tata has opened an instant coffee processing plant in Uganda and a vehicle assembly plant in Zambia (Naidu, 2007: 5). Both benefit the national economies by adding value to raw materials and such diversification (primarily away from primary agriculture) may help affect a nascent new international division of labor. Interestingly, the Tata Group asserts that it has "aligned business opportunities with the objective of nation building" (Tata Group, 2008), so although private, the wider picture of aiding India's rise is seen as an intrinsic aspect of Tata's operations. Such rhetoric, tinged with mercantilist nationalism, contrasts strongly with the individualistic nature of most Western corporations, who rarely subscribe to such mottos.

India's burgeoning middle class is increasingly buying Africa's light manufactured products, household consumer goods, and processed foods and utilizing the continent's back-office services, tourism facilities, and telecommunications (Broadman, 2008). However, a possible fly in the ointment is the fact that despite liberalization, India retains high import tariffs that makes the importation of many high-value-added goods and services from Africa uncompetitive. Here, New Delhi is constrained by its democracy and its diverse constituents, many of whom demand the maintenance of protectionist trade policies.

Meanwhile, African imports from India currently include machinery, transport equipment, paper and other wood products, textiles, plastics, and chemical and pharmaceutical products (Pham, 2007: 346). Indian pharmaceutical manufacturers such as Cipla and Ranbaxy are progressively penetrating Africa's health markets, providing drugs at a fraction of the cost of Western pharmaceuticals. Ranbaxy Laboratories, which has been involved in joint ventures in Nigeria since the late 1970s, are now taking advantage of WTO provisions that permit patents to be broken in the case of national emergencies. This is particularly important in the fight against HIV/AIDS, where the demand for low-cost antiretrovirals is intense. Apart from India's major international companies, smaller Indian businesses are penetrating Africa's markets. In fact, between 2002 and 2005, Indian firms topped the list of foreign direct investments (FDI) projects in Africa at 48, compared to 32 from China (Naidu, 2008: 125).

However, as mentioned above, the trade imbalance between Africa and India is problematic. Not only does SSA import much more manufactured goods from India than India does from Africa, but a sizeable number of consumer goods from India directly compete against Africa's domestic products (Broadman, 2008). Many Indian products, when combined with dynamics already unleashed by the surge in Chinese exports to Africa (not forgetting what already comes from established trade partners), places "huge pressure on small, generally weak industries in the region" (Bonnet, 2006: 16). An example of this would be Kenyan companies' increasing inability to export clothing either to neighboring markets or to the United States because, in part, of the volume of relatively cheap Indian-made garments that now has an increasing market share.

India's investing companies have also been criticized on the grounds that they conduct business in a dishonest manner. In 2006, Transparency International released its Bribe Payers Index which evaluates countries in the propensity of their businesses to pay bribes while operating abroad: India was deemed the worst (Sorbara, 2007). Despite the fact that this may not be an approved method of business, it may be to India's advantage in gaining contracts within the contexts of corrupt neo-patrimonial African systems where power is transmitted through informal channels of reciprocity. It is not just private companies who are looking to skew the deal in their favor; Indian governmental initiatives also aim to manipulate the market to their benefit.

Yet there are also positive aspects of this trading relationship. Although the trade imbalance has grown in recent years (and is likely to continue), the imbalance is not of a major magnitude. More importantly, as many Indian firms active in Africa are multinational corporations, engaging in business with such corporations may help African companies expand their own engagement in network trade (Broadman, 2008). It is often argued that FDI has a general trend to draw trade flows from the host nation as new investors often have little knowledge of local contractors or local human, technical or financial capacity. Consequently, the sourcing of goods and services may take place outside of the host market. Yet "Indian companies are much more integrated into African society and the African economy, hiring locally and emphasizing training Africans how to maintain and repair the plants they build" (Pham, 2007: 348). Such expansion is observable in the food-processing sector in Tanzania, textile sector in Ghana and fishing industry in Senegal.

It should be noted that most of Indian trade is with West and Southern Africa; West Africa primarily due to the ongoing discoveries of oil reserves, and Southern Africa because of South Africa's developed markets—South Africa is India's largest trading partner in SSA. In fact, India's imports from South Africa account for more than 50 percent of India's total African imports, while Indian exports to South Africa make up about 25 percent of total Indian exports to SSA (ibid.). It has been asserted that Indian companies see South Africa as "the gateway into the rest of Africa" (ibid.). This perhaps explains why India has entered into negotiations for a preferential trade agreement with South Africa.

The South African relationship actually demonstrates the two-way nature of Indo-African commerce. For instance, Airports Company South Africa (ACSA) won the bid in India for the modernization of Mumbai airport, and in 2006 South African Breweries announced that they would invest US$225 million in India over the next five years. The supermarket chain Shoprite Checkers has a presence in India with the first franchisee, Shoprite Hyper Mulund, open in Mumbai. The South African insurance giant Sanlam has entered into a joint venture with the Shriram Life Insurance Company for the provision of long-term insurance, and India's state-owned Power Grid Corporation appointed Eskom of South Africa to set up 800 kV substations. However, outside of South African corporate activity, overall African investment in India at present remains limited.

Energy

With over one billion people, India ranks sixth in the world for energy demands, and "future projections are that by 2030 India is expected to become the world's largest consumer of energy, bypassing Japan and Russia" (Naidu, 2007: 3). Currently, roughly 30 percent of India's energy needs are met by oil (70 percent of which is imported). "The International Energy Agency (IEA) estimates that in order to stay on its current growth trajectory, India will have to increase its energy consumption by at least 3.6 percent annually. This will lead India's energy demand to double by 2025" (Haté, 2008: 1). It is projected that India will need to import 90 percent of its gas and crude oil in a few years (Beri, 2005: 372). In light of these energy needs, India is looking for new and diversified oil sources. Africa is an extremely attractive option; African oil is high quality, and, with many new discoveries outside of conflict zones, it is open for foreign participation. Additionally, only Nigeria is a member of the Organization of the Petroleum Exporting Countries (OPEC), which sets limits on member countries' output levels. According to one Indian analysis, "the discovery of vast energy sources has raised the strategic importance of the continent" (ibid.: 371).

It is in the oil sector where Indian investment perhaps poses the greatest risk for ordinary Africans. This is not specific to Indian corporations; the oil industry, in general, has often been accused of a disregard for poor governance in favor of rewarding contracts and Indian commentators have made this point alongside their international peers (see Sharma and Mahajan, 2007). An example of Indian disregard for ethical concerns might be seen in the case where the overseas division of Oil and Natural Gas Corporation Limited (ONGC), namely, the ONGC Videsh Limited (OVL), an Indian public sector petroleum company invested US$750 million to acquire two oil blocks in Sudan. Canadian company Talisman had previously sold the blocks due to pressure from human rights groups who had argued that the investment in these blocks fuelled conflict in Sudan (Beri, 2005: 378).

However, there are some ethical considerations in Indian corporations' presence in the African oil sector. In Nigeria, for instance, ONGC has "not only carried out exploration and production successfully in very difficult terrains, but has also been responsive to the needs of local population in terms of development of healthcare facilities and education centers etc." "Corporate social responsibility projects undertaken by ONGC in and around its project sites . . . have been immensely appreciated by the local community" (*This Day* [Lagos], February 15th, 2009). OVL has invested US$10 million in railway construction in Nigeria, a valuable investment in the country's dilapidated public infrastructure (Agrawal, 2007: 5). Of course, such investments are both tactical and no doubt with an eye on the bottom line. They do nonetheless contribute to development and arguably contrast with the activities of many Western corporations.

Interestingly, Indian efforts to gain access to African oil shows less of the somewhat reckless attributes found in much of the Chinese efforts to do the same. For instance, in January 2006, ONGC put in a winning US$2 billion bid for an offshore Nigerian oil field, only to see the Indian Cabinet block the deal on the grounds that it was not commercially feasible. Consequently, China National Offshore Oil Corporation (CNOOC) bought a 45 percent working interest in the field (*This Day* [Lagos], April 21, 2006). What was interesting here was that the Indian government deemed the deal as too risky, with potential political repercussions. Yet for the Chinese oil company, such concerns did not appear to be paramount—an interesting reflection on the comparative risks Beijing and New Delhi are willing to take to gain access to oil supplies.

Indian oil companies are expanding in Ghana; OVL and the Ghana National Petroleum Corporation (GNPC) agreed in October 2004 to begin joint oil exploration (Beri, 2005: 384). Indian rhetoric of the developmental spin-offs of such ventures is often underlined by official pronouncements: Indian minister of external affairs has asserted that "investment in this [oil] sector should directly assist in the building up of a trained and skilled workforce" (quoted in Sharma and Mahajan, 2007: 42).

OVL is also working in the Ivory Coast, Libya and Egypt while Indian Oil Corporation (IOC), another Indian state-owned entity, has invested US$1 billion in an offshore block in the Ivory Coast (Pham, 2007: 344) and possesses a Nigerian oil refinery worth US$3.5 billion (Naidu, 2007). Other African countries where Indian oil companies are seeking contracts include Burkina Faso, Chad, Equatorial, Guinea, Guinea-Bissau, Niger, Democratic Republic of Congo and Senegal. India's energy footprint in Africa is becoming increasingly noticeable as Indian companies aggressively search for new sites of exploration and investment.

The Indian presence in SSA's oil industries obviously has mixed connotations for indigenous locals. However, the activities of Indian corporations are probably no worse than other international actors whose companies are equally involved with less than salubrious regimes. In fact, the ability of the Indian state to influence (even curtail) deals done by the state-owned OVL perhaps gives Indian activity an ethical edge over the strictly private (and profit-driven) activities of Western corporations. Certainly, community development projects seem to be an integral component of Indian activity in the sector, no doubt informed by political considerations emanating from New Delhi.

Where there are possible factors that may undermine such trends is in the ongoing competition with Chinese companies in Africa for energy contracts. Chinese companies already have a strong market presence in poorly governed states. The question is, will this reduce the likelihood of negative Indian involvement in such economies, or induce Indian companies to follow suit? Indian companies have already been subject to attempts by Chinese corporations to block access to certain African oilfields—the classic example being the ability of the Chinese to prevent the April 2004 agreement between Shell and OVL in Angola. Of note, the Indian government continued its economic aid programs in Angola in spite of such developments. Explaining such a position, New Delhi has claimed that, unlike the US and China, India's energy security policy is based on "an integrated set of policies to balance foreign policy, economic, environmental, and social issues with the rising demand for energy" (Naidu, 2007: 2). This, of course, is for public consumption, but it does also reflect a desire by Indian policymakers not to be seen to be too nakedly mercenary in India's dealings with Africa, a stance that fits with overall Indian foreign policy toward Africa as noted above.

Land

A controversial aspect of growing Indo-African ties is the increasing number of private Indian companies who are purchasing large areas of African farmland to grow agricultural produce to export to India. Indian companies have signed a number of deals in Ethiopia, Kenya and Madagascar to produce a wide range of food crops, including rice, sugarcane, maize, pulses, oilseeds, tea and even vegetables. Some Indian firms are also investing in Africa to grow the biofuel crop *jatropha* (Sharma, 2008). The Gambella Agriculture Project by the Bangalore-based Karuturi Global Limited involves acquiring 8,50,000 acres of land in Ethiopia for cultivation of food grains, sugarcane, palm oil and other crops. The company has acquired land in Kenya too.

Of note, New Delhi provides cheap credit lines to Ethiopian entities to generate agricultural exports to India, supporting such investments through schemes such as the "Duty Free Tariff Preference Scheme," under which Ethiopian agro-products can enter India on lower tariffs. Clearly, the motive behind Indian investments in Ethiopia is to boost agricultural products meant for export to India. This springs from the domestic situation in India, where most of India's farms are small and fragmented and inappropriate for large-scale commercial farming. The Indian government encourages Indian companies to engage in such outsourcing as an alternative to purchasing expensive food from international markets.

However, the Food and Agriculture Organization (FAO) has dubbed such deals as "land grabbing," with Devinder Sharma of the Forum for Biotechnology and Food

Security stating that "It is unfortunate that the Indian government is supporting such acts. Such deals are bound to result in civil strife in host countries in coming days" (ibid.). Sharma points out that there are serious ethical and environmental concerns involved in the land acquisitions: "Outsourcing food production will ensure food security for investing countries but would leave behind a trail of hunger, starvation and food scarcities for local populations. The environmental tab of highly intensive farming—devastated soils, dry aquifer, and ruined ecology from chemical infestation—will be left for the host country to pick up" (ibid.). Yet a number of African governments seem keen to encourage such investments—reflecting the short-termism and lack of vision of many African administrations.

Conclusion

While Indian activity in Africa is multifaceted and New Delhi's official policies are clearly not purely altruistic, the renewal and upsurge in the Indian presence in Africa arguably does benefit many of the continent's economies by helping to provide new communication and transportation networks that are necessary for economic growth. Indirectly, an emerging India within the international system is of great political significance for the developing world as New Delhi increasingly uses its nascent economic and political muscle to advance improved trade and political conditions for itself, but also for developing nations more generally.

Currently, Indian activity in Africa may be said to constitute a middle ground between China's "hands-off" stance and the intrusive conditionalities associated with Western policies. Indian activities arguably provide an alternative option to Africa between the two extremes. Media representations of India's role in Africa have argued that "India's strategy and strengths in Africa are quite different. China concentrates on resources-based investment, while India has focused on capacity building" (Ramachandran, 2007). While not wishing to romanticize Indian ties with Africa, there is an element of truth here. Overall, mutual political and economic cooperation (as well as aid) in exchange for increased economic interaction and political support for India's rise on the global stage helps us to understand current Indo-African ties. As one analysis put it, "India is . . . cultivating a global relationship with the United States, and it is interacting in Africa with other global powers such as China. Africa is still a relatively small part of India's foreign policy, far less significant in commercial or political terms than the Middle East or Southeast Asia. But as India cultivates its global role, this is an area where it can position itself as a leader, a supplier of investment, and an aid donor" (Haté, 2008: 3).

The question here though is, is India a "scrambler or a development partner?" (Corkin and Naidu, 2008). While Indian academics forcefully assert that it is a true partnership (see Sharma, 2007), the answer to such a question remains very much open. Observers of Africa's international relations will need to check carefully as India's engagement in Africa unfolds. Naturally, much will depend upon African agency. African governments *could* use the opportunity of an increased Indian corporate presence in Africa as sources of appropriate technology, skills and advice for economic development. The key issue here is, how can (or will) African leaders seek to leverage the newfound Indian investment and interest in SSA so that Africa's place in global trade networks becomes more proactive and beneficial to the continent's citizens? As ever, it remains a priority for African elites to "accelerate efforts at getting [their] own house in order and to implement the policies, institutions, and trade-enabling physical infrastructure that will be the critical foundations" that will make African recovery possible (Corkin and Naidu, 2008: 115).

India's growing activity in Africa certainly presents an opportunity for a number of African economies to move away from being export-only and has the potential to help African companies become more efficient by exposing them to competition, new advances in technology and modern labor skills (Broadman, 2008: 105). As one commentator has noted, Indian (and Chinese) demand for African exports "is good news, because the boom is a potentially pivotal opportunity for African countries to move beyond their traditional reliance on single-commodity exports and move up from the bottom of the international production chain, especially if growth-enhancing opportunities for trade with the North continue to be as limited as they have been historically" (ibid.).

However, what many analysts missed prior to the global credit crunch was that Indian overseas acquisitions in Africa and elsewhere have been made possible not because Indian companies are particularly wealthy or dominant in their industries, but because it was very easy to borrow:

> Indian companies are the beneficiaries, for now, of the same global liquidity bubble that is producing multibillion-dollar private equity takeovers and has helped the Indian stock market rise fourfold since 2003. Thus, Indian companies are investing more overseas than foreigners are investing in India. Of course some acquisitions are in fields where India does lead—software and generic pharmaceuticals. Some are driven by business logic. But others do more to swell Indian pride than boost the Indian economy. (*New York Times* [New York], February 8, 2007)

As noted, India is unique among developing countries in that its FDI outflows are greater than its FDI inflows. Indian investors have been aided by an unsustainable rate of growth in bank credit, but India is a capital-short country and the global recession of 2009 will no doubt impact upon the ability and/or willingness of Indian companies to continue their buying spree in Africa.

Of course, bureaucratic links between the Indian Ministry of Commerce and the Ministry of External Affairs are indirect (Beri, 2005: 390), and Indian economic involvement in Africa is not controlled by New Delhi but by Indian corporate actors. Such activity is thus less influenced by normative concerns. It is therefore imperative for African states to recognize that while Indian official policy toward Africa talks the rhetoric of solidarity, Indian corporations generally only pursue the bottom line. Controlling and managing Indo-Africa relations is thus crucial for the continent if it is to benefit from the opportunities that increased Indian attention to Africa affords. Indian commentators like to assert that there "exists enormous goodwill for India in Africa and India should take advantage of it to further strengthen ties through a new partnership" (Beri, 2003). It is up to Africans to negotiate with Indian actors to ensure that the benefits accrued from Indo-African ties are evenly shared and that Indian interest in the continent, alongside others, may help serve as a catalyst for renewal.

CHAPTER SIX

The Empire(s) Strike Back? The European Union and Africa

Due to the colonial legacy, Europe as a continent has a special and peculiar relationship with Africa. As Chabal (2009: 20) notes, "it is in Africa that [the Europeans] most clearly revealed their own vision of mankind, extolled most loudly their own colonial (missionary) project, deployed most skillfully their own justification for enslaving and exploiting 'others', justified most casuistically their own sense of racial superiority and, today, revel in their most self-serving display of guilt and regret." As the EU has developed as a supra-national organization, this particular past and present encounter with Africa has been continually negotiated.

Despite repeated protestations by many African elites since independence to break free from the colonial past and the ties that bind Africa and Europe together, it remains a fact that for most SSA countries, the EU remains the main trading partner and the EU absorbs around 85 percent of Africa's agricultural exports and 75 percent of SSA's overall trade. Even with the rise of interest in the continent by the United States, China and India (the latter two eagerly seized upon in some quarters as finally proffering up the chance to move on from Europe), the EU continues to be Africa's key partner and a major source of developmental assistance. The EU is thus a most important factor in Africa's international relations and will remain so for at least the short- to medium-term.

Of note, the EU officially presents itself as a qualitatively distinct actor in global affairs (see Söderbaum and van Langenhove, 2007). Indeed,

> [t]he underlying assumption of this self-perception is that the EU, in its global action, follows values and approaches that are somehow different from those of nation states—especially the USA, but also individual EU member states—which are mainly or exclusively concerned with their national interests. In the same vein the EU would also be different from international institutions such as the IMF or the World Bank, and from regional organizations, such as Mercosur, which are chiefly concerned with economic policies. (Fioramonti and Poletti, 2008: 167; see also Smith, 2003)

However, "In spite of this self-representation, the EU's international action in policy sectors such as trade and investment, as well as in democracy promotion, is quite controversial, multifaceted and, often, inconsistent" (ibid.). This chapter seeks to outline some of the reasons why this is so, with particular reference to EU-SSA relations. In doing so, some caveats are in order. First, this chapter focuses on SSA and not relations with North Africa (see Gillespie and Youngs, 2002; Gomez, 2003). Secondly, this chapter chiefly concerns itself with economic issues and does not discuss the increasing emergence of the EU's role in conflict prevention (see Olsen, 2002; Stewart, 2006; Merlingen and Ostrauskaite,

2008). Finally, it should be understood that throughout the chapter the term "European Union" is used although, in fact, between 1957 and 1993, the organization's predecessor was the European Economic Community (EEC) and, in addition, the EU is actually made up of three pillars: the European Community (EC), the Common Foreign and Security Policy (CFSP), and the Police and Judicial Co-operation in Criminal Matters (Bomberg, Peterson and Stubb, 2008).

Understanding EU-Africa Relations

Since the end of the Cold War, momentous changes within the international system have impacted on EU-SSA relations. The collapse of the Soviet Union and the break up of the socialist bloc has led to the creation of over 150 million "new poor" in Eastern Europe and arguably a loss of geopolitical importance for many African countries. The subsequent failure of the "peace dividend" to materialize, and the escalation of conflicts in Africa in the 1990s led to a sharp increase in EU humanitarian aid, but this led to a diversion of scarce resources away from long-term development. And perhaps crucially, European integration and enlargement has arguably continued to push African development concerns into the background (Zielonka, 2001). The EU's membership increased from 15 countries to 25 on May 1, 2004, then 27 in 2007, with hundreds of thousands of migrants from within Europe every year now seeking employment, primarily in Western Europe, and often in competition with African migrants (Tsebelis, 2008). At the same time, the cost of enlargement has been calculated at US$93 billion, while all of the new members have no colonial heritage in Africa and need persuading why the EU should divert resources to that continent. Colonial guilt on the part of some member states of the EU perpetually encounters the notion that EU-Africa ties have moved into a postcolonial phase (Khadiagala, 2000: 83). So, EU-SSA relations are going through a process of flux.

According to Hurt (2004), a number of different approaches to the relationship between the EU and SSA exist. The officially sanctioned EU view springs from liberalism and seeks to advance the notion that the relationship is based on mutually beneficial terms grounded in cooperation and interdependence (see Gruhn 1976; Zartman 1976). This in itself is derivative of liberal understandings vis-à-vis integration (Chivvis, 2003). From this viewpoint, exploitative relations are absent and, rather, Africa's development is dependent upon greater integration into the global economy, which the EU can help facilitate, on mutually advantageous conditions for both parties. As the EU's *Strategy for Africa* put it:

> The purpose of the EU's action is to work in partnership with the nations of Africa to promote peace and prosperity for all their citizens. . . . The Strategy will further reinforce the basic principles that govern this relationship, most prominently *equality, partnership and ownership* . . . Key to the success of the partnership will be its ability to cement the bonds between the two continents beyond the formal political and economic interaction . . . objectives should be supplemented, especially for those countries closer to the EU, by support for economic integration and political cooperation with the EU. Taken together, these measures constitute the EU's common, comprehensive and coherent response to Africa's development challenges. (European Commission, 2005: 3)

A radically different interpretation of the EU's relationship with SSA emerges from Dependency Theory, a critique particularly strong in the 1970s and early 1980s (see Galtung, 1976). This approach sees the relationship as being emblematic of typical core-periphery relations and springing from the historical colonial relationship between Europe and Africa—a process that some authors see as having left a legacy of under-development on the African continent (Rodney, 1972). In short, the colonization process resulted in Africa's economies being oriented more toward the needs of European capital than the requirements of the local. This was the quintessential definition of dependency. Rather than picture an ahistorical "level playing field," as favored by liberalism, whereby each social formation needed to simply go through the ideal-type stages of growth, Dependency Theory rather asserted that Europe had an advantage from the start in that they never had to—at least in modern times—experience colonial rule, nor had to attempt to integrate themselves into a global economy already replete with richer and more powerful competitors. Comparing then the experiences of Europe and Africa, certainly at the early stages of development, was a futile exercise.

Critically, Dependency Theory also pointed out that the relationships of dependency crafted during the Age of Expansionism by the European metropoles were continued long after "official" rule by the colonizers was over. This was recognized early on by some African elites—Nkrumah (1965) being a famous example. According to Dependency theorists, only by recognizing this can a true appreciation of Europe-Africa relations be realized. Such a position asserts that the main obstacles to real autonomous development were not internal (such as Rostow's caricature of "traditional" societies, or the *Economist's* innate "African culture"), but were rather external in origin and contingently bound up with the historical experiences of the spread of international capitalism (Frank, 1967; 1975). As Hurt (2004) notes, this approach has placed particular emphasis on agreements such as the Lomé Convention and how this sustained Africa's role as a primary commodity exporter to Europe through the System for the Stabilization of Export Earnings (STABEX) and the Stabilization Scheme for Mineral Products (SYSMIN). On the other hand, core-periphery ties were cemented by the failure to permit duty-free access for manufactured products from Africa, preventing industrialization. While this approach is helpful in understanding key characteristics of the global capitalist system and how Africa was (unequally) inserted into the world economy, its structuralism serves to deny Africa of any agency and, not least, reduces African elites to the status of willing dupes, something which the evidence of extraversion does not support.

Indeed, while development cooperation itself should be seen as encapsulating particular political and economic relationships, rather than constituting some kind of "apolitical" or "technical" assistance (Brown, 2000: 368), it should not be seen as a one-way street of neocolonial impositions. The dialectical role between political and economic elites *on both sides* shapes the relationship. While structures are vital to comprehend, the agency of actors within such structures is equally important. Consequently, the role of resources (political and economic) that emanated from the relationship with Europe was invariably utilized by extant elites for their own purposes (primarily regime survival) and often ran counter to the expressed aims of the Europeans when disbursing such material. As Brown (2000: 371) notes, "for particular regimes, power lay in the clientelist links and the patronage that occupation of state positions made possible, and access to external resource flows (from both aid and trade) were a major element in this." Ignoring the extraversion strategies of African elites when discussing EU-SSA ties thus makes little sense.

EU-Africa Relations in Historical Perspective

The EU history with postcolonial Africa is long and has been progressively formalized—and politicized—as relations have unfolded (Lister, 1997; Brown, 2002; Holland, 2002). The Treaty of Rome (1957) first established a formalized relationship with Europe's colonial territories (including those outside of Africa), with Article 131 of the Treaty stating that "the Member States agree to associate with the Community the non-European countries and territories which have special relations with Belgium, Denmark, France, Italy, the Netherlands and the United Kingdom." It further stated that "the purpose of association shall be to promote the economic and social development of the countries and territories and to establish close economic relations between them and the Community as a whole." Of note, France made the association of its African colonies with the EEC a precondition for signing the Rome Treaty and becoming a member of the Community. Later, following independence in the 1960s, the first Yaoundé Convention was negotiated with 18 largely Francophone former colonies, the Associated African States and Madagascar (AASM), in 1963, primarily to safeguard French interests.

The Yaoundé Conventions of 1963 (Yaoundé II in 1969 saw the agreement renewed for another five years) "provided both aid and trade access to the EU market—although the latter was given only on a reciprocal basis and therefore did not match the 'special treatment' in terms of nonreciprocal trade benefits that developing countries were establishing in the General Agreement on Tariffs and Trade (GATT) at a global level. It also showed that Europe would play a role in the international support that was afforded to the development and stability of the new states. While the move represented something of a 'multilateralization' of postcolonial ties in that the agreements were with the whole EEC rather than simply the former colonial power it also reflected French priorities in North-South relations, protecting as it did France's postimperial ties with Africa" (Brown, 2000: 372). As Brown infers, the relationship between the EU and SSA has had to negotiate a perpetual tension: that of balancing the wider, multilateral, interests of the EU, with the more immediate (and often more compelling) interests of individual members, primarily the ex-colonial powers. This tension has, in fact, continually weakened attempts at constructing a unified EU stance toward Africa.

After the United Kingdom joined the EC in 1973, a new agreement had to be established in order to accommodate those countries that were members of the Commonwealth. Thus the Lomé Treaty of 1975 was established, maintaining a separate cooperation agreement between the then 46 ACP states (Africa, the Caribbean and the Pacific) and the EU. The objective of Lomé was "to promote the economic, cultural and social development of ACP countries" and was founded on three official principles: equality of the partners, sovereignty in decision-making and the security of relations. The Treaty aimed to bolster trade between the EU and ACP states, support the structural adjustment efforts of ACP countries, facilitate access to capital markets and support direct investment, in addition to compensating fluctuations in export earnings (see Brown, 1999; Montana, 2003).

A key article of the Lomé Convention(s) was nonreciprocal trade access, which allowed approximately 90 percent of ACP exports to enter the EU's markets duty free.

Protocols that managed bananas, beef, rum, sugar and veal exports from the ACP states to the EU were added, fixing an annual import quantity and price. Economic developmental assistance to the ACP states was also central, mediated through the European Development Fund (EDF) and disbursed according to requirements and based on per capita income. In June 2006, the 10th EDF was agreed for the period 2008 to 2013, with an overall budget of €23,966 billion [US$33,398 billion] (de Bergh, 2006: 1). Compensation for fluctuations in export earnings was covered by two commodity insurance schemes: the stabilization of exports (STABEX) of Lomé I, and the system of minerals (SYSMIN), introduced by Lomé II. These insurance schemes were calculated to aid in the alleviation of negative impacts stimulated by shortfalls in export receipts. Industrial and technical cooperation was also a feature of Lomé, with the aim that ACP countries could access EU expertise in aiding the industrialization and development of their economies.

It is absolutely crucial to situate Lomé within its broader global context. With the growth in membership in the UN of states of the South, combined with a steady disillusionment with an ever-apparent unequal world, a strategic space opened up for the ex-colonial nations to question the extant global order. This was particularly so as this was an order in which the new states had had no hand in crafting. As the 1970s progressed, the South began to push for an agenda that sought to deal primarily with the issue of trade with the North. This call for a New International Economic Order (NIEO) symbolically culminated at the Sixth Special Session of the United Nations in 1974 where, under the NAM's then leader (Algeria's Houari Boumedienne), the South deployed NAM and G-77 (a permanent group representing the interests of the South within the United Nations) texts in successfully pushing for a comprehensive normative declaration detailing the aspirations of the South's elites. This in essence reflected responses to real problems experienced by states in the South, particularly as a result of the Bretton Woods system's creation and operation (Laszlo et al., 1979).

Emboldened by the demonstration of economic power by OPEC during the crisis of 1973–4, Southern elites clamored for greater development finance, an increase in the percentage of gross national product (GNP) allocated by the North as aid, and development issues to be placed centrally at the IMF and World Bank. Overall, these were the heydays of the South's role in world affairs as active agents and Lomé reflected this. During this period, "there were fears of a permanent global power shift" within the West (Whiteman, 1998: 31). The sorts of concessions granted by Europe at Lomé reflect this. Arguably, since the ascendancy of neoliberalism and the subsequent demise of Third Worldism, what we have witnessed regarding EU-SSA relations is a process whereby the EU has sought to claw back such concessions and the ACP nations have sought to defend them.

The Convention was subsequently renegotiated and signed in 1980 (Lomé II), 1985 (Lomé III), and 1990 (Lomé IV). These saw, progressively, new additions to the Treaty, namely nonreciprocal trade concessions (Lomé I), the "globalization" of EU-ACP cooperation (Lomé II) and economic, social, and cultural rights (Lomé III). Human rights, regionalization, structural adjustment policies, liberal democratization and the rule of law were added at Lomé IV, reflecting the hegemony of neoliberalism as the Cold War ended (Olsen, 2001). A midterm review of Lomé IV was embarked on in 1995 (Crawford, 1996; Parfitt, 1996; Olsen, 2001). The Lomé Conventions expired on February 29, 2000, to be replaced by the Cotonou Agreement.

The Cotonou Agreement

The Cotonou Agreement was signed on June 23, 2000 in the capital of Benin between the then 15 members of the EU and 77 ACP countries. The Agreement was the result of protracted and controversial discussions between the two sides that had begun in September 1998 (Martenczuk, 2000; Forwood, 2001). The new agreement marked a deep change in the nature and spirit of the relationship, when compared to earlier EU-ACP conventions. Indeed, Cotonou is in many ways a departure from the provisions of Lomé and can be seen to reflect the hegemony of neoliberal thinking vis-à-vis the link between development and economic policies. The more interventionist nature of Lomé, reflecting the thrust of the NIEO of the 1970s had had to fight a continual rearguard action as successive Lomé agreements emerged, but by the 1990s neoliberalism had all but extinguished such sentiments (Hurt, 2003: 163). The wider ideational and structural context of Cotonou is thus crucial.

It was the EU that commenced proceedings toward a post-Lomé accord with the publication of a Green Paper on the future of EU-ACP relations (see Commission of the European Communities, 1996). In contrast, the ACP generally favored a modification of the accord—but no more. The Libreville Declaration, issued by the first Summit of ACP Heads of State and Government in 1997, called on the EU to maintain nonreciprocal trade preferences and market access in a successor agreement and maintain the preferential commodity protocols and arrangements (ACP Heads of State and Government, 1997). However, the EU advanced a wholesale overhaul. Consequently, a compromise was reached, though slanted in favor of the EU due to its preponderant economic muscle. The failure of Lomé to promote broad-based development within the ACP countries, even after a quarter of a century of privileged concessions and market access to Europe, made many EU actors question the apparent inability of ACP societies to respond favorably to the diverse economic incentives offered by Brussels. Indeed, during the Lomé time frame, the ACP countries' shares in the EU's market fell from 6.7 percent in 1976 to 3 percent in 1998, while 60 percent of the total ACP export concentrated on only 10 products. There was also an appreciable rise in poverty in many ACP countries (NEPRU, 2001: 2).

Dissatisfaction with Lomé then coincided with two developments outside the control of the EU-ACP framework. First, the conclusion of the Uruguay Round of the General Agreement on Tariffs and Trade (GATT) and the establishment of the WTO in 1994 had profound implications for Lomé. Fundamentally, the WTO provisions of nondiscrimination made many of the preferential provisions of Lomé unsustainable: the nonreciprocal trade regime of Lomé was illegal within WTO rules as it was granted to only and all ACP countries, regardless of their level of economic development. In 1996 Lomé's provisions came before the WTO and the exclusive and preferential trade relationship between the EU and the ACP states fell foul of WTO statutes. Thus the EU proposed free trade agreements, or Economic Partnership Agreements (EPAs), with individual as well as groups of ACP countries. Brussels' ambition was that such EPAs would substitute for Lomé's nonreciprocal trade preferences.

Secondly, the continuing planned process of EU enlargement, as well as the launching of the Single European Market in 1993 and the inauguration of a single European currency, meant that agreements entered into with non-EU sides needed to be renegotiated to reflect such new developments. Indeed, the Cotonou Agreement had to be negotiated within a wider context whereby the EU had emerged as a major global actor in its own right and where concerns about managing its relationships with its ex-colonies was but one part of an ever-expanding portfolio of foreign policy concerns (Bretherton and Vogler, 1999). By the time that Cotonou was negotiated, it could be argued that the EU had moved on from its fixation with its ex-territories that had been so starkly exemplified by the Yaoundé concords. Equally, the ACP countries now had to negotiate in an environment where other parts of the world were clamoring for attention and in competition for the EU's scarce resources. Not least, of course, were the emerging economies of Central and Eastern Europe, many of whom were aspiring members of the EU and certainly desired—and demanded—increased attention (and expenditure) from Brussels.

Cotonou can be described as resting on three pillars: the political dimension, development cooperation and trade cooperation. The overlapping interconnectedness of these three pillars will be described below. First, embedded in all national development strategies and within the framework of EU development cooperation with an individual ACP country, the key political activities are linked to the promotion of institutional, political and legal reform processes, as well as capacity building programs for public and private actors and civil society. Secondly, development cooperation ranges from the promotion of the private sector, to regional cooperation, as well as "mainstreaming" gender, the environment, and HIV/AIDS into EU-ACP aid partnerships. The European Development Fund acts as a special funding mechanism, with EU member states negotiating their contributions to it every five years. Thirdly, trade is envisioned as the strongest pillar of the Cotonou Agreement, as it is conceived as the engine of sustainable development. Yet the ability of the EU to promote "sustainable development" in Africa has arguably been constrained by domestic pressures within the EU itself that lead to highly unequal sets of relationships between the EU and SSA, most graphically symbolized with the EU's systems of subsidies and the Common Agricultural Policy.

The Common Agricultural Policy

"More than thirty years after the signing of the first Lomé Convention (1975), the ACP still exports primarily raw materials to Europe and provides a ready market for European finished goods. Conventional procedures have not promoted diversification, competitiveness, growth or poverty reduction in any sustainable manner. Although regional integration has belonged for decades to the declared aims of both the EU's and the ACP's own development strategies, it has been applied with little success" (Kohnert, 2008: 12). This reflects a degree of failure that both the EU and Africa's elites cannot escape from. Arguably key in explaining some of the factors behind this situation is the Common Agricultural Policy (CAP) of the EU.

The CAP has its roots in postwar Western Europe, where agriculture had been crippled and food security was problematic. The CAP was initially aimed at encouraging better agricultural productivity as a means of guaranteeing stable supplies of reasonably priced food and also help rebuild Europe's agricultural sector. The CAP provided subsidies and structures guaranteeing high prices to farmers and provided incentives for them to increase production. The CAP was highly successful in facilitating the EU's self-sufficiency in food production from the 1980s onwards. However, as part of the processes stimulated by the CAP, permanent surpluses of major farm commodities (the infamous "butter mountains" and "wine lakes"—see Cottrell, 1987) developed. Some of these surpluses were exported, with the aid of export subsidies, which massively distorted world markets, while at the same time being expensive to EU taxpayers (see Mackel, Marsh and Revell, 1984).

Due to mounting pressure within the EU, a series of reforms, particularly at the beginning of the 1990s, were introduced. Production limits reduced surpluses for instance. Farmers were encouraged to rely more on the market, although they still received direct income aid. A ceiling was also put on the CAP's budget and in 2003 a further fundamental reform was agreed. Currently, the majority of aid to EU farmers is disbursed independently of their levels of production; under the new system (the Single Farm Payment), EU farmers receive direct income payments to keep them in business, but the link to production has been removed.

The EU makes much of these reforms. However, Charles Crawford, the British ambassador to Poland (correctly) described the CAP as "The most stupid, immoral state-subsidized policy in human history," which amounted to little more than "a program which uses inefficient transfers of taxpayers money to bloat rich French landowners and so pump up food prices in Europe, thereby creating poverty in Africa, which we then fail to solve through inefficient but expensive aid programs" (cited in *Sunday Times* [London], December 11, 2005). In 2007, the EU spent US$58.5 billion on untargeted support to agriculture, and US$13 billion on targeted payments under the rural development program. All CAP expenses amounted to slightly more than 40 percent of the EU budget (European Commission, 2008).

Within the EU there is deep division regarding the CAP. The British state that they would like to abolish tariffs and all other measures that maintain EU agricultural prices above world market levels. They would also like to stop the direct payments that farmers receive irrespective of their production output. However, Germany, France and other states where the agricultural lobby is strong wish that the CAP be strengthened, with the French claiming that the CAP is so effective that it should be exported to developing countries! This French claim needs contextualizing; according to one analysis, CAP reform:

[I]s supporting the expansion of exports through enhancing its price competitiveness and shifting patterns of exports away from basic agricultural products to value-added food products. As the process of CAP reform is rolled out to more and more sectors, the cumulative effect on the price competitiveness of EU value-added food products will be greatly enhanced . . . further fuelling the expansion of EU exports of value-added food products. This is particularly the case for simple value-added food products, where the price of the agricultural raw materials is proportionally far more important to the price of the final product than for more sophisticated value-added food products. Unfortunately, "it is precisely these simple value-added food products that have been the starting point for agriculture-based industrial development." (Goodison, 2007: 292)

Consequently, "The EU approach to agricultural reform thus has serious implications for African food and agricultural production. Indeed, it could well serve to lock African agricultural production into an externally oriented system of production where prices received are either stagnant or declining" (ibid.: 295). Critics have equally argued that the replacement of nonreciprocal trade preferences as provided by Lomé by *reciprocal* trade agreements known as EPAs will likely continue in these same trajectories.

Economic Partnership Agreements

The EPAs have proven to be highly controversial aspects of the EU's ongoing relationship with SSA. As part of any EPA, the domestic markets of the ACP countries have to be opened up to EU products and all barriers to trade have to be removed—conformity with the WTO is mentioned several times in the Cotonou Agreement. This necessarily introduces high levels of unfair competition into African economies as European producers are granted access to overseas markets while benefiting immensely from price competitive exports due to high levels of direct income support from the EU to enhance EU international competitiveness. For instance, the elimination of unfair cotton subsidies paid by the USA, China and the EU to their farmers would increase the income of West African cotton producers by US$250 million per annum. According to Overseas Development Institute (ODI) estimates, EU cotton subsidies alone account for up to 38 percent of annual income losses of cotton farmers in West and Central Africa; their elimination would increase the cotton export earnings of Benin and the Republic of Chad by US$9 million and US$12 million, respectively (Gillson et al., 2004).

Furthermore, Cotonou extends economic relations to include trade in services and other trade related matters, e.g. product standards, intellectual property rights. The push to include these in EPAs has been particularly controversial, as the EU has succeeded in inducing concessions on the liberalization of "new generation" areas or "Singapore Issues," such as government procurement, health, services, competition policies and investment. Including such "Singapore Issues" is not required for an EPA to be compliant with WTO strictures, but it *is* considered central by the EU in its interpretation of the reciprocity principles of the Cotonou Agreement. However, such nontariff liberalization threatens to reify, if not extend, the domination of ACP economies by EU corporations and any liberalization of such "new generation" issues will be mostly unidirectional in the EU's favor.

Equally problematic is the most-favored nation (MFN) clause. The MFN decree automatically confers any trade benefits under future agreements with other countries onto the EU as long as it concerns a country that contributes 1.5 percent or more to the global economy. The practicalities of this is that any ACP country that signed a trade deal with developing economies such as Brazil, China or India would have to extend exactly the same terms to the whole of the EU. Given the rise of interest by such countries in Africa, the MFN seems designed to prevent such emerging economies from establishing trade pacts with African nations without the EU benefiting. Once they are signed, EPAs will be separate trading arrangements either with regional economic blocs (the EU's preference) or bilaterally.

The advent of EPAs has generated widespread opposition within European circles. Of note, the British Department of Trade and Industry and the DFID issued a joint position paper that critiqued the EU's promotion of reciprocity within EPAs, arguing that EPA negotiations should not be exploited as a means to forcibly open up the markets of the ACP countries, pointing out that "ACP regional groups have maximum flexibility over their own market opening," with over 20 years time for market opening (cited in Goodison, 2007: 296). In turn, the then EU's trade commissioner Peter Mandelson, himself British, rejected this "major and unwelcome shift" in London's stance to EPAs and criticized the influence of campaigning NGOs and celebrities, asserting that Britain's position "could well make progress with EPA negotiations more difficult by reinforcing the views of the more skeptical ACP states and raising the prospect of alternatives that are, in reality, impractical" (*Guardian* [London], May 19, 2005). Such "impractical" demands have been spearheaded by a variety of European civil society organizations such as the STOP-EPA campaign.

In the context of the continuing crisis in the WTO's negotiations on further trade rounds, the EU's project to promote reciprocity as a key element of its EPAs is a main target of the organizations, with claims that they are neocolonial in nature and nakedly in the interest of EU-based multinational corporations. Raffer (2001), in fact, has asserted that "Free Trade Areas (FTAs) must . . . be expected to reflect mainly if not solely European interests—to soften the pressures of globalization on Europe, as the Commission formulated, giving European exporters an advantage over other industrialized countries. This does not suggest development considerations as the main reason." The STOP-EPA organization has stated that "The EU has narrowed down the Cotonou objectives of poverty eradication and sustainable development to a self-serving trade and investment liberalization agenda. EPAs will increase the domination and concentration of European firms, goods and services" (www.stopepa.org).

Meanwhile, Oxfam's position is that "The European Commission clearly wants to use EPAs as a tool to open markets and further its own interests." This is not good. EPAs in their current form would be detrimental to development. They are free trade agreements by any other name and are currently designed to get the most for Europe without the necessary consideration of the negative effects on weaker developing country partners (*Guardian* [London], May 19, 2005). Even the European Parliament has joined in the criticisms, noting in 2007 that it was "very concerned that too rapid a reciprocal trade liberalization between the EU and the ACP could have a negative impact on vulnerable ACP economies" and that "liberalizing trade between unequal partners as a tool for development has historically proven to be ineffective and even counterproductive" (European Parliament, 2006: 1).

From the African side, "There are increasing anxieties on the part of the African partners about the outcome of the EPA negotiations. During the EU-Africa Summit in Lisbon in December 2007, African statesmen such as Senegalese president Abdoulaye Wade and South Africa's Thabo Mbeki made it clear that they considered the EU proposals for EPAs a dead letter which had to be renegotiated by extending the deadline" (Kohnert, 2008: 13). "In addition, the AU Commission president Alpha Oumar Konaré insisted on Africa's right to protect its infant industries. He accused the EU of playing the old divide-and-rule game in Africa by luring more advanced economies such as Kenya, Côte d'Ivoire, and Ghana . . . into signing stop-gap interim bilateral agreements (IEPAs)" (ibid.).

The controversial nature of the EPAs might be seen as part and parcel of a continuing trend to both "open up" ACP markets for the EU's corporate interests as well as an attempt to reconfigure the Global South to accord with the accumulation strategies of capitalist interests. Since "capitalism encompasses the entire globe, its architects require a universal vision, a picture of a globally conceived society, to join classes in different countries . . . [in order] to institutionalize global capital accumulation by setting general rules of behavior and disseminating a developmentalist ideology to facilitate the process" (Mittelman and Pasha, 1997: 51). The political aspect of EU-SSA relations seems to fit with such analysis.

Politics, Conditionalities and EU-SSA Ties

Conditionalities have always existed in EU-SSA relations; the first condition is to join up to any Convention promoted by the EU. As Crawford (2001: 2) notes, "development aid has always been political . . . with implicit conditionality." Initially, however, the first Lomé Convention at least *claimed* that the respect of state sovereignty and the self-determination of partners were paramount. Yet as the EU's policies toward Africa have developed, they have become steadily more politicized (Carbone, 2007). Since around the mid-1980s, explicit references to political norms favored by the Union began to be included in pacts. Carl (1999: 116) states that it was the ACP countries who actually initiated this process by asking that a reference to the respect of human rights as a common "belief" be inserted into Lomé III in 1985 as a means of shaming the Netherlands and the United Kingdom for their economic and political ties to apartheid South Africa (Carl, 1999: 116). Due to British and Dutch objections, human rights were reduced to the annex of the text.

As the Cold War ended and as the "wave of democratization" swept over the developing world, the tables were turned and the EU adopted a proactive stance in advocating political matters as prerequisites for the EU-ACP relationship (Olsen, 1997). Human rights, liberal democracy and the rule of law were all clauses inserted into the text of Lomé IV Convention, and the revised Lomé IV Convention of 1995 actually saw these norms elevated to the status of "essential" as to what the EU-ACP countries were striving to arrive at as part of the Convention. The Cotonou Agreement pushed this further by developing a framework whereby punishment for misdemeanors, in the form of aid suspension for gross abuses of human rights, was introduced.

In contrast to Lomé, Cotonou also established an apparatus for the reduction of aid through possible modifications of Country Strategy Papers (Santiso, 2003). Cotonou also made aid and resource redistribution possible, with mechanisms to reward compliant countries, and limit or deny unspent funds to poor performers. This sent "the message that it is possible to re-allocate the second tranche to other countries that do perform well and take more account of EU priorities" (Crawford, 1996: 509). This followed a broader pattern whereby "the introduction of explicit political conditions to aid was additional to the prevailing economic conditionality that had dominated aid policy in the 1980s, with multilateral lending and much bilateral aid dependent on the adoption of International Monetary Fund/World Bank-led structural adjustment programs" (Crawford, 2001: 2).

In this sense, political conditionalities have become part of the EU's development cooperation regime and this fits with the progressive efforts by all major Western donors to use aid as a tool to advance particular understandings of "good governance" (see Abrahamsen, 2000). "The 1990s witnessed a dramatic increase in interest among western liberal democracies and international organizations in promoting democracy, human rights and good governance as the global gold standards for states" (Burnell,

2000: 3). A remarkable consensus was achieved on both the ends and the means that were declared in the policy statements of donors in the immediate post–Cold War period. Indeed, all intergovernmental organizations, as well as OECD states and other donor agencies, more or less accept as commonsense the self-evident virtuosity and truth of the liberal project. This hegemony is reinforced and amplified by the fact that liberalism is the foundation upon which the IFIs operate.

Such a normative agenda is equally dominant within the EU, with a broad consensus on what is "good" economic policy linked to what constitutes the fundamentals of any governance structures. All of this fosters an intellectual climate at the EU's policy level in which the basic assumptions of liberalism go unproblematized: "Untrammeled international competition, the celebration of the market, of wealth and self, anti-communism and anti-unionism; all these are no longer propagated as 'revolutionary' in the sense of challenging a prevailing consensus of a different content, but they are now part of normal every day discourse; self-evident, near impossible to contradict or even doubt" (Overbeek and van der Pijl, 1993: 2). "We are given to understand that the laws of the market will inevitably embrace the whole world, so there is really no point in fighting them" (Wood, 2006: 15). The EU's relationships with the ACP countries fit such a portrayal.

This is important, as on the EU's part, "In addition to the general goal of forging good relations with (potential) political and economic partners across the globe, the Union also wishes to use its place in international relations as a vehicle for advocating some of the values it considers important. Among these values are democracy, social welfare, human rights and liberalism" (Arts and Dickson, 2004: 1). It should be noted that the EU does not generally make an explicit distinction between the promotion of human rights and the promotion of liberal democracy; they are assumed to be one and the same thing. Indeed, "the promotion of democracy and human rights has become an increasingly central feature of EU external relations policy over the past 15 years, including in Africa. It is a prominent characteristic both of the EU's development co-operation policy and of its foreign policy more generally" (Crawford, 2004: 3).

Hurt (2004) notes the EU's policy approaches to achieve its objectives vis-à-vis liberal democracy and "good governance" were twofold: first, provide positive support for specific aid projects and programs aimed at strengthening respect for human rights and liberal democratic practices and institutions. Secondly, as noted, introduce sanctions when there are perceived breaches of human rights, a lack of democracy/democratization, or serious state corruption (Portela, 2009). This fits with the notion that the key element of conditionality is "the use of pressure, by the donor, in terms of threatening to terminate aid, or actually terminating or reducing it, if conditions are not met by the recipient" (Stokke, 1995: 11).

An EU Council of Ministers meeting in 1991 established much of the framework for the implementation of such measures. The adoption of the resolution of the Council of Ministers on "Human Rights, Democracy and Development" in November 1991 "was, and remains, the pivotal policy statement" as it "made promotion of human rights and democracy both an *objective* and a *condition* of development co-operation" (Crawford 2000: 92). And as the 1990s progressed, various African regimes fell foul of the EU. Aid was suspended to The Gambia in 1994 following the military coup that deposed President Dawda Jawara, to Liberia in 1998 in objection to President Charles Taylor's support for the Sierra Leonean Revolutionary United Front, and to Togo in 1998 in protest against sham presidential elections. Reflecting the power disparities between the

EU and its erstwhile ACP "partners," the ACP-EU Joint Assembly was not conferred with when political questions were deployed as a means to trigger and justify the suspension of aid. This is perhaps unsurprising given that the Maastricht Treaty on the European Union made the promotion of liberal democracy and human rights a key objectives of the newly created second pillar, theCFSP. In other words, from Brussels' perspective, liberal conceptions of democracy and human rights were nonnegotiable. In fact, since May 1995, human rights and democracy clauses have been inserted into all EU-ACP agreements and allow for the use of conditionality mechanisms.

Criticism of the EU's use of conditionalities to promote reforms center on the suspicion that the EU utilizes political reform as a means to promote economic liberalization, and political conditionality and democracy promotion as means of promoting dominant relationships. Yet, according to Uvin (1993: 68), "conditionality can be said to have been effectively exercised only if a recipient country undertakes a policy change that would not have undertaken by itself, that is, without the pressure made to bear upon it by the donor." Following on from this, a number of constraints on the effectiveness of conditionalities can be outlined (Olsen, 1998). First, in comparison to other sources of revenues, such as trade and foreign investment, aid is largely insignificant in most countries, reducing the power to delay aid suspension as a viable political instrument. Secondly, there is no clear definition of what constitutes the priorities for aid and other considerations are often deemed more important, such as economic or geopolitical objectives.

Thirdly, most of the EU's ex-colonial powers have their client states and "pets" and work hard at defending these from predation by other EU member states and/or punishment from the EU as a whole. A somewhat cynical "gentlemen's agreement" is in fact in operation, which shields miscreants. Ethiopia and Zaïre, for instance, "enjoyed continued EC financial support [and were] prominent recipients of EC aid even though their human rights [were] clearly abysmal" (Nwobike, 2005: 1395). Generally, those African elites who have the temerity to challenge the ex-colonial power *or* who have no active patrons within the EU are the most vulnerable to sanctions. Witness the cases of Côte d'Ivoire, Sudan and Zimbabwe's relations with the EU. It is rare that this tacit agreement is breached, although France did just that in 2003 when President Robert Mugabe was invited to the Franco-African Summit, provoking apoplexy in London.

Conclusion

As a means of furthering EU interests, the European Council adopted in December 2005 a new Strategy for Africa. This was the first EU concept paper with a *continental* focus and aimed to provide an integrated framework for EU-Africa relations. The plan of the Strategy for Africa is that the various foreign, security, trade and development policies will be coordinated under this new framework. This is in part a response to the long-standing criticism that the EU's "actorness" is limited by its divergent members' various—and often contesting—interests and the concomitant overlapping and duplication of policies (see Manners and Whitman, 2001). The Strategy emphasizes the notion of "partnership" with Africa and explicitly links its emergence to the new institutional dynamics within Africa, such as the establishment of NEPAD and the AU. However, the disjuncture between the EU's self-perceived role and that of others' views on the organization is again highlighted by the very concept of "partnership." Though a fashionable term among all main development agencies and IFIs, the possibility of genuine equality in the relationship has long been in doubt, reducing the term "partnership" to mere rhetorical status (see Hurt, 2003; Raffer, 2001).

In fact, the notion of "partnership" is undermined by other conceptions of the EU as being a mercantilist actor in global trade (Wolf, 1995: 335–6). Here, the EU is seen as primarily an economic power that utilizes its commercial muscle to force open foreign markets while maintaining a (relatively) closed domestic market. Critics point to the EU's agricultural sector and the CAP as examples of the latter; the EPAs as examples of the former. From this perspective, it could be argued that the concessions granted at Lomé were historical anomalies that sprang from a specific temporal conjuncture, i.e. the rise of Third Worldism and the NIEO moment. The preferential market access that was granted to the ACP countries on the basis of nonreciprocity is, in this view, under a process of correction with the planned rolling out of the EPAs. Here, the EU's deft deployment of the WTO's prescriptions as being both fixed and also beyond the control of the EU (despite the fact that the EU, collectively, is a weighty component of the WTO) is a useful alibi for Brussels. Critics argue that this attempt to shift the blame to the WTO is actually a premeditated effort by the EU to clear itself of any responsibility for policy decisions that are in fact its own (Hurt, 2003: 174).

Intriguingly though, such negative observations of the EU as a hypocritical protectionist power are not coupled with a wider negative assessment of its role in the broader international system. Indeed, the EU's role in promoting multilateralism and its ostensible willingness to promote a new multipolar global order goes down well in most African capitals, particularly within the context of recent American foreign policy. Criticism of the EU's role in international trade issues is often mitigated by other evaluations of the EU. And, of course, the importance of the EU as a "model" for regional integration is something that has considerable purchase across the continent and which the EU has been active in promoting via technical assistance to various regional economic communities in Africa, however unrealistic this may be.

Yet it remains that "the EU is often described as an inconsistent actor which, while reiterating the importance of the fight against poverty and the quest for sustainable development in its public statements, continues to perpetuate poverty in the so-called developing world through unfair practices and double standards in some of the most sensitive sectors for developing economies" (Fioramonti and Poletti, 2008: 168). Having said that, as Effeh (2008: 88) reminds us, "by overemphasizing the issue of protectionism in Western markets, commentators on Africa often ignore one of the region's defining problems: its lack of basic infrastructural and institutional capacity . . . In a sense, it could be argued that the region's inability to create the necessary institutions and infrastructure is a direct function of resource constraints. Yet, this would ignore the fact that in many cases, resources are either stolen by the ruling elite, or diverted into inappropriate projects, while public institutions are constantly undermined by what media commentators sometimes describe as 'bad politics.'"

To summarize, the evolution of the EU's relations with SSA remain dominated by notions of partnerships via development cooperation and inconsistencies regarding economic dealings that often exert powerfully negative images of the EU as a collective unit that gives with one hand but that takes back with the other. Handicapped by the divergent interests of its various members, the question remains whether the EU can move from individual actions to a genuinely common set of policies toward SSA (Vorrath, 2005). Indeed, the standard of EU policy coherence has been the subject of controversial debates within the EU, particularly with regard to Brussels' ability to speak with a unified voice in international affairs (see Carbone, 2009). "Despite being institutionalized in the Treaty of Maastricht, policy coherence for development . . . which implies taking into account the needs and interest of developing countries in non-aid policies, failed to make headway in the EU, remaining the unheeded concern of some NGOs and a small group of member states" (Carbone, 2008). In fact, policy coherence in the developmental realms has been dubbed "a 'mission impossible' for whoever attempts it due to the interplay of various issues and interests, the different commitment to international development of the member states, and the EU's institutional framework" (ibid.).

Certainly, movement on policies is excruciatingly slow while the EU as an institution is notorious for its bureaucratic inertia (Olsen, 2005). Paradoxically, it is probably in SSA where the EU has the greatest potential space to maneuver and overcome its failure to develop as a truly coherent global political actor (see Söderbaum and Stålgren, 2009). However, Brussels has historically not been able to achieve this, despite the colonial inheritance and the long-standing ties between key EU members and much of the continent. Currently, the hegemony of neoliberalism within the EU serves the broad interests of outwardly orientated fractions of the EU's ruling elites and navigating the tensions that this creates in any consistent set of development policies remains a key challenge to the EU-SSA relationship, particularly when these same actors practice de facto mercantilism and protectionism in certain areas of policy while proclaiming their commitment to liberalization. Such hypocrisy invites scorn and resentment within Africa. Of course, with the steady emergence of new actors in Africa's international relations, such as China and India, time may be running out for the EU to fashion a more unambiguous Africa policy.

CHAPTER SEVEN

Why Do We Need Political Scientists? Africa and the International Financial Institutions

The IFIs, primarily the World Bank and the IMF, have been actively involved in Africa's international relations since the heady days of independence. Initially, both Bretton Woods institutions had quite particular (and balancing remits); the IMF's mission was to avert macroeconomic insecurity through the stabilization of exchange rates, while the World Bank was to foster (initially European) economic recovery and development via the provision of low-interest loans (Calvert and Calvert, 2007: 176). Yet in the decades that followed, "mission creep" slowly changed the remits of IFIs far beyond their original mandates. It is important to note here that the institutions' roles at their founding was to provide temporary liquidity to existing economies and provide low-interest loans, rather than attempt to wholesale restructure them along particular economic lines.

Not only has Africa received over US\$1 trillion in development-related aid over the past 50 years (Moyo, 2009: xviii), but SSA has probably been the region that has undergone the most concentrated and continuous applications of IFI prescriptions over an increasingly diverse range of policy areas for over two decades, with generally disappointing results (Thomas, 2004). Indeed, the role of the IFIs in Africa has been highly controversial, with the institutions being variously accused of incompetence, destabilizing regimes, causing Africa's economic downturn and being an instrument of neo-imperialism.

This is particularly problematic in the context of the MDGs, which were adopted by the UN General Assembly in September 2000. The eight MDGs range from halving extreme poverty to halting the spread of HIV/AIDS and providing universal primary education. The goal is to achieve the MDGs by 2015. However, currently, the MDGs have no chance of being met if the present trajectories continue. Primary education for all will be delivered not as the Goals pledged in 2015, but, at the current rate, in 2130. The halving of poverty will be met not by the promised 2015 but by 2150, and the elimination of preventable infant deaths not by the target year of 2015 but by 2165 (*Fabian Review*, January 2005). Thus the role of the IFIs is an extremely important aspect of Africa's contemporary political economy, as is studying the dialectical relationship between the IFIs and Africa's elite classes.

The Development Debate: Initial African Responses

Early postcolonial economic proposals were generally motivated by the desire (at least rhetorically) to surmount what were regarded as problems emanating from the legacy bequeathed by colonialism. Thus stress was laid on accelerated projects to develop infrastructure and education while import-substitution, encouraged at the time by development agencies and the IFIs, was meant to stimulate industrialization (Anyang'Nyong'o and Coughlin, 1991). However, this strategy fell apart before the twin problems of the collapse in the price of primary commodities and the debilitating effect of malgovernance eroded the resources and capacity of a great many African states to pursue such policies. On the "purely" economic front, the collapse of the value of primary commodities on the global market meant that import substitution policies became more and more untenable as the public fiscus increasingly accrued ruinous external debt, increasing a debilitating dependence on exogenous actors. And as the capacity of the state declined, alongside the collapse of what infrastructure that existed that might have facilitated exports, combined with destructive domestic policies that disadvantaged agricultural producers, SSA lost out more and more to other competitors for the supply of commodities onto the global economy.

Having said that, it would be wrong to ascribe responsibility for the continent's decline to solely exogenous factors, such as the collapse of commodity prices or the oil crisis (or even the pernicious effects of the IFI's prescriptions). Proponents of such a position have perhaps forgotten that

[b]y April 1970, Liberia and Somalia had already received seven stand-by agreement loans from the IMF to help them address balance of payments and budgetary crises; Burundi had received five such loans; Ghana, Mali, and Rwanda four loans; Sierra Leone and Sudan three; Congo/Zaïre had completed its first IMF supervised devaluation. The granting of multiple stand-by agreements in less than a decade of independence suggests an almost immediate deterioration in management. (van de Walle, 2001: 121)

By the late 1970s, African development had begun to manifestly stall on a continental level and solutions and explanations for the emerging crisis of development were required and necessary. Certainly by the mid-1970s much of Africa was no longer experiencing the golden days of the immediate postindependence period. During the 1960s, for instance, African agriculture performed relatively adequately and only 17 out of 45 sub-Saharan states suffered negative annual growth rates in their per capita food production. However, by 1976 the number of countries experiencing negative rates was 29 (Onimode, 1988). The continent's average annual growth also declined precipitously. Between 1965 and 1973 the 45 countries of Black SSA enjoyed an average annual growth rate of 2.9 percent (although if one excludes Nigeria then that growth rate was only 1.2 percent).

However, between 1973 and 1980, i.e. the beginning of Africa's "lost decade," Africa's annual growth rate had declined to a minimal 0.1 percent or, if we take Nigeria out of the equation, a disastrous −0.7 percent (World Bank, 1989: 221). Simultaneously, Africa's foreign debts were increasing exponentially. Thus, in 1970, Kenya had an external public and private debt of US$406 million but by 1980 this had become US$2675. Other countries had equally depressing debt burdens: Zaïre went from US$311 million in 1970 to US$4294 million by 1980; Zambia from US$653 million to US$2274 million; Ghana from US$497 million to US$1138 million. Even a tiny country such as The Gambia, which in 1970 only had a total debt of US$5 million, had, a decade later, one of US$106 million (World Bank, 1989: 256). Clearly something had to be done and competing internal and external narratives contended for supremacy.

From the African elites' side, the Lagos Plan of Action was the major response to Africa's stalled development. Initially meeting in Monrovia, Liberia, in July 1979, African leaders advanced the idea that the continent's development could not be contingent on simply waiting for benefits to accrue from the types of special relationships crafted with Europe through the Yaoundé and Lomé agreements, nor could Africa progress without actively tackling the legacy of underdevelopment left by Africa's insertion into the global capitalist economy by colonization. Autocentricity and the continued demand for an NIEO were intrinsically wrapped up in this thrust (Mathews, 1989: 52–7).

The Monrovia meeting determined that a number of strategic tasks were necessary in order for Africa to develop and overcome the impasse that the continent was experiencing by the mid-1970s. Among other resolutions, Monrovia pronounced that the creation of national and regional bodies was necessary to pursue autocentricity and that Africa had to develop self-reliance in food production while engaging in developmental-oriented planning. The lofty aim at the time was to create modern and developed, or at least discernibly developing—if economic growth rates are measured—economies by the year 2000. Borrowing from the Europeans, a Common Market was deemed necessary to be in place by 2025. The Monrovia Declaration closed with the decision to direct the OAU's secretary general and the executive secretary of the United Nations Economic Commission for Africa (UNECA) to formulate a program to stimulate such development.

This process continued in July 1980 with the Second Extraordinary Session of the heads of states and governments, which was held in Nigeria and produced the much-vaunted Lagos Plan of Action and the Final Act (OAU, 1980). Essentially, the Lagos Plan of Action was a clarification of the broad philosophy that Monrovia had indicated and was a document that sought to arrive at strategies that might promote growth on a continent that was disengaged and less influenced by the vagaries of the global market. An emphasis on inter-African trade and investment through regional cooperation was central to the Lagos Plan of Action (LPA), despite, or perhaps because, "by 1980—when the LPA was adopted—almost all the economic co-operation schemes optimistically launched in the 1960s—the halcyon days of African integration—had become largely moribund" (Asante, 1985: 82). The reduction in external debt, import-substitution policies and a general goal of autocentric development further underpinned the Lagos Plan.

Perhaps unsurprisingly given both the Dependency Theory that provided the framework for its analysis and (and this is perhaps the most important) the fact that it was African elites themselves conducting the exercise, the LPA's conclusions were "a classic dependency interpretation of the African condition" (Owusu, 2003; 1657). It exonerated African leaders and blamed the historical injustices experienced by Africa and the persistent dependence on external forces for the crisis. Certainly, the LPA went out of its way to absolve the postcolonial elites of any responsibility for Africa's predicament. Indeed, the LPA quite explicitly stated that "despite all efforts made by its leaders, [the continent] remains the least developed" (OAU, 1980: 7). In general, "the tendency of the Lagos Plan was to list the problems that African countries were facing, suggest [solutions] without even a vague hint of how these could be financed, and then recommend the creation of numerous international institutions to help African countries" (Herbst, 1993: 139).

That the LPA failed is incontrovertible. Based on faulty assumptions about Africa's economic condition, and ignoring systematic malgovernance, its prescriptions were described as "economically illiterate" by Clapham (1996a: 176). Primarily, the LPA strategy was based on a continuation of import substitution and hinged on three conditions that Africa simply did not possess. The assumptions made by the LPA were that "the actual surplus extracted from the agricultural sector is, in fact, invested in the industrial sector, where it will be converted into additional manufacturing capacity . . . Second, peasants must continue to produce—indeed expand production—despite conditions that clearly work against them. Third, certain (heavy) industries need specialized manpower and relatively large markets to be efficient and viable. None of these conditions were really met in Africa" (Ergas, 1987: 309). Indeed, "why these measures should be taken and what priority should be given to them [were] never stated because the Lagos Plan [did] not suggest how the agrarian crisis the African states [were] facing originated" (Herbst, 1993: 139). To do so, it is suggested, would have involved apportioning degrees of blame, which would have inevitably led to African leaders having to take their fair share, something which was scrupulously avoided and dodged by the Plan and its architects.

The Era of Structural Adjustment

A year later, in 1981, the World Bank responded to the LPA with its own analysis. Entitled *Accelerated Development in Sub-Saharan Africa: An Agenda for Action* (also known as the "Berg Report" after its main author, Professor Elliot Berg), the Bank came out strongly against most of the LPA's positions, in particular the notion that the state should be the main engine of growth and the absolution by the LPA of the malevolent role played by African elites in their continent's demise (World Bank, 1981). Meddling by the state in the supposed free running of the market was particularly criticized and was seen as a main reason for Africa's declining growth record, coupled with malgovernance (Arrighi, 2002: 5–35). The perceived overambitious targets of the LPA, such as a pan-continental Common Market *á la* the European Community, were also critiqued. But "such analyses challenged the evidently self-serving perceptions of African elites and their sympathizers [captured in the LPA] and aroused the hostility of institutions such as the United Nations Economic Commission for Africa" (Clapham, 1996b: 811).

In essence, the Berg Report was a rebuttal of the Dependency-tinged LPA and the opening salvo in a decade-long campaign to shape developmental discourse in Africa along lines favored by the key global economic players (Browne and Cummings, 1985). In this regard it should be noted that the Monrovia Declaration and the LPA were launched on the eve of the election to government of conservative neoliberals in Britain and the United States, and the Plan of Action in particular advanced a vision at sharp variance with the gathering thrust of global capitalism and the views of key elites in the developed world. Indeed, separate from the failure of African elites to really do anything about Africa's declining situation, the demise of the Plan's vision played itself out as an integral part of the reassertion of Western-centered hegemony—"America's quest for supremacy [over] the Third World" as Augelli and Murphy (1988) have put it. This was coupled with the steady demise, though not outright extinction, of a protesting voice in Africa's relations with the developed world.

Although various adjustment packages had been implemented in Africa before the 1980s, the Berg Report was to usher in a new era in African politics and development, the era of Structural Adjustment Programs (SAPs). Just as the LPA had skated over the behavior of African elites, the Berg Report remained relatively uncritical of donor activities. The Report advanced a dual strategy for the continent: privatization and liberalization. Reform packages that were rolled out in the 1980s by the IFIs, as well as donors, contained these two basic elements as essential conditionalities for disbursements. A structural adjustment package, granted in 1981 to Côte d'Ivoire and soon to become the first of what would eventually become 26 SAPs to that country, captures the basic ingredients:

> The reforms envisaged by the program are designed to improve the level of public savings and the efficiency in the use of public resources; restructure the agricultural planning system and associated development institutions so that an expanded, well-designed investment program yielding high returns can be mounted in the sector; reflect the costs of providing public services to the sector; assure that rational prices and world market conditions would guide decisions to invest and produce; restructure public enterprise, management, financing and accountability to ensure efficient market oriented operations; restructure incentives, to promote efficient export-oriented industrial investments. (World Bank, 1981)

These elements staked out both an economic and political project and came at a historical juncture when financial indebtedness and economic mismanagement were acting to drastically undermine the continent's development trajectory. At the same time, leaders within Africa began to realize that agreeing to the ongoing restructuring process as promoted through SAPs, even if their commitment was only rhetorical, was necessary for the continuation of the flow of resources via aid (van de Walle, 2001).

The means to overcome Africa's crisis was identified (even if unconsciously) as a return to two old theoretical approaches: neoclassical economics, and Modernization Theory (Mengisteab and Logan, 1995). Within SAPs was an implicit echoing of the modernizers' argument that the "fundamentals" had to be in place to assure economic development. Not bringing such "fundamentals" in place was blamed for the lack of success of SAPs in many African countries (Harvey, 1996). Indeed, the failure to implement SAPs has been held to be a contributing factor in explaining Africa's continued demise, even after SAPs were introduced (van de Walle, 2001). In other words, there was a considerable disparity between rhetorical and practical commitments to economic and political reform. In fact, new loans disbursed by the IFIs as part of a SAP were often seen simply as new sources of largesse to distribute to supporters and clients, with minimal intention to fulfill signed commitments. Yet, the pretence that both donor and recipient were engaged in serious reform was often played out for public consumption. As van de Walle (2001: 224) noted:

> Meetings between the government and its creditors, UN summits, and the annual meetings of the IFI were replete with communiqués and announcements "commending" African governments for the "hard work" they had demonstrated. Governments complained about the austerity that was demanded of them and complained of the socio-political difficulties involved with implementing reform programs. The impression was given that adjustment was a kind of favor that governments' were extending to the West, at tremendous cost.

However, the supposed "one-size-fits-all" approach, which characterized much of the IFIs engagement with Africa, generated a counterreaction in the form of the Africa's Priority Program for Economic Recovery 1986–1990 (APPER). Later transformed and repackaged as the *United Nations Program of Action for Africa's Economic Recovery and Development* (UN-PAAERD), the aim of both initiatives were to ostensibly attempt to work with SAPs through projects that might allow African states to connect with the global market through "shared commitments" and joint efforts (OAU, 1986). Essentially, the debt issue and the scant levels of domestic investment were seen as major stumbling blocks to any successful implementation of the SAPs. An injection of capital was deemed necessary if the continent was to be developmentally kick-started and if the SAP-affected countries were to be cushioned from the more negative effects of the programs. Thus assisting African states to put into practice policy reforms in line with the IFIs' prescriptions was deemed essential to the whole recovery project.

Responding to Structural Adjustment

The impact of SAPs on Africa and African elites' positions, particularly as glasnost and perestroika made Africa's strategic position less and less clear, resurfaced in July 1989 with the UNECA's *African Alternative Framework to Structural Adjustment Programs for Socio-Economic Recovery and Transformation* (AAF-SAP) (OAU, 1989). The Framework sprang from studies by Adebayo Adedeji and other African economists, frustrated at the perceived sidelining—by both African elites and their industrialized partners—of the LPA. The AAF-SAP started out from the basis that "Up to this day, this blueprint [the LPA] contains a valid analysis and the right prescriptions for African countries to transform their economies" (OAU, 1989: 3). Thus the AAF-SAP maintained that huge capital investment in Africa was necessary to spur economic growth while questioning the insistence by donors that Africa should increase its exports as a means of escaping the crisis of development. Rather, the AAF-SAP asserted that a change in consumption patterns to favor locally or regionally produced goods over imported products was required while internationally, the Framework demanded that the donors should support programs designed and implemented by African governments themselves and aimed at tackling specific national problems, rather than seeking to impose the perceived blanket programs associated with the IFIs.

Yet, the assertion that there should be some sudden change in consumption patterns, without addressing the fundamental problem of rapacious elites (who were the main source of such distortions), was bound to fail as was the idea that capital resources should be simply handed over to African leaders to spend as how they saw fit. Certainly, "the claim that no changes were required in the management of African states themselves was unsustainable" (Clapham, 1996a: 176). In fact, the AAF-SAP "was especially critical of reliance on foreign experts and managers in national economic decision making in Africa. Indeed, it seemed to blame the presence of foreigners more than . . . external factors as the debt burden for Africa's crisis" (Herbst, 1993: 141). This suggests that the AAF-SAP was perhaps little more than a nationalist counter-reaction against the perceived overbearing presence of the IFIs.

Indeed, the AAF-SAP's understanding of the African crisis was limited in scope, "dangerously simplistic" as Herbst (1993: 143) puts it, and largely restricting itself to commenting that "the crisis that struck Africa in the 1980s had many causes. The drought resulted in one of the worst famines Africa has known this century. The fall in the prices of Africa's major commodities made foreign exchange to become very scarce and very expensive" (OAU, 1989: 12). Thus, just as the LPA did, African leaders effectively absolved themselves from any responsibility, finding in the weather, foreign experts and external factors such as falls in commodity prices, alibis for the continent's demise.

Problematically, the AAF-SAP "seem[ed] not at all concerned about the performance of African states even though over the last two decades, all evidence suggest[ed] that this performance ha[d] been abysmal" (Herbst, 1993: 145).

The AAF-SAP of 1989 was, however, adopted by the UN General Assembly. A resolution invited the General Assembly to consider the Framework as a basis for "constructive dialogue" and "fruitful consultation." This, despite the observation that it was "a warmed-over version of the Lagos Plan of Action with vague and contradictory, largely statist, policy proposals that could not be implemented under the best of conditions, all of which [were] linked to renewed demands for substantially increased external resource flows and debt relief" (Callaghy, 1991: 55). However, like almost all previous plans in Africa, the AAF-SAP never got off the ground, primarily due to the lack of commitment by both those African leaders who had signed the Framework (thus echoing the fate of the LPA) and the IFIs and Western governments. After all, Zimbabwe adopted an IMF-tailored SAP within a year of African finance ministers rushing to pledge support for the AAF-SAP and supposedly rejecting SAPs!

The IFIs Respond

Interestingly, just as the Berg Report had followed the Lagos Plan, the AAF-SAP was rapidly followed by a new World Bank document in 1989, *Sub Saharan Africa: From Crisis to Sustainable Growth*. This report argued that sound incentives and a decent infrastructure were required to construct an enabling environment for African growth to develop. The Report also, however, argued that "African governments and foreign financiers (commercial banks and export credit agencies as well as donor agencies) must share responsibility [for the continent's crisis]. Foreign financiers and suppliers promoted capital exports with attractive credits, and poor coordination among donors caused duplication and waste" (World Bank, 1989: 27). Interestingly, the Report also touched on malgovernance as a major cause of Africa's impasse, asserting that "foreign aid has greatly expanded the opportunities for malfeasance exacerbated by the venality of many foreign contractors and suppliers" (World Bank, 1989: 27).

Henceforth, the issue of "good governance" would ostensibly be a major focus of the IFIs engagement with Africa. Yet one should not over-exaggerate how serious the IFIs were on this score. As Weaver (2008: 103–4) notes:

> From *Crisis to Sustainable Growth: Sub-Saharan Africa: A Long-Term Perspective Study* argued that the region's difficulties were due to an entrenchment of kleptocratic elites who enriched themselves and their clans by looting public funds rather than striving to alleviate poverty. The first draft of the report strongly criticized the Bank's management for its blindness to these political realities. After an initial vetting, the report was strongly opposed by senior managers and member state representatives on the grounds that the language was too political . . ., contained unflattering connotations for developing countries . . . and smacked of "socialism" . . . The second draft of the report . . . thus strategically adopted the language of "good governance", defined as "the exercise of political power to manage a nation's affairs" . . . [It] was neutral enough to avoid the kind of reactions that the language of kleptocracy had invoked in the first draft.

Somewhat signaling a shift from its previous hard-nosed stance toward the role of the state, the report asserted that human resource development was required (a role that the state could perform) and that a social safety net was also needed. But the IFIs continued to maintain an interpretation of governance as something that restrains state action in the economy rather than generating space for a proactive role. In the IFI's understanding, a state that possesses "good governance" is a state that is effectively a passive actor, supplying public goods, a positive policy milieu (from the perspective of capital, particularly foreign capital), macroeconomic stability, and investment in human resources and physical infrastructure. This understanding thus essentially maintained the principle goals of the neoliberal policies and SAPs of the 1980s.

Good Governance: When Economists "Do" Politics

When and where the IFIs speak regarding "governance," this has been in a technical sense and misses the *political* dimensions and problems. Indeed, the IMF's own prescriptions for designing "good governance" structures draws upon what the body refers to as "broadly agreed best international practices of economic management" (IMF, 1997). According to Keet, by pushing a particular vision of governance, the IMF and World Bank express "a clear bias towards the assumption that it is free market governments with 'sound macro-economic policies' which are 'more reliable' . . . There is also a clear inclination to emphasize, or even equate good governance with the technical qualities of efficient management and the main accountability of client governments to funders/creditors and other external agencies" (Keet, no date).

The turn to "good governance" by the IFIs can be related to both the institutional need to find a role and the refusal (again institutional) of the IFIs to acknowledge that their policies have not worked (Moyo, 2009: 22–6). Role-wise, with the demise of regulated exchange rates in the 1970s, the IMF "lost" its main *raison d'être*. This has provoked a constant reinvention by the IMF to find a new role, if not justify its very existence. In essence, there has been an active promotion of new ideas to secure and advance institutional hegemony within the global economy. This has increasingly stimulated the institution to involve itself in affairs that are beyond the remit of its original mandate—to indulge in "mission creep." Defining and then advocating "good governance" is part and parcel of this process. According to one analysis, "this has been done with grave consequences: the IMF, staffed with macroeconomists, does not have the expertise to provide the kind of advice that it is dispensing today. Nor is the IMF, which has no independent evaluation unit and has been labeled one of the most secretive public institutions in the world, held accountable for the policy advice that it gives" (Welch, 1998).

The refusal by the IFIs to acknowledge that their policies have not worked is also central to the emergence of the "good governance" discourse (Moyo, 2009: 22). This springs from a concern that the SAPs that had attempted to reconfigure the South had been hampered, if not sabotaged, by "poor governance." As George and Sabelli (1994: 142) assert:

> If sustainable poverty reduction turn[ed] out to be just another mirage, institutional responsibility for failure must not be seen to be the fault of the [international financial institutions (IFIs)]. The only other possible culprits [were] the [IFIs'] partners . . . Governance provide[d] a new tool-kit, an instrument of control, an additional

conditionality for the time when the traditional blame-the-victim defense again becomes necessary. It further offer[ed] the opportunity both to instill Western political values in borrowing countries and to fault them if things go wrong.

Instead of questioning their own prescriptions, the IFIs instead sought to advance "good governance" as a necessary precondition for neoliberal reforms to *finally* work. This in itself reflected the conviction among the institutions that neoliberalism was the only way forward and that what was wrong, or had been going wrong, was not the ingredients of the adjustment programs, but rather their implementation and wider institutional setting in the borrowing states. Why this emerged sprang from the institutional culture and specifically the hegemony of narrow-minded economists. As Weaver (2008: 115) notes regarding the World Bank, "governance and anticorruption issues ran head-first into the economistic, technocratic, and apolitical features of the Bank's intellectual culture". After all, there existed "the dominance of neoclassically trained economists within the Bank . . . [many] recruited from academia with little or no experience in government and with little interest in or appreciation of noneconomic factors affecting development" (ibid.: 102).

Within the IFIs there in fact exists "pervasive cynicisms regarding 'social and political scientists'. In the words of one economist in the research department [of the World Bank], 'Why do we need political scientists? We're not interested in voting behavior'" (ibid.: 115). In fact, why the IFIs desperately need political scientists (and sociologists, anthropologists, economic historians, etc.) is answered by Fatton, who notes that their economism is "based on a series of deeply flawed assumptions":

[The IFIs] posit that development can be "private-driven," and that African bourgeoisies can suddenly have a change of heart and become the engine of the take-off, whereas these bourgeoisies have never shown any commitment to sustained productive investment. They posit that privatization leads necessarily to rational economic decisions and that private agents are inherently more virtuous and efficient than public servants, whereas revenues derived from the sale of state assets can be stolen and squandered, and private agents are bent on defending their own selfish interests rather than the collective good. They posit that democratic governance is compatible with the imposition of fiscal austerity in an environment that is already suffering from acute material deprivation, whereas SAPs' huge social costs are unlikely to be tolerated by docile and passive populations. Finally, they posit that trade liberalization will promote more efficient African economies whereas Africa's small industrial base is incapable of withstanding and surviving foreign competition without public protection. (Fatton, 1999: 4)

Africanist social and political scientists know this; narrow-minded economists seemingly do not, despite the fact that the IMF's own Independent Evaluation Office has recommended that "the IMF should strengthen the ability of its staff to analyze political economy issues in order to achieve a better understanding of the forces that are likely to block or enhance reforms and to take these into account in program design" (IMF, 2002). Yet "the traditional predominance of the economics profession in IFI staffing . . . has been [a major] factor in the undervaluation of country-specific knowledge . . . [T]he economist's . . . aversion to country specificity will prove an obstacle to the IFI effort to tackle governance problems" (Kapur and Webb, 2000: 10). As Zeleza (2006: 19) warns us, "there is a danger that unless backed by truly interdisciplinary modes of analysis, economists who are poorly trained to understand historical, political, cultural, and geographical factors may continue devising perilous policies based on simplistic variables."

As noted previously, the World Bank took the lead in this naïve and technocratic approach to governance, with its report in 1989 entitled *Sub-Saharan Africa: From Crisis to Sustainable Growth* (World Bank, 1989). Admittedly, this report took a more holistic view than previous Bank documents and argued that institutional change was necessary if reforms were to be effective. But the Bank continued to advance neoliberal solutions, arguing that what was characterizing the economic crisis in Africa was not unequal trading relations with the North, or massive debt, or the negative effects of liberalization, etc., but rather a "crisis of governance" (ibid.: 60). Critically, the "hegemony of economic ideas explains much of the narrow focus on the effects of governance on growth and aid's impact, rather than a wider concern with equity and justice. Moreover, it explains why research thus far has been dominated by quantitative, cross-national studies and quantifiable measures of governance with surprisingly few qualitative case studies. Because governance reform requires high levels of social and political knowledge about the borrowing countries, the Bank's ideologically driven choice of . . . staff and research agendas has impeded the ability of operational staff to translate ideas about governance into viable reform projects" (Weaver, 2008: 117).

Quite simply, the dominance of rational choice methodologies and the false claim to "objective" and "scientific" economic "laws" has made the IFIs' capture by neoclassical ideologues, arrogantly dismissive of anything but Economics (and a very specific sub-type within that discipline), a disaster for Africa as the institutions explicitly linked good governance to neoliberalism in a wholly apolitical, ahistorical and extremely naïve fashion. Yet "good governance" was advanced as "necessary for the creation of the consent for the new order which structural adjustment could not usher in; and, unsaid, is also needed to implement a sufficient quota of repression as the still unchanged policies of neo-liberalism are implemented" (Bernstein, 1990: 23).

Although such ideas were outside of the IMF's actual remit, the Fund also began to take an increasing interest in "good governance." In September 1996 a declaration entitled *Partnership for Sustainable Global Growth* was adopted by the IMF's Interim Committee and in August 1997 a report, promulgated by the IMF's Executive Board, asserted that the IMF must henceforth assist member countries in creating systems that "limit the scope for ad hoc decision making, for rent seeking, for undesirable preferential treatment of individuals or organizations." This followed the World Bank's earlier pronouncements and henceforth the IMF cast itself as also a promoter of "good governance." The IMF now boldly stated that it was "legitimate to seek information about the political situation in member countries as an essential element in judging the prospects for policy implementation" (James, 1998: 35).

The ability of the IFIs to advance its new ideas on governance was considerably compounded by the structural features of the global economy. As one analysis asserts, the power of the IMF over developing countries "was made all the more formidable since, in the aftermath of the debt crisis, all other potential sources of credit, bilateral or otherwise, required an IMF stamp of approval . . . before any credit was extended" (Adams, 1997: 162). Developing countries increasingly required the IMF's approval in order to secure new aid flows in order to help avoid defaulting on outstanding existing loans. Obviously, this gave the IFIs an incredible amount of potential influence over the economic policies of debt-ridden administrations. State administrations were repeatedly "advised" that economic recovery was dependent upon what was vaguely termed "business confidence," and that this in itself hung on a disciplined labor force and a state that pursued "good governance."

Such advice has been part and parcel of the Structural Adjustment Facility (SAF) and Enhanced Structural Adjustment Facility (ESAF) programs of the institution. These entail the IMF granting medium-term loans to countries. The conditions attached to such loans can include the dismantling of labor regulations, increasing foreign investment incentives, and privatization schemes. Yet, such conditionalities and negotiations between the IMF and the host state frequently posit what is essentially the interest of particular fractions, both national and international, as being in the interests of the wider populace. Concessions, such as the (limited) advancement of what are termed "social issues" allow the IFIs and the negotiating state parties to pass off conditionalities as being concerned with protecting the poorest. O'Brien et al. (2000: 178) remark that such interventions allow the IMF to cast general interests as paramount, thus strengthening the legitimacy of IMF prescriptions and maintaining political support for them. One such tactic is to stress "ownership" of prescriptions by implementing states and portray IFI strictures as being voluntarily followed by administrations pursuing the general interest:

> [M]anagement and staff at the IMF have gone some way to accepting the importance of ownership, at least in so far as it may be an indispensable ingredient for successful policy implementation . . . That said, the change in rhetoric has not to date always translated into substantially different behavior at the Fund. . . . For the IMF, "ownership" has tended to mean acceptance by the borrowing government and its citizens of Fund prescriptions. As one official has typically put it, "we have to persuade the population that an adjustment package is legitimate." (O'Brien et al. 2000: 187)

One way this has been done is for the IFIs to move even further beyond their original mandates—now the institutions are involved in the promotion of "good governance." Although SAPs have in the past few years been replaced with Poverty Reduction Strategy Papers (PRSPs), the theme of "good governance" along neoliberal lines continues.

"Doubling Aid to Halve Poverty": New Spin in Broken Bottles

At the same time as the IFIs have pursued governance prescriptions, albeit unevenly, a consensus of sorts has emerged centered around the massive increase of aid. The premise behind this appears to be the idea that a lack of aid has somehow produced or at least exacerbated Africa's situation *and* that aid and growth are linked. Thus the IFIs now actively advance a position to increase aid and explicitly argue that this will reverse SSA's maldevelopment if coupled with "good governance" prescriptions.

It is important to understand why there has been a sudden upsurge within the IFIs in the idea that aid needs to be massively increased. Interestingly, this idea stems from an academic paper that filtered through into policy-making and became cited as "evidence" for why aid should be boosted. A study by Craig Burnside and David Dollar on aid and growth was published in the high-profile *American Economic Review* (Burnside and Dollar, 2000). The summary of the paper was that "aid has a positive impact on growth in developing countries with good fiscal, monetary, and trade policies." From this came the now familiar refrain that 1 percent of gross domestic product in aid given to a poor but well-managed country increases the growth rate of that country by a sustained 0.5 percentage points. Organizations such as the World Bank began citing this study and soon the international nongovernmental aid community/industry joined in, although the paper's findings that overall, aid has no positive impact on growth were systematically ignored/misinterpreted. This is strange given that the World Bank's own figures speak for themselves (see chart 7.1 below).

The paper's findings played an important role at the 2002 conference on "Financing for Development" in Monterrey, Mexico, which produced the so-called Monterrey Consensus on how to reach the MDGs through more aid. All this, despite the fact that empirical support for the Burnside and Dollar model of aid working even in well-governed countries came from a study of a data set which only covered about 30 percent of the existing observations for aid and growth (something which the aid boosters curiously neglected to mention).

Yet more detailed studies, utilizing Burnside and Dollar's data sets, but expanding them in both breadth and longitude, found that "the coefficient on the crucial interaction term between aid and policy was insignificant in the expanded sample including new data [thus] indicating no support for the conclusion that 'aid works in a good policy environment'" (Easterly, 2003: 27; see also Easterly, Levine and Roodman, 2003). It has been found that at low levels of aid, the positive effect of aid on growth is marginal, while with high levels of aid the negative effect was clear. Jensen and Paldam conducted a study of the robustness of the aid-growth model within Burnside and Dollar's 30 percent sample and tested whether it was replicated in the remaining 70 percent of the data.

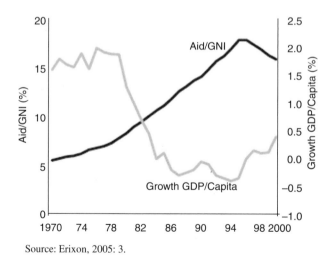

Source: Erixon, 2005: 3.

Chart 7.1 Aid and Growth in Africa (10-Year Moving Average)

They found that "findings are . . . consistent with the possibility that the recent [positive] discussion of aid effectiveness builds upon the mining of a fluke in a particular subset of the data" (Jensen and Paldam, 2003: 19). Yet this is ignored and, as Birdsall, Rodrik and Subramanian (2005) note, aid is continually oversold by the IFIs and donors as a way of lifting people out of poverty, overlooking the more mundane fact that it is heterodox policy innovations that have promoted development in diverse places around the world.

In recent years, the IFIs' message was bolstered by the energetic activities of celebrity economist Jeffrey Sachs and his promotion of the mantra that doubling aid would solve Africa's ills (see Sachs, 2005). In his book, Sachs refused to consider that institutional failure or corruption could undermine the grand plan of doubling aid, stating that "Africa shows absolutely no tendency to be more or less corrupt than any other countries at the same income level." Sachs arrived at this conclusion by using an assortment of qualitative indicators regarding governance that rather remarkably resulted in Cameroon, Central African Republic, Chad, Congo-Brazzaville, Nigeria, Sierra Leone and Togo being scored as having "average" standards of governance, while Burkina Faso and Malawi are "well-governed" (2005: 313–14). The fact was, Sachs' index *presumed* that poor African countries were badly governed and thus his methodology rated them relative to one another, using the level of poverty as a main variable. This is obviously a ridiculous way in which to evaluate whether or not African countries are well governed. Yet it was seized upon by supporters for more aid to argue that African countries are not badly managed (and thus aid would not be wasted).

There has been considerable unease at Sachs' (and the IFIs') position. One reviewer of Sachs' book noted that "The warm reception given to this book by people who should know better is a testament to the decline of political understanding among progressives after two decades of neo-liberal victories. A bleeding heart is a good complement to, but no substitute for, a hard-headed analysis of social structure and the deployment of power" (*Age* [Melbourne], July 2, 2005). Of course, the very discourse of "good governance" ignores hardheaded analyses of social structures. Instead, "the relatively neutral language of institutional economics as a means of attributing past economic failures throughout the developing and transitional world to 'poor governance' and 'institutional deficiencies'" dominates (Weaver, 2008: 99). Indeed, "the governance and anticorruption discourse that finally emerged in the middle to late 1990s in the [World] Bank was overtly driven by a economistic theoretical framework that lacked, in the words of one staff member, a 'real working theory of the state'" (ibid.: 93).

Other commentators have remarked that Sachs "won the emotional, if not the intellectual, argument" (Wrong, 2009: 205). Experts on Africa "might shake their heads at Sachs's simplistic formula for the continent's recovery, but he had successfully wooed pop-star campaigners like Bono and Sir Bob Geldof" (ibid.). As Tony Blair realized, the approval of celebrities in the West's celebrity-obsessed cultures was far more of a vote winner than any hardheaded (and "boring") analysis of the actual issues (Moyo, 2009: 27). An academic critique of Sachs, in fact, asserted that Sachs (and Thomas Friedman) had "hijack[ed] the development debate." Through their "prominent exposure in the US media, and endorsements by celebrities like Bono," Friedman and Sachs "narrowed the debate with simplistic slogans of 'more aid' and 'more trade'. They have done so by putting forward myths about the poor, economic development, and the global economy. In many ways, Friedman and Sachs are leading us backward to the era that began with the ascendancy of Ronald Reagan, Margaret Thatcher, and Helmut Kohl in the early 1980s" (Broad and Cavanagh, 2006: 21).

The IFIs' Institutional Cultures: Part of the Problem

Why the work of Sachs, Burnside and Dollar et al. were seized on as "evidence" as to why aid has to be continually increased is answered by one report on the aid industry, which found that aid organizations define their output as money disbursed rather than service delivered, produce many low-return observable outputs like glossy reports and "frameworks" and few high return activities such as ex-post evaluation, engage in obfuscation, spin control, and amnesia (such as always describing aid efforts as "new and improved") and learn very little from the past (Easterly, 2002: 5). Certainly, "in eagerness to get projects 'sold' to borrowing governments and approved by internal management, staff members [within IFIs] are often over simplistic about the capacity and willingness of governments to sustain governance reform" (Weaver, 2008: 120). In fact, "within the approval culture of the [World] Bank it is very difficult to get staff to scrutinize the sincerity of a government's commitments, and even more difficult for staff to take action that might put approval of a project in jeopardy" (ibid.: 120). After all, "the amount of money which is disbursed [is] the only yardstick of progress, hardly a situation likely to encourage discrimination amongst the officials who are responsible for approving projects" (Wrong, 2009: 207). "No one gets . . . points back at head office for closing down a program or putting a relationship with a client government on ice, even if this was, in fact, the most constructive course of action" (ibid.: 189).

One analysis has remarked on the aid debate, that "evidence gets in the way of the preferences of politicians (and the publics which stand behind them)" (Killick, 2004: 5). Meanwhile, as one former World Bank staff member framed it, "the Bank's approach to fighting corruption could be described as the 'three-monkey policy': 'see nothing, hear nothing, say nothing'" (quoted in Weaver, 2008: 122). Problematically of course, financial inflows in the absence of economic and governmental reforms are unlikely to lead to sustainable economic growth and development. Indeed, such flows may just serve to strengthen the neo-patrimonial nature of the African state (see Mwenda and Tangri, 2005).

Institutions such as the IMF and World Bank must be understood to be relatively autonomous and to possess their own dynamics and self-interests that may undermine any serious application of efficient developmental assistance. One analysis argues that IFI should be understood as bureaucracies, and "can become autonomous sites of authority, independent from the state 'principals' who may have created them, because of power flowing from . . . the legitimacy of the rational-legal authority they embody, and . . . [their] control over technical expertise and information" (Barnett and Finnemore, 1999: 704). Such organizations can be susceptible to pathologies that assume a life of their own, usually springing from institutional cultures that may actually subvert the official remit of the organizations themselves. Consultants hired to construct feasibility studies and project evaluations have major interests in getting the contracts for the project and no interest in seeing them cancelled. They have little interest in exploring possible factors that might complicate or undermine the project's effectiveness (Moyo, 2009). Equally, elements of IFI culture that promote institutional inefficiency include pressures to move money out the door, the reliance on short-term consultants, and, perhaps most perniciously, the cultivation of close relationships between IFI staff and the recipient states, particularly at the higher echelons. This sociological explanation of much IFI activities should not be underestimated:

> World Bank directors are hardly average citizens. Often former government ministers in their former lives, they belong to an international elite that automatically turns left on entering a plane, rarely does its own driving, and expects lodgings to come with staff quarters attached . . . [M]ost regard the African politicians and central bank governors they meet in wood-paneled offices to discuss the fate of the nation as social equals. (Wrong, 2009: 190)

Problematically, "Staffers show an alarming tendency to lose their critical distance, over-identify with their clients and start regarding the interests of the local government and the World Bank as one and the same . . . Back at [the World Bank's] headquarters, they dubbed the syndrome 'governmentitis', or being 'captured' by the host state" (ibid.).

Conclusion

Past experience has shown that the role of the IFIs in Africa has often not only provided substantial resources to predatory elites, thus solidifying their political power, but it has also served to grant the illusion of compliance and cooperation (the partial reform syndrome). Alarmingly, the donor community seems not to particularly care too much about this. After all, the IFIs are at the center of an aid industry in which half a million employees rely on "development assistance" for their salaries and expatriate lifestyles (see Hancock, 1994). This creates an almost relentless momentum to keep the aid money flowing. The actual effectiveness of such aid and whether ordinary Africans benefit is seemingly immaterial.

One commentator writes that donor country reports that give much aid a stamp of approval are spurious. According to him, "supposedly independent [reports on aid] have been financed, sponsored or executed directly by the staff of multilateral and bilateral aid agencies that have vested interests in ensuring increased aid. None of these studies are genuinely independent" (Mistry, 2005: 668). As William Easterly (2003: 35) remarks, "Even when economic performance is clearly deteriorating despite important and rising aid, as in the case of Africa . . . the aid bureaucracies try to finesse the issue by promising that better times are 'just around the corner'." Such rhetoric has now been a consistent feature of this particular aspect of SSA's international relations for nigh on 50 years (Moyo, 2009). The World Bank, for example, has been singing this refrain about Africa for over two decades. Easterly (2003: 35–6) in fact wryly notes the following passages from various World Bank reports:

> From a 1981 World Bank report, *Accelerated Development in Sub-Saharan Africa* (p. 133): "Policy action and foreign assistance . . . will surely work together to build a continent that shows real gains in both development and income in the near future". From a 1984 World Bank report, *Toward Sustained Development in Sub-Saharan Africa* (p. 2): "This optimism can be justified by recent experience in Africa . . . some

countries are introducing policy and institutional reforms". From a 1986 World Bank report, *Financing Growth with Adjustment in Sub-Saharan Africa* (p. 15): "Progress is clearly under way. Especially in the past two years, more countries have started to act, and the changes they are making go deeper than before". From a 1989 World Bank report, *Sub-Saharan Africa: From Crisis to Sustainable Growth* (p. 35): "Since the mid-1980s Africa has seen important changes in policies and in economic performance". From a 1994 World Bank report, *Adjustment in Africa* (p. 3): "African countries have made great strides in improving policies and restoring growth". From a 2000 World Bank report, *Can Africa Claim the 21st Century?:* "Since the mid-1990s, there have been signs that better economic management has started to pay off". From a 2002 World Bank press release on *African Development Indicators*, "Africa's leaders . . . have recognized the need to improve their policies, spelled out in the New Partnership for African Development."

There is in fact a dangerous assumption common within the IFIs "that Africa's problems have been caused by bad policies in the past and that if the 'right' policies can be discovered all will be well" (Dowden, 2004: 142). It is absolutely vital to note that the malady affecting the continent is not simply economic, it is political. As the Nigerian political scientist Claude Ake put it, "we are never going to understand the current crisis in Africa . . . as long as we continue to think of it as an economic crisis" (Ake, 1991: 316). In such circumstances, a huge injection of aid resources may simply bolster the existing situation, rather than contribute to positive change (see Moyo, 2009). Furthermore, refusing to confront the reality of how politics in Africa is practiced is, like the old adage regarding the elephant in the living room, denying its existence in the hope that it will somehow go away. It will not.

Problematically, Africa's economic predicament has remained for now over two decades because, in large part, state elites have fallen short of executing thoroughgoing economic and political reforms and, particularly, overseeing a capable developmental state. This is because the continent's leaders have continued with clientelistic politics, which safeguard their advantaged positions within society and provide access to resources, even while development remains trapped and the broad masses suffer. There is very little evidence, despite the routinely optimistic pronouncements from the IFIs, that this situation has fundamentally changed, even if the democratization waves of the late 1980s/early 1990s have created—in part—somewhat different environments within which elites on the continent must navigate their control. Characterized by continued economic crises and typified by enduring patrimonialism and ongoing foreign aid the continent's leaders continue business pretty much as usual, even if they have had to learn new skills to do so.

A major problem in many African countries is not the absolute quantity of resources but instead rather how what resources that exist are disseminated and utilized. As William Easterly (2003: 33) noted of one Commonwealth nation, "If Zambia had converted all the aid it received since 1960 to investment and all of that investment to growth, it would have had a per capita gross domestic product (GDP) of about $20,000 by the early 1990s. Instead, Zambia's per capita GDP in the early 1990s was lower than it had been in 1960, hovering under $500." A commitment to a more realistic engagement between the IFIs and the true nature of the state in Africa is needed. It also requires a far more sanguine approach to the effectiveness of aid and a recognition that "The 'financing gap' model in which aid increases investment and then that investment increases economic growth has dubious theoretical foundations and numerous empirical failings" (ibid.).

The implications are immense, notably that the attainment of "development" can only be found *inside* Africa, not externally, although there are ways in which the outside world can help. If the IFIs wish to help in this regard, a far more *politicized* raft of development policies will be required. This might include some of the following, drawn from Cromwell and Chintedza (2005). First, they must get a much firmer understanding on the political economy within recipient countries. Sadly, "the path-dependent effect of neo-liberalism in the Bank's theory, reinforced by the dominance of economists in key intellectual positions, led to a peculiar articulation and justification of 'good governance' work that to many (including some operational staff) avoided the kind of blunt political language and analytical tools necessary to put the new ideas [of good government] into practice" (Weaver, 2008: 11). Yet if the relationship between giver and receiver is to be a factor in taming rather than exacerbating neo-patrimonial tendencies, this needs prioritizing.

Secondly, the IFIs should seek to endow civil society with greater effectiveness in the policy process, while being aware that patronage and clientelism exists within civil society and that the danger of elite capture is real (Platteau, 2004). Thirdly, the IFIs need to bear in mind the patronage potential of various policy instruments—and formulate assistance accordingly. The IFIs have to accept the reality that they can be part of the problem by channeling large aid flows through malfunctioning government systems. However, it should be noted that the World Bank's stance toward governance "does not dwell on the more intangible (and analytically difficult) social foundations that determine state legitimacy and authority, without which the best of designs for improving state capability are bound to flounder" (Kapur, 1998: 8).

Fourthly, given that the absence of a bourgeoisie with a stake in economic and political stability characterizes a number of African countries, encouraging policies that would build up a prosperous middle class (while safeguarding the interests of the poor) seems sensible. In short, the IFIs need to focus much more on the *political context* of underdevelopment in Africa and on the support that the IFIs can give for alleviating poverty and promoting development. The inference of this analysis is that the cozy charade of denial and mirage between African heads of state and the IFIs would have to be replaced by a much more fraught set of relationships and interactions. After all, "in the global scheme of things we assume that the state apparatus exists largely to protect the security of its citizens. Across much of Africa . . . this is simply not so" (Cornwell, 2000: 95). Given "persistent features of the operational culture [within the IFIs], most critically the pressure to keep lending" (Weaver, 2008: 11–12), one wonders whether the IFIs can bring themselves to recognize this.

CHAPTER EIGHT

Oil and Its Impact on Africa's International Relations

In today's globalized world economy, oil provides the foundation for commerce and industry, the means for transportation, and provides the ability to wage war. It is, *the* prize to capture (Yergin, 1991). In recent times, there has been growing international interest in Africa as a source for such a vital resource. So much so that there is now talk of a "scramble for Africa's oil," redolent of the nineteenth century's Scramble for Africa (Klare and Volman, 2006a; Watts, 2006; Ghazvinian, 2007; Clarke, 2008). It is important to remember that though this unprecedented attention is relatively new, the presence of oil in Africa is not; oil extraction on the continent began in the 1950s, while exploration was started much earlier (Soares de Oliveira, 2007a). Yet Africa has now emerged as a hugely important source of oil in the global economy. This is largely due to new discoveries—"in the years between 2005 and 2010, 20% of the world's new production capacity is expected to come from Africa" (Ghazvinian, 2007: 12) *and* the instability of oil markets in the Middle East, which compels the search for alternative supply locations.

These and other factors have resulted in major oil corporations from around the world increasingly focusing their attention toward diversifying oil supplies and looking toward SSA. It has been argued that there is nothing particularly new about the new "Scramble." Frynas and Paulo (2007: 233–5) assert that the "key characteristics of the nineteenth century scramble are missing from the current expansion of interests in Africa. For instance, there are no clear spheres of interest or spheres of control today." Yet an identifiable configuration is clearly emerging vis-à-vis the rush for the continent's oil (as Frynas and Paulo themselves admit). American oil corporations largely control the oil fields of those economies that have recently discovered oil reserves, such as Equatorial Guinea and São Tomé and Príncipe, while British and American oil interests dominate Nigeria and French companies lead in Gabon and Congo-Brazzaville. Chinese corporations dominate the oil sector in Sudan. Meanwhile, actors from Brazil, India, Japan, Malaysia, South Korea, etc. are aggressively competing and seeking access across the continent. As Cyril Obi (2007b: 8) notes, "the intensified struggle for oil in Africa is not a re-play of the partition of the 19th century, yet the continent is haunted by the ghost from the past, as the continent's natural resources are being increasingly exploited by competing transnational actors, that simultaneously incorporate, and marginalize people within the various African countries."

With a new energy policy in the United States bent on diversifying Washington's sources of oil (see Chapter One) and with the increased activities of new actors such as Chinese and Indian oil corporations in Africa (see Chapters Four and Five respectively), alongside "traditional" exploiters of Africa's oil (the British, French, etc.), a perceived rush for Africa's oil is now a feature of the continent's international relations.

While analyses indicate that the entire African continent holds only about 10 percent of the world's total oil reserves (Roberts, 2004: 257), by 2015 the United States is predicted to source 25 percent of its oil imports from Africa (Ghazvinian, 2007: 8). In fact, according to the US Department of Energy, the combined oil output by all African producers is projected to rise by 91 percent between 2002 and 2025 (from 8.6 to 16.4 million barrels per day) (Volman, 2006: 611). Thus within oil circles, there is growing excitement about the "alluring global source of energy in Africa" (Shaxson, 2007a: 24). Indeed, as the only region in which oil production is actually rising, Africa has been identified as the "final frontier" in the quest for global oil supplies (Klare and Volman, 2006a).

The burgeoning oil fields in SSA, particularly in the Gulf of Guinea, have become of major geo-strategic importance to the oil-dependent industrialized economies. In fact, it might now be stated that the United States does not just buy oil from Africa, "in many ways it is *dependent* on African oil" (emphasis added) (Barnes, 2005: 236). As Walter Kansteiner, the assistant secretary of state for Africa noted, "African oil is critical to us, and it will increase and become more important as we go forward" (cited in Obi, 2005: 39). Thus today, African oil has become a "matter of US national strategic interest" (Obi, 2005: 38), granting the Gulf of Guinea "major strategic relevance in global energy politics" (Alao, 2007: 168). To the American ambassador to Chad's surprise, "for the first time, the two concepts—'Africa' and 'US national security'—have been used in the same sentences in Pentagon documents" (quoted in Volman, 2003: 76).

Concomitantly, Africa has now emerged as a major site for competition between various oil corporations from diverse nations. Within the next few years, perhaps the largest investment in the continent's history will be seen as billions of dollars are poured into exploration and oil production in Africa. For instance, three of the world's largest oil corporations (Shell, Total and Chevron) are targeting 15 percent, 30 percent and 35 percent respectively of their global exploration and production budgets on Africa (Ghazvinian, 2007: 7). Meanwhile, it is estimated that Sub-Saharan economies will gather over US$200 billion in oil revenue receipts over the next decade (Gary and Karl, 2003: 1). Obviously, for a continent often seen as being marked by grinding poverty and declining standards of living, the questions are: Will this upsurge in income represent real potential for progressive change for Africans? Will the new "Scramble for Africa" result in positive development? And will Africa's international relations be qualitatively reconfigured by the continent's new status as a major supplier of energy to the global political economy?

The Nature of the Scramble

The characteristics of the new Scramble present the broader framework for answering some of the above questions and stimulate some of the dynamics that underpin this new rush into Africa's oil fields by external actors. First, at the global level there is mounting anxiety that future oil supplies will not meet global demand, particularly within a wider context where emergent economies such as Brazil, China and India are rapidly increasing oil consumption to feed their growing economies. The gap between global supply and demand may be reached as early as 2025, according to some analyses (Klare and Volman, 2006a: 609). Thus although the actual quantity of African oil reserves are low in comparison to those presently found in the Middle East—proven oil reserves at the end of 2008 were 117 billion barrels in Africa, compared to 746 billion barrels in the Middle East—in a context marked by deep anxiety over future supplies, Africa's reserves (c. 9 percent of the world's total) are extremely significant (*National Post* [Toronto], July 12, 2008).

Another characteristic of the Scramble is that while it is not solely a race between Chinese and American corporations, the Scramble's dynamics are heavily influenced by the roles and activities of actors from these two states (Frynas and Paulo, 2007: 230). Policymakers in both nations have identified African oil as vital to their respective nations' national interest, albeit for different motives. It is apparent that policy analysts in Beijing see the broader global political milieu as being intrinsically linked to Chinese energy security and feel that in the current environment China is vulnerable until and unless it can diversify its oil sourcing and secure greater access to the world's oil supplies (Taylor, 2006b: 937). Between 2002 and 2025 it is estimated that Chinese energy consumption will rise by 153 percent (Klare and Volman, 2006b), and China is now the second largest consumer of oil globally, after the US, using 7 million barrels of oil a day, expected to rise to 9 million by 2011 (Shinn, 2008). In order to fuel such a growing demand, Chinese oil corporations have entered into the competition for African oil. In fact, China's economic and diplomatic strategy has for the most part focused on oil-rich SSA countries lacking American investment; 85 percent of Chinese African oil imports come from the oil-rich states of Angola, Sudan, Equatorial Guinea, DRC and Nigeria (Taylor, 2006b).

From the American perspective, the "war on terrorism and preparations for war against Iraq . . . enormously increased the strategic value of West African oil reserves" (Ellis, 2003: 135). The high level of interest from such major importers has certainly raised the level of competition over Africa's oil. While corporations headquartered in other states—Britain, Brazil, France, India and Malaysia, for example—are playing important roles in the ongoing Scramble and equally striving to build up their oil portfolios in Africa, it is the ostensible Sino-American competition for oil on the continent that has grabbed the most headlines: "There is also little doubt that the interest in Africa's oil and gas resources has spurred a rivalry between international actors in Africa, notably the American and Chinese governments" (Frynas and Paulo, 2007: 230).

Lastly, arguably unlike the colonial Scramble for Africa, African agency is far more present in the contemporary rush for oil. Many African governments are quite proactive in their roles within today's context. While we might aver that the nineteenth-century Scramble "was driven and dictated by European colonial interests," in the current Scramble for oil, "African leaders act in the role of decision-makers" (Frynas and Paulo, 2007: 235). While it is true that many African states are rich in oil but lack sufficient capital to exploit these resources and thus create formative conditions whereby African elites might be seen as dependent upon external actors to facilitate exploitation (Goel, 2004: 482), the ability of the government to negotiate favorable contracts should not be discounted.

In fact, many oil-rich African governments are quite skilful in playing the oil game—albeit for the benefit of the incumbent elites, rather than the broad masses. In Angola, for example, the state-owned oil company, Sonangol, is "an entity that can articulate state interests in the oil sector with comparative prowess, bringing together its scarce human resources and enabling success in negotiations and joint ventures as well as access to oil-backed loans . . .Insulated from the rest of the state apparatus and the incompetence of the civil service, conversant in the languages of high finance, business contracts and oil technology, Sonangol is a strange marriage of the latest expertise and market savvy with the narrow enrichment goals of a failed state leadership, and it works" (Soares de Oliveira, 2007b: 610–11). The agency of African states should not be ignored in any discussion of the new Scramble.

Why Africa?

Apart from the objective amount of new oil discoveries being revealed in Africa on a regular basis, there are a number of factors that make the continent particularly attractive to oil corporations *and* to non-African political policymakers. Technically, what makes African oil particularly of interest to the oil industry is the quality of African crude oil, known as "sweet" crude, which is comparatively unproblematic to refine and lessens the costs involved in the refining process. Most of Africa's crude oil is high quality and has a light, low sulfur grade. This is highly valued, thanks to its high gasoline content and relatively cheap processing outlay—particularly attractive to corporations headquartered in the West, where environmental regulations make it problematic to refine heavier crude without running up relatively higher expenditures. In a profit-driven industry, African oil makes commercial sense.

The second factor in Africa's attractiveness to the global oil industry is the geographic nature of the continent. Entirely enclosed by water, Africa's location reduces transportation costs and time necessary to ship supplies to the prime global markets, with well-developed sea-lanes readymade for facilitating haulage. The Gulf of Guinea, in particular, benefits from a favorable geographical position from the perspective of oil companies, as it consists of a large maritime area lacking in shipping chokepoints i.e. narrow transport routes, such as those found in the Persian Gulf, that are vulnerable to blockade and flashpoints for trouble.

Thirdly, Africa provides a *relatively* favorable environment vis-à-vis contractual agreements. In an environment where local technical expertise and, often, the capital investment required to extract the oil are lacking, foreign oil companies enter into production sharing agreements. Under a production sharing agreement, the contractor (i.e. the foreign oil company) carries the whole cost and risk of exploration, and is rewarded only if exploration is successful. If there is a commercial discovery, the contractor regains its expended costs through the allocation of oil, what is known in the trade as "Cost Oil." Production for royalties is also recovered, after which the rest of any production, "Profit Oil," is shared as per the agreement. In Nigeria, for example, oil companies pay a flat rate of 50 percent tax on petroleum profits and the installations continue to be assets of the government during the contract (Taylor, 2007: 635). Production sharing agreements are attractive to foreign oil corporations as they create conditions where lucrative profits can be made in exchange for relatively low up-front costs. Furthermore, such agreements are far more attractive than having to work with state-owned oil companies in joint ventures, where the local national oil corporation invariably has a monopoly, including in the distribution of petroleum—Saudi Arabia being the prime example whose arrangements oil corporations are trying to move away from.

A fourth plus point for Africa in the eyes of foreign oil companies is that, with the exceptions of Angola and Nigeria, SSA oil-producing countries are not members of the OPEC. OPEC membership places stringent measures on member states regarding output, as a means to maintain an artificially high oil price. This is why "both the US and oil companies operating in Nigeria have been pressuring the Nigerian government to pull out of OPEC to avoid production quotas imposed by the organization" (Montague, 2002: 2). Equally, this is why the emergence of major sources of oil from non-OPEC states is seen by strategists in London and Washington as positive as, with the increase in non-OPEC oil states, who may produce and export at maximum output, it weakens OPEC's ability to keep the price of oil unnaturally high.

Another attraction for corporations investing in African oil is the fact that most of the oil reserves are offshore. The development of new technology within the oil industry has opened up deepwater and ultra-deepwater reserves (5,000 to 10,000 feet) throughout the Gulf of Guinea, making them now commercially feasible. Offshore locations obviously lessen the possibility that violence, civil strife, etc. may interrupt production (Ghazvinian, 2007: 4). This is hugely desirable from the standpoint of the corporations, given the ongoing onshore situation in the Niger Delta, where oil companies must negotiate large-scale illegal bunkering, kidnappings and violence (see Obi, 2005; Rowell et al., 2005) that has created a situation where:

> A presidential committee report says Nigeria lost at least $28 billion to oil theft and sabotage in the first nine months of 2008. Some 1,000 lives were lost within the same period. Bombings of oil pipelines and kidnappings of oil workers by armed gangs in the creeks of the Niger Delta, home to Africa's biggest oil and gas industry, have cut Nigeria's crude oil output sharply over the past three years. (*Voice of America* [Abuja], April 25, 2009)

Offshore locations also, of course, avoid the "two-speed problem," i.e. "pipelines and offshore platforms can be built much faster than capable states" (Gary and Karl, 2003: 49). Clearly, offshore fields, often far from the political instability and conflict found onshore, can be more easily insulated from the endemic turmoil that characterizes many African states (Mañe, 2005: 7). And related to this *relative* safety (from the perspective of the oil companies), Africa is increasingly viewed more favorably than the Middle East, where xenophobic sentiments are high.

The above factors illustrate why Africa has emerged as a prime site of global interest in terms of oil exploration and production. Yet despite the huge influx of capital into Africa following this new Scramble, there is growing unease about the possibilities that such renewed interest in the continent may not facilitate development but rather reify existing conditions of dependency, depredation and corruption. Indeed, past experience from oil-producing states does not exactly give confidence to any feelings of optimism. Oil and gas investments across SSA have largely proven negative in terms of their socio-economic effects and have certainly largely outweighed any benefits that such capital inflows have brought (Obi, 2007a). It is to the "resource curse" that we now turn to in order to contextualize concerns about the continent's fate under conditions associated with the new Scramble.

Oil, Africa and the Resource Curse

"As the world's most sought after commodity . . . oil has an impact more pronounced and more widespread" than most other commodities (Ross, 2008: 1). In Africa, oil has indeed had an intensive impact on the political economy and social order of oil-rich states, albeit generally negative. Studies have demonstrated "the curse of natural resource-ownership is substantial, manifested in such countries growing slower, on average, by about 1% per year during the period 1970–1989" (Sala-i-Martin and Subramanian, 2003: 3). Indeed, the link between oil and maldevelopment, as well as centralized autocracy, is well known and demonstrated wherever oil is found in Africa: "oil-producing communities appear to have suffered more underdevelopment than their non-oil producing counterparts" (Alao, 2007: 173).

Rather than contributing to development, oil is part and parcel of an intrinsically *extractive* and *exploitative* enterprise; only 5 percent of the billions invested into the oil industry have actually been spent *in* Africa, with the majority lining the pockets of those in power (Ghazvinian, 2007). "In 1970, just before the oil boom, 19 million Nigerians lived below the poverty line. Now, nearly $400 billion in state oil earnings later, 90 million people or more live below that line" (Shaxson, 2007b: 4). The oil companies have shown little concern. After all, "their goal is not to reduce poverty and increase democratic participation, accountability and broad-based prosperity; it is the successful extraction of crude oil for sale in the world market with the smoothest and least bothersome relationship possible with the state that owns it . . . Company policies may be changing with CSR [Corporate Social Responsibility], but this is damage control, not reform" (Soares de Oliveira, 2007a: 265).

One analysis has averred that there are three ways linking authoritarianism and oil: the rentier effect, the repression effect and the modernization effect (Ross, 2001: 357). These effects have consistently served to inhibit political reforms in oil-rich states and have allowed the elites of such economies to be insulated from societal pressures through access to resource rents: the state becomes "remarkably autonomous from public pressure outside the elite" (ibid.). The rentier effect allows oil-rich regimes to utilize oil receipts in place of excise from its citizenry. The concomitant lack of taxation generates an appeasement effect on the mostly impecunious, disenfranchised and disengaged population; it also serves to free the government from welfare provisioning. No taxation not only logically means no representation, but also no services either.

At the same time, oil rents facilitate a strong security apparatus, which in turn creates the repression effect if and when the elites feel challenged: oil "makes authoritarian regimes stronger by funding patronage and repressive apparatuses" (Smith, 2004: 232). A strong security arm is often needed to quell localized (often ethnicized) conflict as oilfields are usually geographically concentrated, while any benefits are diffused—usually back to the capital—and the local communities playing host to a country's oil wealth rarely gain, thus creating resentment and conflict. In such enclave economies, revenue generation is physically confined to small locales, with the prime markets for the products being external (international). This makes "the general economic health of areas outside the enclave quite secondary, if not irrelevant. In enclave economies, then, elites gain little from any deep, growing, economic prosperity of the masses of the population" (Leonard and Straus, 2003: 13). Indeed, oil companies in SSA have often "built their own access roads, provided their own security and, being enclave economies, they relied little on local business linkages" (Frynas and Wood, 2001: 596).

While individuals who have gained access to rents from such enclaves may benefit handsomely, the system fundamentally fails to promote economic growth and development. The Niger Delta would be a classic example. After all, back in 1976, Madujibeya (1976: 294) wrote that "after decades of large-scale oil exploitation, effective economic development [in Nigeria] has remained an ambition." Over 30 years later, very little has changed. Equally, in Angola:

> Neither the oil nor most of the money it brings in ever touches Angolan soil. The country is one of the world's leading oil exporters, producing some one million barrels per day (bpd); this is projected to further rise within the next few years to two million bpd, which is substantially more than the current production in Kuwait. The Angolan government receives something on the order of $5 billion in oil revenue each year. Yet virtually all of the production occurs offshore (and increasingly in very deep water operations); very little of the oil wealth even enters the wider society . . . In spite of some 25 years of booming oil production, Angolans today are among the most desperately poor people on the planet; furthermore, the country ranks near the very bottom of the usual indices of "human development" (161 out of 173 according to the UN Human Development Index . . . The industry imports virtually all its equipment and materials; in addition, it employs very few Angolans, relying for its skilled labor on crews of foreign workers brought in on short-term contracts. These workers live in a gated compound in Cabinda called Malongo, still surrounded by land mines from the civil war that wracked the country from 1975 to 2002. Workers come and go from the airport to their compound in helicopters, bypassing the surrounding town entirely. (Ferguson, 2005: 378)

The modernization effect infers that a dependence on commodity exports retards the social and cultural changes that are deemed necessary for liberal democracy to develop. Economic diversification, through investment in the productivity of other national industries and which might create a bourgeoisie is avoided. The presence of wealth generated by oil within elite circles fails to develop any middles class, yet countries will rarely democratize until they modernize through education, which is not invested in by the overwhelming majority of oil-rich states. The modernization effect here acts in conjunction with the rentier effect, because the state's lack of accountability and lack of service provisions generate low levels of education, which in turn, so the argument goes, decreases optimal conditions for democratization and facilitates autocracy.

In addition to the link between oil and authoritarianisms, other factors might be identified to explain further facets of the resource curse. These are dependence on a single commodity for economic welfare, the Dutch Disease, rent generation and institutional stagnation. Clearly, dependency on one primary resource "exposes countries to volatility, particularly in commodity prices which could have an adverse impact on growth" (Sala-i-Martin and Subramanian, 2003: 2). The fluctuation in receipts garnered from the single commodity can vary wildly year on year and makes planning nigh on impossible. Private investment in turn becomes prohibitively risky and potentially expensive and thus deters most external investment outside of the dominant commodity. Africa's economic collapse in the 1980s can, *in part*, be traced to the vagaries of the international oil market. In order to avoid this aspect of the "resource curse," African economies must shift its current activities in the natural resource sector toward secondary and tertiary production. Yet problematically, the surging demand for oil across the global economy will likely deter diversification attempts as elites will be tempted to seek maximum advantage from the new Scramble.

The Dutch Disease is another negative element that makes up the resource curse associated with oil-rich economies and is a powerful explanation for the "poor performance of oil exporters" (Karl, 1997: 5). The Dutch Disease captures a process whereby a country experiences an export commodity boom which is followed by a decrease in manual exports as policymakers ignore other sectors of the economy, leading to higher inflation and unemployment (McSherry, 2006: 18). The process forces non-oil exports into decline and leaves an economy "dependent on its resource sector and so at the mercy of the volatile international markets" (Ross, 2008: 2). The processes associated with the Dutch Disease are not automatically related to oil—as alternative examples attest: "Norway and Britain used North Sea oil to underwrite their welfare states, while small oil powers like Oman and Brunei found themselves catapulted out of subsistence living in a generation" (Perry, 2007: 6). Rather, they depend largely upon decisions made within the public policy realm and effective governance can minimize any Dutch Disease. A comparative study of Indonesia and Nigeria by Lewis (2007) attests in part to this analysis.

Finally, "natural resources affect economic growth through their adverse effects on economic institutions" (Sala-i-Martin and Subramanian, 2003: 3). Here, it is understood that the huge incomes generated by oil rents can produce a variety of problems for the state. Rents serve to insulate the leadership, as we have noted, and "strengthen the state's leverage over societal actors by giving the state a non-tax revenue cushion" (Ross, 1999: 311). This serves to undermine any need to invest in either institutions outwith the oil sector or in the nation's human capital. As Soares de Oliveira (2007b: 610) notes with regard to Angola:

A veritable basket case of dysfunctional state experiences, Angola brings together the pathologies of the colonial and postcolonial African state with the ailments of petro-statehood . . . Over the past fifteen years in particular, the decay of state institutions, the privatization of power and the abandonment by state elites of tasks they no longer believe are the state's own, especially the provision of public goods, has had an impact on the lives of Angolans that is difficult to overstate. However, the presence of oil deposits changes the calculus of state survival by preserving the Angolan state and other oil states in the region from Somalia-type demise. Oil guarantees it considerable freedom from the international financial institutions, and a solidly long-term legal engagement (through the sale of the fuel that powers industrial civilization) with the international economy. Oil ensures that whatever the domestic political conditions, there will be an interest by multiple external and internal actors in maintaining a notional central structure, and that enough resources will be available to prop up incumbents, guarantee their enrichment, and coerce or co-opt enemies. This allows them to build a political order that is violent, arbitrary, exploitative but fairly reliable. The resulting political process is and will be unstable and fragmentary, but the structure of politics itself will be stable and viable—while oil lasts.

Related to the above, revenues gained from oil frequently "lead to rapacious rent-seeking" (Sala-i-Martin and Subramanian, 2003: 2). Corruption becomes a modus operandi and further undermines institutional development and effectiveness. In such circumstances, rent seeking is directly related to political power, and equally, there is little interest in governance performance as "rents make officials both myopic and risk averse" (Ross, 1999: 311). With growing dependence on oil linked to the means to stay in political power, elites pursue classical Big Man politics, centralizing power and using violence—or the threat of violence—to maintain domination, all facilitated by easy access to necessary resources provided by oil receipts (McSherry, 2006). For instance, there is an observable 2 to 10 percent increase in military spending in states that discover oil, compared to non-oil possessing African countries (Gary and Karl, 2003). Rentier states undermine avenues for local democratic participation as grossly corrupt and criminalized elites utilize oil rents to maintain power—as the example of Gabon attests (see Yates, 1996). Given that President Omar Bongo of Gabon was in power from 1967 to 2009, the longevity of such arrangements can be startling. Indeed, "large resource revenues can 'pay for stability' and maintain a generally autocratic, stable political order . . . generally characterized by the low accountability of elite groups" (Le Billon, 2005: 6).

So, "petro-states continue to come by petro-dollars that are invested largely in reinforcing the ruling class, tightening its grip on the state, acquiring more weapons and ammunition for 'security purposes' and forcing through policies that favor external constituencies such a donors and foreign investors" (Obi, 2005: 40). Of course, the global system of production and the activities of the multinational corporations in fostering such milieu is an integral aspect of any "resource curse." The conversion of oil into a strategic resource has caused immense wealth in the North and among local elites, but has served to immiserate the bulk of the population wherever oil is extracted in Africa. Avoiding this scenario will be absolutely central to any putative positive outcome from the resurgence of interest in Africa's oil. In such circumstances, however, the adage of pessimism of the intellect, optimism of the will is fitting, particularly when examining how oil-rich nations have fared in recent times in Africa and the role of external actors in such situations.

Equatorial Guinea

Equatorial Guinea is routinely described as a "criminal state" (Wood, 2004). In 1995, the US embassy was closed in Malabo because of serious concerns over corruption and human rights. In 1997, oil was discovered in Equatorial Guinea's waters—"just a few weeks after the embassy closed its doors, several US companies found significant petroleum reserves off the coast. Subsequent discoveries led firms such as ExxonMobil and Chevron, as well as small independents like Ocean Energy, Vanco and Triton to invest a collective $5 billion in Equatorial Guinea. Sweetening the deal for the oil companies is the fact that the Obiang regime gave them as much as 87 percent of the oil receipts" (*Nation* [Washington, DC], April 4, 2002). In 2003, the US reopened its embassy in Equatorial Guinea, despite absolutely no change in the nature of governance in the country. Today, there are direct flights from Houston to Malabo, and when in office, Condoleezza Rice publicly called Equatorial Guinea's president, Teodoro Obiang Nguema, a "good friend" of the United States (*Washington Post* [Washington, DC], April 18, 2006). The intense American involvement in the country highlights some of the dynamics thrown up by the quest for energy sources in Africa.

In Equatorial Guinea oil represents 92 percent of its total exports, and despite a sudden inrush of capital in terms of both investment and receipts from oil, there has been minimal improvement in the economic and social welfare of its citizens (see McSherry, 2006). Billions of dollars of oil revenue investment have gone into the building of an ostentatious second capital city ("Malabo II"), while health and education spending remains a mere 1.23 percent of the government's budget, despite the desperate need for basic infrastructure construction such as roads, schools and hospitals (Frynas, 2004). Meanwhile at least 80 percent of oil revenues are captured by 5 percent of the country's population, who indulge in profligate spending on luxury items. A rentier mentality reigns, while Equatorial Guinea's insertion into the global oil market has created "the ultimate enclave industry," capital rather than labor intensive and requiring foreign technology, investment and expertise, with negligible employment opportunities for local citizens (Ghazvinian, 2007: 14). In 2002, for example, the oil industry in Equatorial Guinea employed roughly only 10,000 people, mostly expatriates or immigrants from the United States, Nigeria, the Philippines and Cameroon (McSherry, 2006).

Oil wealth has allowed the incumbent president to ensure consecutive election victories through intimidation and fear, "winning" the election in December 2002 by a North Korean-style 99 percent (Knight, 2003: 338). Washington has remained mute on such matters. In fact, Equatorial Guinea, which has in the past decade gone from being an insignificant blip on international affairs, with a stagnating economy and a dire reputation for repression and human rights abuses, to being a much sought after political partner, with the fastest growing GDP in the world and one of the largest recipients of FDI in SSA. Recent efforts to overthrow the President, including a high-profile coup attempt in 2004, demonstrate however "that the increased spoils of the recent oil boom have inflamed internal power struggles" (Wood, 2004: 553).

Nigeria

Nigeria is another example of the dangers that any resurgence of interest in Africa predicated on energy resources may have for the continent. Nigeria currently produces 10 percent of the oil consumed by the United States, and currently holds roughly half of the Gulf of Guinea's oil reserves. A World Bank report estimated in 2005 that as much as 80 percent of Nigeria's oil revenues benefited just 1 percent of the country's population (*Boston Globe* [Boston], October 3, 2005). Though the Niger Delta region produces 90 percent of Nigeria's oil and over 75 percent of the country's export earnings, very little of the wealth has been seen by residents in the Delta. Since independence there has never been a Nigerian head of state with origins in any one of the oil-producing states. The Nigerian military officer class have long dominated the federal government and "the northern predominantly Hausa region has benefited in a disproportionate manner from oil resources, contributing to grievances by the rest of the country and ongoing instability" (White and Taylor, 2001: 333).

In fact, Nigeria has the second lowest per capita oil export earnings in the world, at US$212 per person in 2004. The 2004 figure compares to the US$589 per person earned in 1980—a decline of more than 50 percent. "In 2006, life expectancy remained staggeringly low at 46 years and income inequality ranked 159th in the world. Despite the improvements in fiscal management, budgets were not implemented as stated, funds were impounded by the President, and extra-budgetary spending continued" (Gillies, 2007: 576). It is estimated that well-connected political insiders steal over 100,000 barrels of oil per day, which works out to be worth approximately US$1.46 billion a year. At the same time, government budgets are routinely estimated on projected income assumptions that are wildly below the actual revenues collected. It is anyone's guess where the surplus finances from oil sales go—certainly not into government coffers or to the broad mass of Nigeria's citizens (*Vanguard* [Lagos], October 26, 2004).

The conspicuous discrepancy between Nigeria's abundant natural resources and the actual welfare of its citizens is an embodiment of the perennial crises confronting virtually all African oil-producing states. Like most oil-rich states in Africa, those who control Nigeria's government are corrupt, self-serving and uninterested in promoting broad-based development in the country. Nigeria's population "has assumed a pyramidal shape, with a tiny but fabulously rich elite at the apex, a 'disappearing' middle class in the centre, and a huge and ever expanding impoverished mass at the base" (Gambari, 2008: 61). The most populous country in Africa is, it is unfortunate to say, synonymous with corruption and malgovernance—the "open sore of the continent" as Nigeria's Nobel Prize winning author, Wole Soyinka, has put it (Soyinka, 1996). In 2007, it was estimated that at least US$380 billion of Nigeria's oil wealth had been stolen by the country's postindependence elites, *about two-thirds of all economic aid granted to Africa during this period* (Adebayo, 2008: 2).

Nigeria is a country where "government's business is no man's business" and where there is a well-understood dictum that there is "nothing seriously wrong with stealing state funds, especially if they [are] used to benefit not only the individual but also members of his community. Those who [have] the opportunity to be in government [are] expected to use the power and resources at their disposal to advance private and communal needs" (Osaghae, 1998: 21). The party contesting a Nigerian election under the rubric "I Chop, You Chop Party" is a manifestation of this well-known situation and is accepted as normal behavior.

Clientelism, patronage and corruption are absolutely central to the whole political economy of the country (see Barnes, 1986; Reno, 1993; Aluko, 2002; and Smith, 2007). Members of a tiny elite clique, encompassing the military top brass, "has grown fabulously wealthy at the expense of the rest of the population" (*IRIN* [Kaduna] February 23, 1999). "Political elites are impelled by short time horizons and chronic insecurity, giving rise to strategies focused on the expedient redistribution of resources rather than the systematic mobilization of resources for production and growth" (Lewis, 2004: 100). Certainly, "Nigeria's elite is hardly known for its vision and foresight nor for its willingness to accept the sacrifices needed to build a diversified economy that is not dependent on oil for 95 per cent of foreign exchange earnings and three-quarters of government revenues" (Gambari, 2008: 61). Indeed, Nigeria's politics have long been an open scramble for power in which elites, often utilizing the ethnic card and playing up tribalism and religious differences, compete for control of the state in order to capture the mega benefits associated with the country's enormous oil revenues.

Consequently, violence has now become a norm in the oil-rich Delta, where militants from the Movement for the Emancipation of the Niger Delta (MEND) routinely attack the oil industry, including kidnappings, assassinations and car bombings. In early 2006, MEND militias began attacking oil installations and kidnapping foreign oil workers, leading to a 20 percent reduction in Nigeria's oil production. MEND appears to be a more efficient organization than the armed gangs that have sought to extort money from oil companies in the Delta region as well as being engaged in the theft of oil. In an interview with the BBC, a MEND leader stated that his organization "was fighting for 'total control' of the Niger Delta's oil wealth, saying local people had not gained from the riches under the ground and the region's creeks and swamps. He said the Delta had been exploited for the benefit of other parts of Nigeria and foreign companies and ordered all oil companies and Nigerians whose roots lie elsewhere to leave the region" (*BBC News Online* [London], April 20, 2006). Any upsurge in interest in Nigeria's oil as part of the broader resurgence in Africa's natural resources is only likely to exacerbate problems.

Conclusion

According to Soares de Oliveira (2007a: 5), "the catapulting of the Gulf of Guinea from strategic neglect to geopolitical stardom in the last few years is illustrative of how space is easily re-conceptualized by capital and politics." The resurgence of politico-economic interest in African oil poses a complicated array of negative pressures on the continent and its international relations that very much outweigh any limited opportunities for progressive change. Hazards spring from both the behavior of external actors, be they corporate or state, as well as the actions of comprador elites in control of rentier economies. As one analysis put it, "the new scramble for Africa risks bringing more misery to the continent's impoverished citizens as Western oil companies pour billions of dollars in secret payments into government coffers throughout the continent. Much of the money ends up in the hands of ruling elites or is squandered on grandiose projects and the military" (*Guardian* [London], June 17, 2003). Indeed, ruling elites continue to impede the process of sharing political and economic power, reform efforts fail and the end result is Africa's subjugation in the global community.

Furthermore, with the upsurge of interest in oil by industrialized and emerging economies, there is the very real possibility that African elites may chose to ignore blandishments about the necessity to practice good government (however defined). As one analysis remarked on Angola, but which is equally applicable to all oil-rich states in SSA, "interest in engaging with the transparency rhetoric may already have peaked amidst all-time high oil prices and a new business partner, China, which has essentially replaced conditionality-ridden OECD donors and Bretton Woods institutions as the source of credit for Angola's 'reconstruction', and is unruffled by fashionable Western good governance agendas" (Soares de Oliveria, 2007b: 613). While we should by no means overestimate how serious the IFIs have been in promoting "good governance," these sort of dynamics unleashed by the resurgence of interest in Africa cannot be a good thing in such circumstances.

The insertion of resource-rich African economies into the global political economy has stimulated the development of rentier states dependent on oil-based revenues but highly susceptible to volatile international markets. Hand in hand with this process has gone, without exception, a manifest failure by African oil-rich governments to constructively reinvest receipts into the promotion of sustainable development. This environment springs not simply from structural systemic circumstances associated with the oil industry (crucial though this is), but also from the decisions made by and for the interests of ruling comprador elites: "no necessary link exists between the accumulation of wealth and a particular social outcome. The windfall profits of petroleum exports do not translate into a politically quiescent population" (Okhrulik, 1999: 295). The discovery of oil, however, has fostered gross economic underdevelopment, largely down to political mismanagement (Frynas, 2004).

From the outside in—and contradicting the self-proclaimed discourse that foreign actors promote democracy and good governance in Africa—kleptocratic and authoritarian trends have been remarkably tolerated by external players, be they autocracies such as China, self-proclaimed democracies as found in the West or institutions ostensibly grounded in self-perceived "sensible" economic policies, such as the IFIs. In fact, the political makeup of the external actor makes very little concrete difference in the processes of engagement by international actors with oil-rich African spaces. The need for oil has in fact accelerated a long-existent trend of forgetting the rhetoric about good governance in favor of naked geopolitics (Schraeder, 2001). As Condoleezza Rice admitted, "nothing has really taken me aback more as secretary of state than the way that the politics of energy [are]—I will use the word 'warping'—diplomacy around the world" (*New York Times* [New York], April 5, 2006).

Of prime concern is that this new interest in African oil may reify in Africa what one analysis has termed the phenomena of the successful failed state (Soares de Oliveira, 2007a). These entities would, by any normal measure of a state's capabilities and performance, be considered as failed, in that there is chronically poor leadership, weak and undiversified economies, fragile institutions and low levels of human development. Yet while being marginalized by the rest of the world, oil-rich states are inherently engaged with it. And while possessing the attributes of a failed/failing state, there persists a paradoxical sustainability where the presence of oil maintains the interest and attention of the international community who uphold relationships with such states, granting them (or rather, their elites) legitimacy (Soares de Oliveira, 2007a). This "legitimacy" not only can serve to play out in domestic terms, but also at the global level. And in such circumstances, if a state's "success" is determined by their international legitimacy, recognized sovereignty and the ability to interact at the global level (rather than how they serve their citizenries), then the presence of oil has granted success to some fundamentally dysfunctional African states. Angola, Equatorial Guinea, Nigeria and Sudan all spring to mind at this juncture.

Of course, there are possibilities—however remote—that Africans may benefit from the increased interest in the continent's oil, albeit indirectly. The plethora of externally delivered infrastructure built by, for example, Chinese construction companies as part of broader packages to secure oilfields for Chinese oil companies would be one such instance. And it is not *impossible* that accrued oil revenues may help implement constructive change, perhaps in the direction of the welfare reforms pursued by some Middle Eastern oil producers. It is just unlikely.

There have been calls for a "big push" internationally to promote transparency and accountability as a means to positively alter the developmental outcomes of oil-rich states in Africa (Gary and Karl, 2003). However, the current securitization discourse within American foreign policy surrounding resources in Africa (see Chapter One) and the pressing concerns felt by Beijing policymakers to secure oil, arguably at any cost, potentially exacerbates the resource curse threat and also introduces the potential to militarize the region: the "US navy is making a presence in the Gulf of Guinea and the Department of Defense also seeks to establish a modest capacity for fighting any localized, indigenous forces that might threaten the free flow of petroleum exports" (Klare and Volman, 2006a: 303). If this stimulates the development of a security dilemma in West Africa, then oil's role in Africa's international relations really will be a curse.

Regrettably, the pursuit of energy and profit is likely to fit a familiar pattern—and is intimately entwined with consumption and lifestyle patterns outside of the African continent. Indeed, "it is important to remember that the dangerous effects of Africa's oil are not confined to this continent" as its negative effects spread globally, "to tangle secretly with a globalized financial architecture and with the shadow worlds of Western politics" (Shaxson, 2007a: 26). Whether this will lead to actual conflict remains to be seen (see Rowell, Marriott and Stockman, 2005). Either way, the ownership of oil in SSA has, thus far, proven to be detrimental to most of Africa's peoples, with the majority of those consuming Africa's oil (African and non-African) caring very little. Instead, "what is on offer in the name of petro-development is the terrifying and catastrophic failure of secular nationalist development" (Watts, 2006), something whose progress (or lack thereof) we have witnessed over the last 40 years or so. As Obi (2007b: 17) notes, what is needed is the "re-organization of production in the continent in ways that lift it out of its marginal position in the globalized division of labour which since the days of the 'old scramble', has defined it as an object of domination and exploitation by forces from 'outside.'" Yet in the present climate, this situation is not likely to change any time soon.

Bibliography

Abdul-Raheem, T. (2005) 'Gordon's Marshall Plan for Africa: Who Is Helping Whom?', *Pambakuza News*, January 13.

Abrahamsen, R. (2000) *Disciplining Democracy: Development Discourse and Good Governance in Africa* London: Zed Books.

Abrahamsen, R. and Williams, P. (2001) 'Ethics and Foreign Policy: The Antinomies of New Labour's "Third Way" in Sub-Saharan Africa', *Political Studies*, vol. 49, no. 2.

Abrahamsen, R. and Williams, P. (2002) 'Britain and Southern Africa: A "Third Way" or Business as Usual?' in Adar, K. and Ajulu, R. (eds) *Globalisation and Emerging Trends in African States' Foreign Policy-making Process* Aldershot: Ashgate.

ACP Heads of State and Government (1997) *The Libreville Declaration*, http://www.acpsec.org.

Actionaid (2005) *The African Commission for Britain* London: Actionaid.

Adams, N. (1997) *Worlds Apart: The North-South Divide and the International System* London: Zed Books.

Adebayo, A. (1997) 'Folie de Grandeur', *The World Today*, vol. 53, no. 6.

Adebayo, A. (2008) 'Hegemony on a Shoestring: Nigeria's Post-Cold War Foreign Policy' in Adebayo, A. and Mustapha, A. (eds) *Gulliver's Troubles: Nigeria's Foreign Policy after the Cold War* Scottsville: University of KwaZulu-Natal Press.

Adebayo, A. and O'Hanlon, M. (1997) 'Africa: Toward a Rapid Reaction Force', *SAIS Review*, vol. 17, no. 2.

Africa Policy Advisory Panel (2004) *Rising US Stakes in Africa: Seven Proposals to Strengthen US-Africa Policy* Washington, DC: Center for Strategic and International Studies.

Agawu, K. (2003) *Representing African Music: Postcolonial Notes, Queries, Positions* New York, NY: Routledge.

Agrawal, S. (2007) *Emerging Donors in International Assistance: The India Case* Ottawa: IDRC-Partnership and Business Development Division.

Ake, C. (1987) *Democracy and Development in Africa* Washington, DC: Brookings Institute.

Ake, C. (1991) 'How Politics Underdevelops Africa' in Adedeji, A., Teriba, O. and Bugembe, P. (eds) *The Challenge of African Economic Recovery and Development* Portland: Cass.

Akyeampong, E. (2005) 'Diaspora and Drug Trafficking in West Africa: A Case Study of Ghana', *African Affairs*, vol. 104, no. 416.

Alao, A. (2007) *Natural Resources and Conflict in Africa: The Tragedy of Endowment* Rochester, NY: Rochester University Press.

Alden, C. (2000) 'From Neglect to "Virtual Engagement": The United States and Its New Paradigm for Africa', *African Affairs*, vol. 99, no. 396.

Alden, C. and Viera, A. (2005) 'The New Diplomacy of the South: South Africa, Brazil, India and Trilateralism', *Third World Quarterly*, vol. 26, no. 7.

Allen, C. (1998) 'Britain's Africa Policy: Ethical or Ignorant?', *Review of African Political Economy*, vol. 27, no. 77.

Allimadi, M. (2003) *The Hearts of Darkness: How White Writers Created the Racist Image of Africa* New York, NY: Black Star Books.

Aluko, M. (2002) 'The Institutionalisation of Corruption and Its Impact on Political Culture in Nigeria', *Nordic Journal of African Studies*, vol. 11, no. 3.

Antkiewicz, A. and Whalley, J. *China's New Regional Trade Agreements*, National Bureau of Economic Research Working Paper no. W10992, 2005.

Anyang'Nyong'o, P. and Coughlin, P. (1991) *Industrialization at Bay: African Experiences* Nairobi: Academy Science Publishers.

Armah, A. (1986) 'Africa and the Francophone Dream', in *West Africa*, no. 3582, April 28.

Armijo, L. (2007) 'The BRICs Countries (Brazil, Russia, India, and China in the Global System', *Asian Perspective*, vol. 31, no. 4.

Arrighi, G. (2002) 'The African Crisis: World Systemic and Regional Aspects', *New Left Review* 15, May-June.

Arts, K. and Dickson, A. (2004) (eds) *EU Development Cooperation: From Model to Symbol* Manchester: Manchester University Press.

Asante, S. (1985) 'Development and Regional Integration Since 1980'in Adedeji A. and Shaw, T. (eds) *Economic Crisis in Africa: African Perspectives on Development Problems and Potentials* Boulder, CO: Lynne Rienner.

Astier, H. (2007) 'Plus c'est la rupture, plus c'est la même chose ?' Sarkozy's France after 6 months', paper presented to "Sarkozy's France", Cambridge symposium, November 30.

Augelli, E. and Murphy, C. (1988) *America's Quest for Supremacy and the Third World: A Gramscian Analysis* London: Pinter Publishers.

Ayittey, G. (1995) 'Nigeria: The High Cost of Erratic Financial Policies', *Economic Reform Today*, no. 1.

Baker, R. (1999) 'The Biggest Loophole in the Free-Market System', *Washington Quarterly*, vol. 22, no. 4.

Barnes, S. (1986) *Patrons and Power: Creating a Political Community in Metropolitan Lagos* Manchester: Manchester University Press.

Barnes, S. (2005) 'Global Flows: Terror, Oil and Strategic Philanthropy', *Review of African Political Economy*, vol. 34, no. 104/5.

Barnett, M. and Finnemore, M. (1999) 'The Politics, Power, and Pathologies of International Organizations', *International Organization*, vol. 53, no. 4.

Bava, U. (2007) 'New Powers for Global Change? India's Role in the Emerging Global Order', *Dialogue on Globalization Briefing Papers* no. 4, New Delhi: Friedrich Ebert Stiftung.

Bayart, J.-F. (1993) *The State in Africa: The Politics of the Belly* London: Longman.

Bayart, J.-F. (1998) '*Bis repetita*': la politique africaine de François Mitterrand' in Cohen, S. (ed.) *Mitterrand et la sortie de la Guerre Froide* Paris: Presses Universitaire de France.

Bayart, J.-F. (2000) 'Africa in the World: A History of Extraversion', *African Affairs*, vol. 99, no. 395.

Bayart, J.-F., Ellis, S. and Hibou, B. (1999) *The Criminalization of the State in Africa*, Oxford: James Currey.

Beri, R. (2003) 'India's Africa Policy in the Post-Cold War Era: An Assessment', *Strategic Analysis*, vol. 27, no.2.

Beri, R. (2005) 'Africa's Energy Potential: Prospects for India', *Strategic Analysis*, vol. 29, no. 3.

Bermann, C. (2007) 'Resource Sector in Africa and the Brazilian Extractive Natural Resources Industries', speech given to the Expert Roundtable "Resource Governance in Africa in the 21st Century", at the University of Sao Paulo and Brazilian NGO's and Social Movements Forum for Environment and Development, Berlin, March 26–28.

Bernstein, Henry (1990) 'Agricultural Modernisation and the Era of Structural Adjustment: Observations on Sub-Saharan Africa', *Journal of Peasant Studies*, vol. 18, no. 1.

Birdsall, N., Rodrik, D. and Subramanian, A. (2005) 'How to Help Poor Countries', *Foreign Affairs*, July/August.

Blum, S. (2003) 'Chinese Views of US Hegemony', *Journal of Contemporary China*, vol. 12, no. 35.

Boisbouvier, C. (2007) 'Sarkozy et la Françafrique: entre rupture et realpolitik', *Radio France Internationale*, July 28.

Bomberg, E., Peterson, J. and Stubb, A. (2008) *The European Union: How Does it Work?* Oxford: Oxford University Press.

Bonnett, D. (2006) 'India in Africa: An Old Partner, a New Competitor', *Traders Journal*, no. 26.

Bratton, M. and van de Walle, N. (1994) 'Neopatrimonial Regimes and Political Transitions in Africa', *World Politics*, vol. 46, no. 4.

Bratton, M. and van de Walle, N. (1997) *Democratic Experiments in Africa: Regime Transitions in Comparative Perspective* Cambridge: Cambridge University Press.

Breslin, S. (1996) 'China: Developmental State or Dysfunctional Development?', *Third World Quarterly*, vol. 17, no. 4.

Breslin, S. (2005) 'Power and Production: Rethinking China's Global Economic Role', *Review of International Studies*, vol. 31, no. 4.

Breslin, S. (2006) 'Globalization, International Coalitions and Domestic Reform in China' in Rodan, G. and Hewison, K. (eds) *Neoliberalism and Conflict in Asia After 9/11* London: Routledge.

Breslin, S. (2007) *China and the Global Political Economy* Basingstoke: Palgrave.

Breslin, S. and Taylor, I. (2008) 'Explaining the Rise of "Human Rights" in Analyses of Sino-African Relations', *Review of African Political Economy*, vol. 35, no. 115.

Bretherton, C. and Vogler, J. (1999) *The European Union as a Global Actor* London: Routledge.

Brigagão, C. (2009) 'The Strategic Lines of Brazilian Foreign Policy', Norwegian Peacebuilding Centre, May 26.

Broad, R. and Cavanagh, J. (2006) 'The Hijacking of the Development Debate: Why Jeffrey Sachs and Thomas Friedman are Wrong', *World Policy Journal*, Summer, vol. 23, no. 2.

Broadman, H. (2007) *Africa's Silk Road: China and India's New Economic Frontier* Washington, DC: World Bank.

Broadman, H. (2008) 'China and India Go to Africa: New Deals in the Developing World,' *Foreign Affairs*, vol. 87, no. 2.

Brown, W. (1999) 'The EU Structural Adjustment Support: The Case of Zimbabwe', *Review of African Political Economy*, vol. 26, no. 79.

Brown, W. (2000) 'Restructuring North-South Relations: ACP-EU Development Co-operation in a Liberal International Order', *Review of African Political Economy*, vol. 27, no. 8.

Brown, W. (2002) *The European Union and Africa: The Restructuring of North-South Relations* London: I.B. Tauris.

Brown, G. (2004) 'The Challenges of 2005: Forging a New Compact for Africa', *New Economy*, vol. 11, no. 3.

Brown, W. (2006) 'Africa and International Relations: A Comment on IR Theory, Anarchy and Statehood', *Review of International Studies*, vol. 32, no. 1.

Browne, R. and Cummings, R. (1985) *Lagos Plan of Action vs. the Berg Report Lawrenceville*, VA: Brunswick Publishing.

Burnell, P. (2000) 'Democracy Assistance: The State of the Discourse' in Burnell, P. (ed.) *Democracy Assistance. International Co-operation for Democratization* London: Frank Cass.

Burnside, C. and Dollar, D. (2000) 'Aid, Policies, and Growth', *American Economic Review*, vol. 90, no. 4.

Callaghy, T. (1984) *The State-Society Struggle: Zaïre in Comparative Perspective* New York, NY: Columbia University Press.

Callaghy, T. (1987) 'The State as Lame Leviathan: The Patrimonial Administrative State in Africa' in Ergas, Z. (ed.) *The African State in Transition* London: Macmillan.

Callaghy, T. (1991) 'Africa and the World Economy: Caught Between a Rock and a Hard Place' in Harbeson, J. and Rothchild, D. (eds) *Africa in World Politics* Boulder, CO: Westview.

Callaghy, T. (1996) 'Africa Falling Off the Map', *Current History*, vol. 93, no. 579.

Callaghy, T., Kassimir, R. and Latham, R. (eds) (2001) *Intervention and Transnationalism in Africa: Global-Local Networks of Power* Cambridge: Cambridge University Press.

Calvert, P. and Calvert, S. (2007) *Politics and Society in the Developing World* Harlow: Pearson Education.

Campaign Against Arms Trade (2005) *G-8: Arms Dealers to the World* London: Campaign Against Arms Trade.

Carbone, M. (2007) *The European Union and International Development: The Politics of Foreign Aid* London: Routledge.

Carbone, M. (2008) 'Mission Impossible: The European Union and Policy Coherence for Development', *Journal of European Integration*, vol. 30, no. 3.

Carbone, M. (2009) (ed.) *Policy Coherence and EU Development Policy* London: Routledge.

Carl, G. (1999) 'Return to Colonialism? The New Orientation of European Development Assistance', in Lister, M. (ed.) *New Perspectives on European Union Development Cooperation* Boulder, CO: Westview Press.

Carmody, P. (2005) 'Transforming Globalization and Security: Africa and America Post-9/11', *Africa Today*, vol. 52, no. 1.

Castells, M. (2001) *End of Millennium* Oxford: Blackwell.

Césaire, A. (1972) [1955] *Discourse on Colonialism* New York, NY: Monthly Review Press.

Chabal, P. (1994) *Power in Africa: An Essay in Political Interpretation* New York, NY: St. Martin's Press.

Chabal, P. (2009) *Africa: The Politics of Suffering and Smiling* London: Zed Books.

Chabal, P. and Daloz, J-P. (1999) *Africa Works: Disorder as Political Instrument* Oxford: James Currey.

Chafer, T. (2002a) 'Franco-African Relations: No Longer so Exceptional?', *African Affairs*, vol. 101.

Chafer, T. (2002b) *The End of Empire in French West Africa: France's Successful Decolonization?* New York, NY: Berg.

Chafer, T. and Sackur, A. (eds) (2002) *Promoting the Colonial Idea: Propaganda and Visions of Empire in France* Basingstoke: Palgrave.

Chang, G. (2002) *The Coming Collapse of China* London: Random House.

Charbonneau, B. (2006) 'Mastering "Irrational" Violence: The Relegitimization of French Security Policy in Sub-Saharan Africa', *Alternatives*, vol. 31, no. 2.

Charbonneau, B. (2008) *France and the New Imperialism: Security Policy in Sub-Saharan Africa* Aldershot: Ashgate.

Chaturvedi, S. and Mohanty, S. (2007) 'Trade and Investment: Trends and Prospects', *South African Journal of International Affairs*, vol. 14, no. 2.

Chipman, J. (1989) *French Power in Africa* Oxford: Blackwell.

Chiriyankandath, J. (2004) 'Realigning India: Indian Foreign Policy after the Cold War', *Round Table*, vol. 93, no. 372.

Chivvis, C. (2003) 'A Liberal History of European Integration', *International Affairs*, vol. 79, no. 5.

Clapham, C. (ed.) (1982) *Private Patronage and Public Power: Political Clientelism in Modern States* London: Pinter.

Clapham, C. (1985) *Third World Politics: An Introduction* London: Croom Helm.

Clapham, C. (1996a) *Africa and the International System* Cambridge: Cambridge University Press.

Clapham, C. (1996b) 'Governmentality and Economic Policy in Sub-Saharan Africa', *Third World Quarterly*, vol. 17, no. 4.

Clarke, D. (2008) *Crude Continent: The Struggle for Africa's Oil Prize* London: Profile Books.

Coates, D. and Hay, C. (2001) 'The Internal and External Face of New Labour's Political Economy', *Government and Opposition*, vol. 36, no. 4.

Collier, P. (2007) *The Bottom Billion: Why the Poorest Countries are Failing and What Can Be Done about It* Oxford: Oxford University Press.

Collier, P., Hoeffler, A. and Pattillo, C. (2001) 'Flight Capital as a Portfolio Choice', *The World Bank Economic Review*, vol. 15.

Commission for Africa (2005) *Our Common Interest* London: Commission for Africa.

Commission of the European Communities (1996) *Green Paper on Relations between the European Union and the ACP Countries on the Eve of the 21st Century: Challenges and Options for a New Partnership* Luxembourg: Office for Official Publications of the European Communities.

Connell, J. (2004) 'World Music: Deterritorializing Place and Identity', *Progress in Human Geography*, vol. 28, no. 3.

Cook, N. (2006) *AIDS in Africa* Washington, DC: Congressional Research Service.

Cooper, A. (2008) *Celebrity Diplomacy* Boulder, CO: Paradigm Publishers.

Copson, R. (1994) *Africa's Wars and Prospects for Peace*, New York, NY: M.E. Sharpe.

Copson, R. (2007) *The United States in Africa: Bush Policy and Beyond* London: Zed Books.

Corkin, L. and Naidu, S. (2008) 'China and India in Africa: An Introduction', *Review of African Political Economy*, vol. 35, no. 1.

Cornelissen, S. (2004) 'It's Africa's Turn!' The Narratives and Legitimations Surrounding the Moroccan and South African Bids for the 2006 and 2010 FIFA Finals', *Third World Quarterly*, vol. 25, no. 7.

Cornwell, R. (2000) 'A New Partnership for Africa's Development?', *African Security Review*, vol. 11, no. 1.

Cottrell, R. (1987) *The Sacred Cow: The Folly of Europe's Food Mountains* London: Grafton.

Crawford, G. (1996) 'Whither Lomé? The Mid-term Review and the Decline of Partnership', *Journal of Modern African Studies*, vol. 34, no. 3.

Crawford, G. (2000) 'European Union Development Co-operation and the Promotion of Democracy' in Burnell, P. (ed.) *Democracy Assistance. International Co-operation for Democratization* London: Frank Cass.

Crawford, G. (2001) *Foreign Aid and Political Reform. A Comparative Analysis of Democracy Assistance and Political Conditionality* New York, NY: Palgrave.

Crawford, G. (2002) 'Evaluating EU Promotion of Human Rights, Democracy and Good Governance: Towards a Participatory Approach', *Journal of International Development*, vol. 14, no. 6.

Crawford, G. (2004) *The European Union and Democracy Promotion in Africa: The Case of Ghana* POLIS Working Paper No.10, Leeds: University of Leeds.

Cromwell, E. and Chintedza, A. (2005) 'Neopatrimonialism and Policy Processes: Lessons from the Southern African Food Crisis', *IDS Bulletin*, vol. 36, no. 2.

Crook, R. (1989) 'Patrimonialism, Administrative Effectiveness and Economic Development in Cote d'Ivoire' *African Affairs* vol. 88, no. 351, April.

Cumming, G. (1996) 'French Aid to Africa: Towards a New Consensus?', *Modern and Contemporary France*, vol. 4, no. 4.

Cumming, G. (2000) 'Modernisation without Banalisation: Towards a New Era in French African Aid Relations', *Modern and Contemporary France*, vol. 8, no. 3.

Cumming, G. (2003) 'From Realpolitik to The Third Way: British African Policy in the New World Order' in Engel, U. and Olsen, G. (eds) *Africa and the North: Between Globalization and Marginalization* London: Routledge.

Cumming, G. (2004) 'UK African Policy in the Post-Cold War Era: From Realpolitik to Moralpolitik?', *Commonwealth and Comparative Politics*, vol. 42, no. 2.

Cumming, G. (2005) 'Transposing the "Republican" Model? A Critical Appraisal of France's Historic Mission in Africa', *Journal of Contemporary African Studies*, vol. 23, no. 2.

Cumming, G. (2006) 'Exporting the Republican Model: A Critique of France's Civilising Mission in Africa' in G. Raymond and Cole, A. (eds) *Redefining the French Republic*, Manchester: Manchester University Press.

Curtis, M. (2002) 'Blair's Jaw Jaw Means War War', *Red Pepper*, October.

Darby, P. (2002) *Africa, Football, and FIFA: Politics, Colonialism and Resistance.* London: Routledge.

de Arimatiia da Cruz, J. (2005) 'Brazil's Foreign Policy under Luis Inacio "Lula" da Silva: An Early Assessment of a Leftist President', *Politics and Policy*, vol. 33, no. 1.

de Bergh, M. (2006) *Background Note: The 10th European Development Fund: Where do We Stand?* Maastricht: European Centre for Development Policy Management.

Decalo, S. (1989) *Psychoses of Power: African Personal Dictatorships* Boulder, CO: Westview.

Decalo, S. (1990) *Coups and Army Rule in Africa* New Haven: Yale University Press.

DFID (2000) *Eliminating World Poverty: Making Globalisation Work for the Poor* London: DFID.

DFID (2001) *The Causes of Conflict in Africa: Consultation Document* London: DFID.

Dickie, J. (2004) *The New Mandarins: How British Foreign Policy Works* London: I.B. Tauris.

Diop, C. (1987) *Precolonial Black Africa: A Comparative Study of the Political and Social Systems of Europe and Black Africa, from Antiquity to the Formation of Modern States* Westport, CT: L. Hill.

Dirlik, A. (2006) 'Beijing Consensus: Beijing "Gongshi". Who Recognizes Whom and to What End?', mimeo.

Dixon, R. and Williams, P. (2001) 'Tough on Debt, Tough on the Causes of Debt? New Labour's Third Way Foreign Policy', *British Journal of Politics and International Relations*, vol. 3, no. 2.

Dowden, R. (2004) 'The State of the African State: The Past, Present and Future of the Nation State in Africa', *New Economy*, vol. 11, no. 3.

Dunn, K. (2003) *Imagining the Congo: The International Relations of Identity* New York, NY: Palgrave.

Durkheim, E. (1982) [1907] *The Rules of Sociological Method* New York, NY: Free Press.

Duyvendak, J. (1949) *China's Discovery of Africa* London: Probsthain.

Easterly, W. (2002) 'The Cartel of Good Intentions: The Problem of Bureaucracy in Foreign Aid', *Journal of Policy Reform*, no. 4.

Easterly, W. (2003) 'Can Foreign Aid Buy Growth?', *Journal of Economic Perspectives*, vol. 17, no. 3.

Easterly, W., Levine, R. and Roodman, D. (2003) *New Data, New Doubts: A Comment on Burnside and Dollar's "Aid, Policies, and Growth" (2000)*, National Bureau of Economic Research, Working Paper 9846.

Effeh, U. (2008) 'Africa and the Multilateral Trading Regime: Re-examining the "Market Access" Mantra', *Journal of Politics and Law*, vol. 1, no. 1.

Ela Ela, E. (2000) 'La Nouvelle Politique de coopération militaire de la France en Afrique', *Défense Nationale*, vol. 56, no. 2.

Ellis, S. (2003) 'Briefing: West Africa and Its Oil', *African Affairs*, vol. 102, no. 406.

Ellis, S. (2009) 'West Africa's International Drug Trade', *African Affairs*, vol. 108, no. 431.

Embassy of the People's Republic of China in the Republic of Zimbabwe (2000a) 'Strengthen Solidarity, Enhance Co-operation and Pursue Common Development by Zhu Rongji', Harare.

Embassy of the People's Republic of China in the Republic of Zimbabwe (2000b) 'The Beijing Declaration of the Forum on China-Africa Co-operation', Harare.

Ergas, Z. (1987) 'In Search of Development in Africa' in Ergas, Z. (ed.) *The African State in Transition* London: Macmillan.

Erixon, F. (2005) *Aid and Development: Will It Work This Time?* London: International Policy Network.

Ero, C. (2001) 'A Critical Assessment of Britain's Africa Policy', *Conflict, Security, and Development* vol. 1, no. 2.

European Commission (2005) *EU Strategy for Africa: Towards a Euro-African Pact to Accelerate Africa's Development* Brussels: Commission of the European Communities.

European Commission (2008) *EU Budget 2007: Financial Report* Brussels: European Union.

European Parliament (2006) 'EP: Decision of the Committee Responsible', INI/2005/2162, February 21.

Fafowora, O. (2008) 'The Unsung Player: The Nigerian Diplomat and the Foreign Service' in Adebajo, A. and Mustapha, A. (eds) *Gulliver's Troubles: Nigeria's Foreign Policy after the Cold War* Scottsville: University of Kwa-Zulu Natal Press.

Falola, T. (2006) 'Writing and Teaching National History in Africa in the Era of Global History' in Zeleza, P. (ed.) *The Study of Africa: Disciplinary and Interdisciplinary Encounters* Dakar: Codesria.

Fatton, R. (1999) 'Civil Society Revisited: Africa in the New Millennium', *West Africa Review*, vol. 1, no. 1.

Fatton, R. (2002) *Haiti's Predatory Republic: The Unending Transition to Democracy* Boulder, CO: Lynne Rienner.

Ferguson, J. (2005) 'Seeing Like an Oil Company: Space, Security, and Global Capital in Neoliberal Africa', *American Anthropologist*, vol. 107, no. 3.

Fioramonti, L. and Poletti, A. (2008) 'Facing the Giant: Southern Perspectives on the European Union', *Third World Quarterly*, vol. 29, no. 1.

Foot, R. (2006) 'Chinese Strategies in a US-Hegemonic Global Order: Accommodating and Hedging', *International Affairs*, vol. 82, no. 1.

Ford, N. (2006) 'Indian Connection Gathers New Momentum: With the Emergence of China and India, Africa's Traditional Trading Partners are Changing', *African Business*, vol. 235, November 1.

Forwood, G. (2001) 'The Road to Cotonou: Negotiating a Successor to Lomé', *Journal of Common Market Studies*, vol. 39, no. 3.

Frank, A. G. (1967) *Capitalism and Underdevelopment in Latin America: Historical Studies of Chile and Brazil* New York, NY: Monthly Review Press.

Frank, A. G. (1975) *On Capitalist Underdevelopment*. Bombay: Oxford University Press.

Franklin, M. (2005) *Resounding International Relations: On Music, Culture and Politics* Basingstoke: Palgrave.

Fru Doh, E. (2008) *Africa's Political Wastelands: The Bastardization of Cameroon* Bamenda: Langaa Research and Publishing.

Frynas, J. (2004) 'The Oil Boom in Equatorial Guinea', *African Affairs*, vol. 103, no. 413.

Frynas, J. and Paulo, M. (2007) 'A New Scramble for African Oil? Historical, Political, and Business Perspectives', *African Affairs*, vol. 106, no. 423.

Frynas, J. and Wood, G. (2001) 'Oil & War in Angola', *Review of African Political Economy*, vol. 28, no. 90.

Fyson, S. (2009) 'Sending in the Consultants: Development Agencies, the Private Sector and the Reform of Public Finance in Low-income Countries', *International Journal of Public Policy*, vol. 4, nos 3–4.

Gallagher, J. (2009) 'Healing the Scar? Idealizing Britain in Africa, 1997–2007', *African Affairs*, vol. 108, no. 432.

Galtung, J. (1976) 'The Lomé Convention and Neo-Capitalism', *African Review*, vol. 6, no. 1.

Gambari, I. (2008) 'From Balewa to Obasanjo: The Theory and Practice of Nigeria's Foreign Policy' in Adebayo, A. and Mustapha, A. (eds) *Gulliver's Troubles: Nigeria's Foreign Policy after the Cold War* Scottsville: University of KwaZulu-Natal Press.

Ganguly, S. and Pardesi, M. (2007) 'India Rising: What is New Delhi to Do?', *World Policy Journal*, vol. 24, no.1.

Gary, I. and Karl, T. (2003) *Bottom of the Barrel* London: Catholic Relief Services.

George, S. and Sabelli, F. (1994) *Faith and Credit: The World Bank's Secular Empire* Harmondsworth: Penguin.

German Development Institute (2009) 'India's Development Cooperation – Opportunities and Challenges for International Development Cooperation', Briefing Paper, 3/2009.

Ghazvinian, J. (2007) *Untapped: The Scramble for Africa's Oil* London: Harcourt.

Gill, B. and Reilly, J. (2000) 'Sovereignty, Intervention and Peacekeeping: The View from Beijing', *Survival*, vol. 42, no. 3.

Gillespie, R. and Youngs, R. (2002) (eds) *The European Union and Democracy Promotion: The Case for North Africa* London: Routledge.

Gillies, A. (2007) 'Obasanjo, the Donor Community and Reform Implementation in Nigeria', *Round Table*, vol. 96, no. 392.

Gillson, I., Poulton, C., Balcombe, K. and Page, S. (2004) *Understanding the Impact of Cotton Subsidies on Developing Countries* London: Overseas Development Institute.

Gilroy, P. (1993) *The Black Atlantic: Modernity and Double-Consciousness* Cambridge, MA: Harvard University Press.

Glenny, M. (2009) *McMafia: Seriously Organized Crime* London: Vintage.

Global Witness (2009) *Undue Indulgence: How Banks Do Business with Corrupt Regimes* London: Global Witness.

Goel, R. (2004) 'A Bargain Born of Paradox: The Oil Industry's Role in American Domestic and Foreign Policy', *New Political Economy*, vol. 9, no. 4.

Golan, T. (1981) 'A Certain Mystery: How Can France Do Everything that It Does in Africa—and Get Away with It?' *African Affairs*, vol. 80, no. 318.

Goldstein, J. (2008) 'EUFOR Chad: A Step Forward for European Defense', *World Politics Review*, March 27.

Goldstein, A., Pinaud, N., Reisen, H. and Xiaobao Chen (2005)*The Rise of China and India. What's in It for Africa?* Paris: OECD Development Centre Studies.

Gomez, R. (2003) *Negotiating the Euro-Mediterranean Partnership: Strategic Action in EU Foreign Policy* Aldershot: Ashgate.

Goodison, P. (2007) 'What is the Future for EU-Africa Agricultural Trade After CAP Reform?' *Review of African Political Economy*, vol. 34, no. 112.

Grant, J. A. and Taylor, I. (2004) 'Global Governance and Conflict Diamonds: The Kimberley Process and the Quest for Clean Gems', *Round Table: Commonwealth Journal of International Relations*, vol. 93, no. 375.

Gregory, S. (2000) 'The French Military in Africa: Past and Present', *African Affairs*, vol. 99, no. 396.

Green, P. and Ward, T. (2004) *State Crime: Governments, Violence and Corruption* London: Pluto Press.

Gruhn, I. (1976) 'The Lomé Convention: Inching towards Interdependence', *International Organization*, vol. 30, no. 2.

Gu Weiqun (1995) *Politics of Divided Nations: The Case of China and Korea* Westport, CT: Westview.

Gu Xuewu (2005) 'China Returns to Africa', *Trends East Asia*, no. 9, p. 8.

Hale, F. (2005) 'H R Trevor-Roper *vs.* Arnold Toynbee: A Post-Christian Religion and a New Messiah in an Age of Reconciliation?', *Verbum et Ecclesia*, vol. 26, no. 1.

Hancock, G. (1994) *The Lords of Poverty: The Power, Prestige, and Corruption of the International Aid Business* New York, NY: Atlantic Monthly Press.

Han Nianlong (1990) *Diplomacy of Contemporary China* Beijing: New Horizon Press.

Hansen, A. (2008) *Backgrounder: The French Military in Africa* Washington, DC: Council on Foreign Relations.

Hargreaves, J. (1982) Book review of *La Politique africaine du Général de Gaulle, African Affairs*, vol. 81.

Harrison, G. (2002) *Issues in the Contemporary Politics of Sub-Saharan Africa: The Dynamics of Struggle and Resistance*, Basingstoke: Palgrave.

Harvey, C. (ed.) (1996) *Constraints on the Success of Structural Adjustment Programmes in Africa* London: Macmillan.

Haté, V. (2008) 'India in Africa: Moving Beyond Oil', *South Asia Monitor*, no. 119.

Hegel, G. (1975) [1822] *Lectures on the Philosophy of World History* New York, NY: Oxford University Press.

Hentz, J. (2004) 'The Contending Currents in United States Involvement in Sub-Saharan Africa' in Taylor, I. and Williams, P. *Africa in International Politics: External Involvement on the Continent* London: Routledge.

Herbst, J. (1993) *The Politics of Reform in Ghana, 1982–1991* Berkeley: University of California Press.

Hill, C. (2001) 'Foreign Policy' in Seldon, A.(ed.) *The Blair Effect* London: Little, Brown, 2001.

Holland, M. (2002) *The European Union and the Third World* Basingstoke: Palgrave.

Hong Eunsuk and Sun Laixiang (2006) 'Dynamics of Internationalization and Outward Investment: Chinese Corporations' Strategies', *China Quarterly*, vol. 187.

House Committee on International Relations (2001) *Africa and the War on Global Terrorism*, hearing before the Subcommittee on Africa of the Committee on International Relations, One hundred Seventh Congress, First Session, Washington, DC: United States House of Representatives.

Huliaras, A. (1998) 'The "Anglo-Saxon Conspiracy": French Perceptions of the Great Lakes Crisis', *Journal of Modern African Studies*, vol. 36, no. 4.

Hurrell, A. and Narlikar, A. (2006) 'A New Politics of Confrontation? Developing Countries at Cancun and Beyond', *Global Society*, vol. 20, no. 4.

Hurt, S. (2003) 'Co-operation and Coercion? The Cotonou Agreement between the European Union and ACP States and the End of the Lomé Convention', *Third World Quarterly*, vol. 24, no. 1.

Hurt, S. (2004) 'The European Union's External Relations with Africa after the Cold War: Aspects of Continuity and Change' in Taylor, I. and Williams, P. (eds) *Africa in International Politics: External Involvement on the Continent* London: Routledge.

Hutchison, A. (1975) *China's African Revolution* London: Hutchinson.

Impey, A. (1998) 'Popular Music in Africa' in Stone, R. (ed.) *The Garland Encyclopedia of World Music* New York, NY: Garland Publishing.

India-Brazil-South Africa (IBSA) Dialogue Forum *Plan of Action*, Pretoria: Department of Foreign Affairs.

International Monetary Fund (1996) *Partnership for Sustainable Global Growth* Washington, DC: International Monetary Fund.

International Monetary Fund (1997a) *The Role of the IMF in Governance Issues: Guidance Note* Washington, DC: International Monetary Fund.

International Monetary Fund (1997b) *Evaluation of Prolonged Use of IMF Resources* Washington, DC: International Monetary Fund.

International Monetary Fund (2002) *Evaluation of Prolonged Use of IMF Resources* Washington, DC: International Monetary Fund.

Jackson, R. and Rosberg, Carl (1982) *Personal Rule in Black Africa: Prince, Autocrat, Prophet, Tyrant* Los Angeles, CA: University of California Press.

Jackson, R. and Rosberg, C. (1994) 'The Political Economy of African Personal Rule' in Apter, D. and Rosberg, C. (eds) *Political Development and the New Realism in Sub-Saharan Africa* Charlottesville, VA: University of Virginia Press.

James, H. (1998) 'From Grandmotherliness to Governance: The Evolution of IMF Conditionality', *Finance and Development*, vol. 35, no. 4.

Jensen, P. and Paldam, M. (2003) *Can the New Aid-Growth Models be Replicated?* Aarhus: University of Aarhus, Department of Economics, Working Paper, no. 2003-17.

Jobelius, M. (2007) 'New Powers for Global Change? Challenges for International Development Cooperation: The Case of India', *Dialogue on Globalization Briefing Papers*, no. 5, New Delhi: Friedrich Ebert Stiftung.

Kapoor, S. (2005) 'Plugging the Leaks: A Very Short Paper on Curbing Capital Flight, Tax Avoidance and Tax Evasion', paper prepared for International Policy Dialogue 'New Sources of Development Financing', organized by InWEnt and the Federal Ministry for Economic Cooperation and Development (BMZ), August.

Kapur, D. (1998) *The State in a Changing World: A Critique of the 1997 World Development Report* Working Paper No.98-2. Weatherhead Center for International Affairs, Cambridge, MA: Harvard University.

Kapur, R. and Webb, R. (2000) *Governance-related Conditionalities of the International Financial Institutions*, G-24 Discussion Paper Series, Center for International Development, Cambridge, MA: Harvard University.

Kargbo, M (2006) *British Foreign Policy and the Conflict in Sierra Leone, 1991–2001* Oxford: Peter Lang.

Karl, T. (1997) *The Paradox of Plenty: Oil Booms and Petro-States* Berkeley, CA: University of California Press.

Keet, Dot (no date) *Globalisation and Regionalisation: Contradictory Tendencies? Counteractive Tactics? Or Strategic Possibilities?* mimeo.

Kelsall, T. (2002) 'Shop Windows and Smoke-filled Rooms: Governance and the Re-politicisation of Tanzania', *Journal of Modern African Studies*, vol. 40, no. 4.

Khadiagala, G. (2000) 'Europe in Africa's Renewal: Beyond Postcolonialism?' in Harberson, J. and Rothchild, D. (eds) *Africa in World Politics: The African State System in Flux* Boulder, CO: Westview.

Killick, T. (2004) 'Politics, Evidence and the New Aid Agenda', *Development Policy Review*, vol. 22, no. 1.

Koscr, K. (2003) *New African Diasporas* London: Routledge.

Kraxberger, B. (2005) 'The United States and Africa: Shifting Geopolitics in an "Age of Terror"', *Africa Today*, vol. 52, no. 1.

Langton, D. (2006) *Africa: US Foreign Assistance Issues*, Washington, DC: Congressional Research Service.

Lanteigne, M. (2005) *China and International Institutions: Alternate Paths to Global Power* London: Routledge.

Lanteigne, M. (2008) 'The Developmentalism/Globalization Conundrum in Chinese Governance' in Laliberté, A. and Lanteigne, M. (eds) *The Chinese Party-State in the 21st Century: Adaptation and the Reinvention of Legitimacy* London: Routledge.

Lee, S. (2009) *Boom and Bust: The Politics and Legacy of Gordon Brown* Oxford: Oneworld.

Lister, M. (1997) *The European Union and the South: Relations with Developing Countries* London: Routledge.

Li Xing (1996) 'Democracy and Human Rights: China and the West', *Monthly Review*, vol. 48, no. 7.

Khanna, P. and Mohan, C. (2006) 'Getting India Right', *Policy Review*, no. 135, February and March.

Klare, M. and Volman, D. (2006a) 'The African "Oil Rush" and US National Security', *Third World Quarterly*, vol. 27, no. 4.

Klare, M. and Volman, D. (2006b) 'America, China and the Scramble for Africa's Oil', *Review of African Political Economy*, vol. 33, no. 108.

Kleine-Ahlbrandt, S. and Small, A. (2008) 'China's New Dictatorship Diplomacy: Is Beijing Parting with Pariahs?', *Foreign Affairs*, January/February.

Knight, R. (2003) 'Expanding Petroleum Production in Africa', *Review of African Political Economy*, vol. 30, no. 96.

Kohnert, D. (2008) *EU-African Economic Relations: Continuing Dominance Traded for Aid?* GIGA Working Paper, no. 82, Hamburg: German Institute of Global and Area Studies.

Kroslak, D. (2004) 'France's Policy towards Africa: Continuity or Change?' in Taylor I. and Williams, P. (eds) *Africa in International Politics: External Involvement on the Continent* London: Routledge.

Kurlantzick, J. (2006) 'China's Charm: Implications of Chinese Soft Power', Carnegie Endowment Policy Brief, no 47.

Kurlantzick, J. (2007) *Charm Offensive: How China's Soft Power is Transforming the World* New Haven, CT: Yale University Press.

Labouret, H. (1940) 'France's Colonial Policy in Africa', *African Affairs*, vol. 39.

Lai, K. (2006) 'India-Brazil-South Africa: The Southern Trade Powerhouse Makes Its Debut', *Panama News*, vol. 12, no. 6, March 19–April 8.

Laszlo, E., Baker, R., Eisenberg, E. and Raman, V. (1979) *The Objectives of the New International Economic Order*. New York, NY: Pergamon.

Le Billon, P. (2005) 'The Geopolitical Economy of "Resource Wars"', in Le Billon, P. (ed.) *The Geopolitics of Resource War, Resource Dependence, Governance and Violence* London: Frank Cass.

Lechini, G. (2005) 'Is South-South Co-operation still Possible? The Case of Brazil's Strategy and Argentina's Impulses towards the New South Africa and Africa' in Atilio, B. and Lechini, G. (eds) *Politics and Social Movements in an Hegemonic World: Lessons from Africa, Asia and Latin America* Buenos Aires: Consejo Latinoamericano de Ciencias Sociales.

Lemarchand, R. and Eisenstadt, S. (eds) (1980) *Political Clientelism, Patronage and Development* New York, NY: Sage.

Leonard, D. and Straus, S. (2003) *Africa's Stalled Development: International Causes and Cures* Boulder, CO: Lynne Rienner.

LeVine, V. (1980) 'African Patrimonial Regimes in Comparative Perspective', *Journal of Modern African Studies*, vol. 18, no. 4.

Lewis, P. (2004) 'Getting the Politics Right: Governance and Economic Failure in Nigeria' in Rotberg, R. (ed.) *Crafting the New Nigeria: Confronting the Challenges* Boulder, CO: Lynne Rienner.

Lewis, P. (2007) *Growing Apart: Oil, Politics and Economic Change in Indonesia and Nigeria* Ann Arbor, MI: University of Michigan Press.

Lockwood, M. (2005) *The State They're in: An Agenda for International Action on Poverty in Africa* London: ITDG Publishing.

Lyman, P. and Morrison, J. S. (2005) 'The Terrorist Threat in Africa', *Foreign Affairs*, vol. 83, no. 1.

MacFarlane, N. (2006) 'The "R" in BRICs: Is Russia an Emerging Power?', *International Affairs*, vol. 82, no. 1.

MacGaffey, J. and Bazenguissa-Ganga, R. (2000) *Congo-Paris: Transnational Traders on the Margins of the Law* Oxford: James Currey.

Mackel, C., Marsh, J. and Revell, B. (1984) 'The Common Agricultural Policy', *Third World Quarterly*, vol. 6, no. 1.

Madujibeya, S. (1976) 'Oil and Nigeria's Economic Development', *African Affairs*, vol. 75, no. 300.

Maguire, J. and Pearton, R. (2000) 'Global Sport and the migration patterns of France'98 World Cup Finals Players: Some preliminary observations', *Soccer and Society*, vol. 1, no. 1.

Maguire, J. and Stead, D. (1998) 'Border Crossings. Soccer Labour Migration and the European Union', *International Review for the Sociology of Sport*, vol. 33, no. 1.

Mañe, D. (2005) 'Emergence of the Gulf of Guinea in the Global Economy: Prospects and Challenges', panel Presentation before the United States Congress Members held by the Congressional Black Caucus United States Congress, mimeograph.

Manners, I. and Whitman, R. (2001) (eds) *The Foreign Policies of European Union Member State* New York, NY: Palgrave.

Manning, P. (1998) *Francophone Sub-Saharan Africa, 1880–1995* Cambridge: Cambridge University Press.

Marchal, R. (1998) 'France and Africa: The Emergence of Essential Reforms?' *International Affairs*, vol. 74, no. 2.

Marriage, Z. (2006) 'Defining Morality: DFID and the Great Lakes', *Third World Quarterly*, vol. 27, no. 3.

Martenczuk, B. (2000) 'From Lomé to Cotonou: The ACP-EC Partnership Agreement in a Legal Perspective', *European Foreign Affairs Review*, vol. 5, no. 4.

Martin, G. (1995) 'Continuity and Change in Franco-African Relations', *Journal of Modern African Studies*, vol. 33, no.1.

Martin, W. (2004) 'Beyond Bush: The Future of Popular Movements and US Africa Policy', *Review of African Political Economy*, vol. 31, no. 102.

Martin, H. and Schumann, H. (1998) *The Global Trap*, New York, NY: Zed Books.

Mathew, G., Ganesh, J. and Dayasindhu, N. (2008) *How India Is Riding on Globalization to Become an Innovation Superpower: Innovation Geo-dynamics* Oxford: Chandos.

Mathews, K. (1989) 'The Organization of African Unity in World Politics' in Onwuka, R. and Shaw, T. (eds) *Africa in World Politics* London: Macmillan.

Matusevich, M. (1999) 'Perestroika and Soviet Policy Shift in Africa', *Nigerian Forum*, vol. 20, nos 7–8.

Matusevich, M. (ed.) (2006) *Africa in Russia, Russia in Africa: Three Centuries of Encounters* Trenton, NJ: Africa World Press.

McCormick, D. (2008) 'China and Indian as Africa's New Aid Donors: The Impact of Aid on Development', *Review of African Political Economy*, vol. 35, no. 1.

McNulty, M. (1997) 'France's Role in Rwanda and External Military Intervention: A Double Discrediting', *International Peacekeeping*, vol. 4, no. 3.

McSherry, B. (2006) 'The Political Economy of Oil in Equatorial Guinea', *African Studies Quarterly*, vol. 8, no. 3.

Medard, J. (1982) 'The Underdeveloped State in Tropical Africa: Political Clientelism or Neo-patrimonialism' in Clapham, C. (ed.) *Private Patronage and Public Power: Political Clientelism in Modern States* London: Pinter.

Medard, J-F. (2008) 'Crisis, Change and Continuity: Nigeria-France Relations' in Adebajo, A. and Mustapha, A. (eds) *Gulliver's Troubles: Nigeria's Foreign Policy after the Cold War* Scottsville: University of KwaZulu-Natal Press.

Mengisteab, K. (1996) *Globalisation and Autocentricity in Africa Development in the 21st Century* Trenton, NJ: Africa World Press.

Mengisteab, K. and Logan, I. (eds) (1995) *Beyond Economic Liberalization in Africa: Structural Adjustment and the Alternatives* London: Zed Press.

Mercer, C., Page, B. and Evans, M. (2008) *Development and the African Diaspora: Place and the Politics of Home* London: Zed Books.

Merlingen, M. and Ostrauskaite, R. (2008) *European Union Peacebuilding and Policing* London: Routledge.

Mills, G. (2004) 'Africa's New Strategic Significance', *Washington Quarterly*, vol. 27, no. 4.

Ming Xia (2000) *The Dual Developmental State: Development Strategy and Institutional Arrangements for China's Transition* Aldershot: Ashgate.

Mistry, P. (2005) 'Reasons for Sub-Saharan Africa's Development Deficit that the Commission for Africa Did Not Consider', *African Affairs*, vol. 104, no. 417.

Mittelman, J. and Pasha, M. (1997) *Out from Underdevelopment Revisited: Changing Global Structures and the Remaking of World Order* Basingstoke: Macmillan.

Mohan, C. (2006) 'India and the Balance of Power', *Foreign Affairs*, vol. 85, no. 4.

Monson, I. (2003) *The African Diaspora: A Musical Perspective* New York, NY: Routledge.

Montague, D. (2002) 'Stolen Goods: Coltan and Conflict in the Democratic Republic of Congo', *SAIS Review*, vol. 22, no. 1.

Montana, I. (2003) 'The Lomé Convention from Inception to the Dynamics of the Post-Cold War, 1957–1990s', *African and Asian Studies*, vol. 2, no. 1.

Mosher, S. (2000) *Hegemon: China's Plan to Dominate Asia and the World* New York, NY: Encounter.

Moss, T. (2009) *How the Economic Crisis Is Hurting Africa—And What to Do about It* Washington, DC: Center for Global Development.

Moyo, D. (2009) *Dead Aid: Why Aid Is Not Working and How There Is Another Way for Africa* London: Penguin Books.

Mudimbe, V. (1988) *The Invention of Africa: Gnosis, Philosophy, and the Order of Knowledge* Bloomington, IN: Indiana University Press.

Mwega, F. (2007) 'China, India and Africa: Prospects and Challenges', revised version of a paper earlier presented at the AERC-AFDB International Conference on 'Accelerating Africa's Development Five Years into the Twenty-First Century', November 22–24, 2006, Tunis, Tunisia.

Mwenda, A. and Tangri, R. (2005) 'Patronage Politics, Donor Reforms and Regime Consolidation in Uganda', *African Affairs*, no. 104.

Naidu, S. (2007) 'India's African Relations: Playing Catch Up with the Dragon', Los Angeles, CA: Globalization Research Center: African Studies Center, UCLA.

Naidu, S. (2008) 'India's Growing African Strategy', *Review of African Political Economy*, vol. 35, no. 1.

Naidu, S. and Davies, M. (2006) 'China Fuels Its Future with Africa's Riches', *South African Journal of International Affairs*, vol. 13, no. 2.

Naím, M. (2005) *Illicit: How Smugglers, Traffickers, and Copycats are Hijacking the Global Economy* New York, NY: Doubleday.

Nanda, P. (ed.) (2008) *Rising India: Friends and Foes* New Delhi: Lancer Publishers.

Narayan, S. (2005) *Trade Policy Making in India* Singapore: Institute of South Asian Studies, National University of Singapore.

Nayar, B. and Paul, T. (2003) *India in the World Order: Searching for Major Power Status* Cambridge: Cambridge University Press.

N'Diaye, B. (2009) 'Francophone Africa and Security Sector Transformation: Plus a Change . . .', *African Security*, vol. 2, no. 1.

Ndikumana, L. and Boyce, J. (2002) *Public Debts and Private Assets: Explaining Capital Flight from Sub- Saharan African Countries* Amherst, MA: University of Massachusetts.

NEPRU (2001) 'The Lomé Convention, the Cotonou Convention and Namibia', *The Namibian Economy*, no. 34, January.

Nkrumah, K. (1965) *Neo-Colonialism: The Last Stage of Imperialism*. London: Nelson.

Nöthling, F. (1989) *Pre-Colonial Africa: Her Civilisations and Foreign Contacts* Johannesburg: Southern Book Publishers.

Nwobike, J. (2005) 'The Application of Human Rights in African Caribbean and Pacific-European Union Development and Trade Partnerships', *German Law Journal*, vol. 6, no. 10.

Obi, C. (2001) 'Global, State and Local Intersections: Power, Authority, and Conflict in the Niger Delta Oil Communities' in Callaghy, T., Kassimir, R. and Latham, R. (eds) *Intervention and Transnationalism in Africa* Cambridge: Cambridge University Press.

Obi, C. (2005) 'Globalization and Local Resistance: The Case of Shell versus the Ogoni' in Amoore, L. (ed.) *The Global Resistance Reader* London: Routledge.

Obi, C. (2007a.) 'Oil and Development in Africa: Some Lessons from the Oil Factor in Nigeria for the Sudan' in Patey, L. (ed.) *Oil Development in Africa: Lessons for Sudan after the Comprehensive Peace Agreement* Copenhagen: Danish Institute for International Affairs.

Obi, C. (2007b) 'Scrambling for Oil in West Africa?', mimeo.

Obiorah, N. (2007) 'Who's Afraid of China in Africa?' in Manji, F. and Marks, S. (eds) *African Perspectives on China in Africa* Cape Town: Fahamu.

Oborne, P. (2005) *The Rise of Political Lying* London: Free Press.

O'Brien, R., Goetz, A., Scholte, J. and Williams, M. (2000) *Contesting Global Governance: Multilateral Economic Institutions and Global Social Movements* Cambridge: Cambridge University Press.

Okruhlik, G. (1999) 'Rentier Wealth, Unruly Law, and the Rise of Opposition: The Political Economy of Oil States', *Comparative Politics*, vol. 31, no. 3.

Olsen, G. (1997) 'Western Europe's Relations with Africa since the End of the Cold War', *Journal of Modern African Studies*, vol. 35, no. 2.

Olsen, G. (1998) 'Europe and the Promotion of Democracy in Post-Cold War Africa: How Serious is Europe?', *African Affairs*, vol. 97, no. 388.

Olsen, G. (2001) 'Europe and Africa in the 1990s: European Policies towards a Poor Continent in an Era of Globalisation', *Global Society*, vol. 15, no. 4.

Olsen, G. (2002) 'The EU and Conflict Management in African Emergencies', *International Peacekeeping*, vol. 9, no. 3.

Olsen, G. (2005) 'The European Union: "European Interests", Bureaucratic Interests and International Options' in Engel, U. and Olsen, G. (eds) *Africa and the North: Between Globalization and Marginalization* London: Routledge.

Ong, R. (2007) '"Peaceful Evolution", "Regime Change" and China's Political Security', *Journal of Contemporary China*, vol. 16, no. 53.

Onimode B. (1988) *A Political Economy of the African Crisis* London: Institute for African Alternatives.

Organization of Africa Unity (1980) *The Lagos Plan of Action for the Economic Development of Africa, 1980–2000* Addis Ababa: OAU.

Organization of African Unity (1986) *Africa's Economic Recovery and Development (UN-PAAERD)* Addis Ababa: OAU.

Organization of African Unity (1989) *The African Alternative Framework to Structural Adjustment Programme for Socio-Economic Recovery and Transformation (AAF-SAP)*. Addis Ababa: OAU.

Osaghae, E. (1998) *Crippled Giant: Nigeria since Independence* London: Hurst and Company.

Overbeek, H. and van der Pijl, K. (1993) 'Restructuring Capital and Restructuring Hegemony: Neo-liberalism and the Unmaking of the Post-war Order' in Overbeek, H. (ed.) *Restructuring Hegemony in the Global Political Economy: The Rise of Transnational Neo-Liberalism in the 1980s* London: Routledge.

Owusu, F. (2003) 'Pragmatism and the Gradual Shift from Dependency to Neoliberalism: The World Bank, African Leaders and Development Policy in Africa', *World Development*, vol. 31, no. 10.

Parfitt, T. (1996) 'The Decline of Eurafrica? Lomé's Mid-Term Review', *Review of African Political Economy*, vol. 23, no. 67.

Park, R. (1965) 'Indian-African Relations', *Asian Survey*, vol. 5, no. 7.

Pepy, D. (1970) 'France's Relations with Africa', *African Affairs*, vol. 69, no. 275.

Perry, A. (2007) 'Africa's Oil Dreams', *Time*, May 31.

Pham, P. (2007) 'India's Expanding Relations with Africa and Their Implications for US Interests', *American Foreign Policy Interests*, vol. 29, no. 5.

Platteau, J-P (2004) 'Monitoring Elite Capture in Community-Driven Development', *Development and Change*, vol. 35, no. 2.

Poddar, T. and Yi, E. (2007) 'India's Rising Growth Potential', *Goldman Sachs Global Economic Paper*, no. 152.

Portela, C. (2009) *European Union Sanctions and Foreign Policy* London: Routledge.

Porteous, T. (2005) 'British Government Policy in Sub-Saharan Africa under New Labour' *International Affairs* vol. 81, no. 2.

Porteous. T. (2008) *Britain in Africa* London: Zed Books.

Prior, C. (2007) 'Writing Another Continent's History: The British and Pre-colonial Africa, 1880–1939', *eSharp*, issue 10.

Qian Qichen (2005) *Ten Episodes in China's Diplomacy* New York, NY: HarperCollins.

Raffer, K. (2001) 'Cotonou: Slowly Undoing Lomé's Concept of Partnership', European Development Policy Study Group, Discussion Papers, no. 21, October.

Ramachandran, S. (2007) 'India Pushes People Power in Africa,' *Asia Times,* July 13.

Ramo, J. (2004) *The Beijing Consensus* London: Foreign Policy Centre.

Reed, M. (1987) 'Gabon: A Neo-Colonial Enclave of Enduring French Interest', *Journal of Modern African Studies*, vol. 25, no. 2.

Reno, W. (1993) 'Old Brigades, Money Bags, New Breeds, and the Ironies of Reform in Nigeria', *Canadian Journal of African Studies*, vol. 27, no. 1.

Reno, W. (1999) *Warlord Politics and African States* Boulder, CO: Lynne Rienner.

Reno. W. (2001) 'How Sovereignty Matters: International Markets and the Political Economy of Local Politics in Weak States' in Callaghy, T., Kassimir, R. and Latham, R. (eds) *Intervention and Transnationalism in Africa*, New York, NY: Cambridge University Press.

Reno, W. (2009) 'Illicit Commerce in Peripheral States' in Friman, R. (ed.) *Crime and the Global Political Economy* Boulder, CO: Lynne Rienner.

Rice, S. (2000) 'The Clinton-Gore Administration Record in Africa: Remarks to the Foreign Affairs Braintrust Annual Congressional Black Caucus', Washington, DC, September 15.

Rice, S. (2001) 'Testimony of Dr. Susan E. Rice before the House International Relations Committee Subcommittee on Africa – "Africa and the War on Global Terrorism", November 15, Washington, DC: Committee on International Relations.

Roberts, P. (2004) *The End of Oil: The Decline of the Petroleum Economy and the Rise of the New Energy Order* London: Bloomsbury.

Rodney, W. (1972) *How Europe Underdeveloped Africa*. London: Bogle L'Ouverture Publications.

Rosenberg, J. (1990) 'A Non-Realist Theory of Sovereignty?: Giddens' *The Nation State and Violence*', *Millennium*, vol. 19, no. 2.

Ross, M. (1999) 'The Political Economy of the Resource Curse', *World Politics*, vol. 51, no. 2.

Ross, M. (2001) 'Does Oil Hinder Democracy?', *World Politics*, vol. 53, no. 3.

Ross, M. (2008) 'Blood Barrels: Why Oil Wealth Fuels Conflict', *Foreign Affairs*, vol. 87, no. 3.

Rothchild, D. and Emmanuel, N. (2005) 'United States: The Process of Decision-making on Africa' in Engel, U. and Olsen, G. (eds) *Africa and the North: Between Globalization and Marginalization* London: Routledge.

Rowell, A., Marriott, J. and Stockman, L. (2005) *The Next Gulf: London, Washington and Oil Conflict in Nigeria* London: Robinson Publishing.

Sachs, J. (2005) *The End of Poverty: Economic Possibilities for Our Time* New York, NY: Penguin Press.

Saferworld (2007) *The Good, the Bad and the Ugly: A Decade of Labour's Arms Exports* London: Saferworld.

Sahni, V. (2007) 'India's Foreign Policy: Key Drivers', *South African Journal of International Affairs*, vol. 14, no. 2.

Sala-i-Martin, X. and Subramanian, A. (2003) *Addressing the Natural Resource Curse: An Illustration from Nigeria*, NBER Working Paper June, New York, NY: National Bureau of Economic Research.

Sandbrook, R. (1985) *The Politics of Africa's Economic Stagnation* Cambridge: Cambridge University Press.

Santiso, C. (2003) 'Responding to Democratic Decay and Crises of Governance: The European Union and the Convention of Cotonou', *Democratization*, vol. 10, no. 3.

Sanyal, S. (2008) *An Indian Renaissance: How India Is Rising after a Thousand Years of Decline* New Delhi: World Scientific Publishing.

Sarkozy, N. (2007) *Testimony: France in the Twenty-first Century* London: Pantheon.

Schmidt, E. (2007) *Cold War and Decolonization in Guinea, 1946–1958* Athens, OH: Ohio University Press.

Schraeder, P. (2001) 'Forget the Rhetoric and Boost the Geopolitics: Emerging Trends in the Bush Administration's Policy towards Africa, 2001', *African Affairs*, vol. 100, no. 400.

Scott, D. (2007) *China Stands Up: The PRC and the International System* London: Routledge.

Sharma, A. (2007) 'India and Africa: Partnership in the 21st Century', *South African Journal of International Affairs*, vol. 14, no. 2.

Sharma, D. (2008) 'India Cultivates Africa', *Daily Mail* (London), June 25.

Sharma, D. and Mahajan, D. (2007) 'Energizing Ties: The Politics of Oil', *South African Journal of International Affairs*, vol. 14, no. 2.

Shaw, M. (2001) 'The Political Economy of Crime and Conflict in Sub-Saharan Africa', *South African Journal of International Affairs*, vol. 8. no. 2.

Shaxson, N. (2007a) *Poisoned Wells: The Dirty Politics of African Oil* Basingstoke: Palgrave.

Shaxson, N. (2007b) 'Oil, Corruption and the Resource Curse', *International Affairs*, vol. 83, no. 6.

Shaxson, N. (2008) 'The Biggest Secret in Africa?', *Tax Justice Network*, January 18.

Shinn, D. (2008) *Responding to China in Africa* Washington, DC: American Foreign Policy Council.

Shubin, V. (2004) 'Russia and Africa: Moving in the Right Direction?' in Taylor, I. and Williams, P. (eds) *Africa in International Politics: External Involvement on the Continent* London: Routledge.

Singh, R. (2006) 'India, Africa Ready to Embrace Global Destiny', press release January, 25, New Delhi: Ministry of External Affairs.

Smith, B. (2004) 'Oil Wealth and Regime Survival in the Developing World, 1960–1999', *American Journal of Political Science*, vol. 48, no. 2.

Smith, D. (2007) *A Culture of Corruption: Everyday Deception and Popular Discontent in Nigeria* Princeton, NJ: Princeton University Press.

Smith, K. (2003) 'The European Union: A Distinctive Actor in International Relations', *The Brown Journal of World Affairs*, vol. 9, no. 2.

Smith, R. (1973) 'Peace and Palaver: International Relations in Pre-Colonial West Africa', *Journal of African History*, vol. 14, no. 4.

Smith, R. (1976) *Warfare and Diplomacy in Pre-colonial West Africa* London: Methuen.

Snow, P. (1988) *The Star Raft: China's Encounter with Africa* London: Weidenfeld and Nicholson.

Soares de Lima, M. and Hirst, M. (2006) 'Brazil as an Intermediate State and Regional Power: Action, Choice and Responsibilities', *International Affairs*, vol. 82, no. 1.

Soares de Oliveira, R. (2007a) *Oil and Politics in the Gulf of Guinea* London: Hurst and Company.

Soares de Oliveira, R. (2007b) 'Business Success, Angola-style: Postcolonial Politics and the Rise and Rise of Sonangol', vol. 45, no. 4.

Söderbaum, F. and Stålgren, P. (eds) (2009) *The European Union and the Global South* Boulder, CO: Lynne Rienner.

Söderbaum, F. and van Langenhove, L. (eds) (2007) *The EU as a Global Player: The Politics of Interregionalism* London: Routledge.

Sorbara, M. (2007) 'India and Africa: It's Old Friends, New Game and Rules', *The Nation*, February 9.

South Bulletin (2003) 'G-20: A Powerful Tool for Convergence in Negotiations', November, 2003.

Soyinka, W. (1996) *The Open Sore of a Continent: A Personal Narrative of the Nigerian Crisis* New York, NY: Oxford University Press.

Spero, J. and Hart. J. (2002) *The Politics of International Economic Relations,* Belmont, CA: Thompson-Wadsworth.

Stewart, E. (2006) *European Union and Conflict Prevention: Policy Evolution and Outcome* Münster: Schleswig-Holstein Institute for Peace Research/Lit Verlag.

Stokke, O. (1995) (ed.) *Aid and Political Conditionality* London: Routledge.

Styan, D. (1996) 'Does Britain Have an African Policy?', *L'Afrique Politique*, no. 26.

Sullivan, M. (1999) 'Developmentalism and China's Human Rights Policy' in Van Ness, P. (ed.) *Debating Human Rights: Critical Essays from the United States and Asia* New York, NY: Routledge.

Sutter, R. (2008) *Chinese Foreign Relations: Power and Policy since the Cold War* Lanham, MD: Rowman and Littlefield.

Tangri, R. (1999) *The Politics of Patronage in Africa: Parastatals, Privatization and Private Enterprise* Trenton, NJ: Africa World Press.

Tangri, R. and Mwenda, A. (2001) 'Corruption and Cronyism in Uganda's Privatization in the 1990s', *African Affairs*, vol. 100, no. 398.

Tata Group (2008) 'About Us: Tata Group Profile', www.tata.com.

Taylor, I. (1997) *China's Foreign Policy towards Southern Africa in the "Socialist Modernisation" Period* East Asia Project Working Paper 18, Dept. of International Relations, University of the Witwatersrand.

Taylor, I. (1998) 'China's Foreign Policy towards Africa in the 1990s', *Journal of Modern African Studies*, vol. 36, no. 3.

Taylor, I. (2003) 'Conflict in Central Africa: Clandestine Networks and Regional/Global Configurations', *Review of African Political Economy*, vol. 30, no. 95.

Taylor, I. (2004a) 'Blind Spots in Analyzing Africa's Place in World Politics', *Global Governance*, vol. 10, no. 4.

Taylor, I. (2004b) 'The "All-weather Friend"? Sino-African Interaction in the Twenty-first Century' in Taylor. I. and Williams, P. (eds.) *Africa in International Politics: External Involvement on the Continent* London: Routledge.

Taylor, I. (2005a) *NEPAD: Towards Africa's Development or Another False Start?* Boulder, CO: Lynne Rienner.

Taylor, I. (2005b) '"The Devilish Thing": The Commonwealth and Zimbabwe's Denouement', *Round Table: Commonwealth Journal of International Relations.* vol. 94, no. 380.

Taylor, I. (2005c) 'Advice Is Judged by Results, Not by Intentions: Why Gordon Brown is Wrong about Africa', *International Affairs,* vol. 81, no. 2.

Taylor, I. (2006a) *China and Africa: Engagement and Compromise* London: Routledge.

Taylor, I. (2006b) 'China's Oil Diplomacy in Africa', *International Affairs,* vol. 82, no. 5.

Taylor, I. (2007) 'China's Relations with Nigeria', *Round Table: The Commonwealth Journal of International Affairs,* vol. 96, no. 392.

Taylor, I. (2009) *China's New Role in Africa* Boulder, CO: Lynne Rienner.

Taylor, I. and Mokhawa, G. (2003) 'Not Forever: Botswana, Conflict Diamonds and the Bushmen', *African Affairs,* vol. 102.

Taylor, I. and Nel, P. (2002) '"Getting the Rhetoric Right", Getting the Strategy Wrong: "New Africa", Globalisation and the Confines of Elite Reformism', *Third World Quarterly,* vol. 23, no. 1.

Taylor, I. and Williams, P. (2001) 'South African Foreign Policy and the Great Lakes Crisis: African Renaissance Meets Vagabondage Politique?', *African Affairs,* vol. 100, no. 399.

Taylor, I. and Williams, P. (2002) 'The Limits of Engagement: British Foreign Policy and the Crisis in Zimbabwe', *International Affairs,* vol. 78, no. 3.

Taylor, I. and Williams, P. (2004) 'Understanding Africa's Place in World Politics' in Taylor, I. and Williams, P. (eds.) *Africa in International Politics: External Involvement on the Continent* London: Routledge.

Thomas, C. (2004) 'The International Financial Institutions' Relations with Africa' in Taylor, I. and Williams, P. (eds) *Africa in International Politics* Abingdon: Routledge.

Titley, B. (2002) *Dark Age: The Political Odyssey of Emperor Bokassa* Montreal: McGill-Queen's University Press.

Touati, S. (2007) *French Foreign Policy in Africa: Between Pré Carré and Multilateralism,* Chatham House Briefing Papers.

TRALAC (2009) *The African Trading Relationship with Brazil* Stellenbosch: TRALAC.

Transparency International (2003) *Clean Money, Dirty Money: Corruption and Money Laundering in the UK* London: Transparency International.

Tsebelis, G. (2008) 'Thinking About the Recent Past and the Future of the EU', *Journal of Common Market Studies,* vol. 46, no. 2.

UNODC (2005) *Transnational Organized Crime in the West African Region* New York, NY: UNODC.

UNODC (2007) *Cocaine Trafficking in West Africa: The Threat to Stability and Development* Vienna: UNODC.

US Department of Commerce, 2007 *Summary of AGOA I* Washington, DC: Department of Commerce.

Utley, R. (2002) '"Not to Do Less but to Do Better . . .": French Military Policy in Africa', *International Affairs,* vol. 78, no. 1.

Utley, R. (2005) 'Franco-African Military Relations: Meeting the Challenges of Globalization?', *Modern and Contemporary France,* vol. 13, no. 1.

Uvin, P. (1993) 'Do as I Say, Not as I Do": The Limits of Political Conditionality' in Sorensen, G. (ed.) *Political Conditionality* London: Frank Cass.

van de Walle, N. (2001) *African Economies and the Politics of Permanent Crisis, 1979–1999* Cambridge: Cambridge University Press.

Verschave, F-X (1998) *La Françafrique, le plus long scandale de la République* Paris: Stock.

Vilby, K. (2007) *Independent? Tanzania's Challenges Since Uhuru* Dar es Salaam: E and D Vision Publishing.

Vines, A. and Sidiropoulos, E. (2008) 'India and Africa: India Calling', *World Today*, vol. 64, no. 4.

Visentini, P. (2009) 'Prestige Diplomacy, Southern Solidarity or "Soft Imperialism"? Lula's Brazil-Africa Relations (2003 Onwards)', paper presented to African Studies Centre, Leiden, Netherlands, April 16, 2009.

Volman, D. (2003) 'The Bush Administration and African Oil: The Security Implications of US Energy Policy', *Review of African Political Economy*, vol. 30, no. 98.

Volman, D. (2006) 'The African Oil Rush and US National Security', *Third World Quarterly*, vol. 27, no. 4.

Vorrath, J. (2005) *From Individual Action to a Common Strategy? EU Policy on Sub-Saharan Africa*, SEF Project Series, "Development and Failing States", Second Expert Workshop, Bonn: Stiftung Entwicklung und Frieden.

Wang Chaohua (ed.) (2003) *One China, Many Paths* London: Verso.

Wang Hongying (2003) *China's New Order: Society, Politics and Economy in Transition* Cambridge, MA: Harvard University Press.

Wang Jian-ye (2007) *What Drives China's Growing Role in Africa?* IMF Working Paper WP/07/211, Washington, DC: International Monetary Fund.

Ware, Z. (2006) 'Readdressing Labour's Relationship with Sub-Saharan Africa', *Round Table*, vol. 95, no. 383.

Waters, M. (1998) 'An Open Letter from Congresswoman Maxine Waters: Why We Must Now Oppose the Omnibus Fast Track/Africa Trade Bill', July 30.

Watts, M. (2006) 'Empire of Oil: Capitalist Dispossession and the Scramble for Africa', *Monthly Review*, vol. 58, no. 4.

Weatherley, R. (1999) *The Discourse of Human Rights in China: Historical and Ideological Perspectives* London: Macmillan Press.

Weaver, C. (2008) *Hypocrisy Trap: The World Bank and the Poverty of Reform* Princeton, NJ: Princeton University Press.

Weiss, T. and Hubert, D. (2002) *The Responsibility to Protect: Supplemental Volume: Research, Bibliography, Background* Ottawa: IDRC Books.

Welch, C. (1998) 'In Focus: The IMF and Good Governance', *Foreign Policy in Focus*, vol. 3, no. 33.

White, G. and Taylor, S. (2001) 'Well-oiled Regimes: Oil and Uncertain Transitions in Algeria and Nigeria', *Review of African Political Economy*, vol. 28, no. 89.

Whiteman, K. (1998) 'Africa, the ACP and Europe: The Lessons of 25 Years', *Development Policy Review*, vol. 16, no. 1.

Williams, P. (2004) 'Britain and Africa after the Cold War' in Taylor, I. and Williams, P. (eds) *Africa in International Politics External Involvement on the Continent* London: Routledge.

Williams, P. (2005) *British Foreign Policy under New Labour* Basingstoke: Palgrave.

Wolf, M. (1995) 'Cooperation or Conflict? The EU in a Liberal Global Economy', *International Affairs*, vol. 71, no. 2.

Wood, E. (2006) 'Democracy as Ideology of Empire' in Mooers, C. (ed.) *The New Imperialists: Ideologies of Empire* Oxford: Oneworld Publications.

Wood, G. (2004) 'Business and Politics in a Criminal State: The Case of Equatorial Guinea', *African Affairs*, vol. 103, no. 413.

World Bank (1981) *Accelerated Development in Sub-Saharan Africa: An Agenda for Action* Washington, DC: World Bank.

World Bank (1989) *Sub-Saharan Africa: From Crisis to Sustainable Growth* Washington, DC: World Bank.

World Bank (2007) 'World Bank Officials Engage African Diaspora in Development Efforts', Washington, DC, December 3.

World Bank (2009) *Regional Fact Sheet from the World Development Indicators, 2009: Sub-Saharan Africa* Washington, DC: World Bank.

World Development Movement (2005) *Heading for Failure: How Water Privatisation Threatens the Millennium Development Goals* London: World Development Movement.

Wrong, M. (2000) *In the Footsteps of Mr. Kurtz: Living on the Brink of Disaster in the Congo* London: Fourth Estate.

Wrong, M. (2009) *Our Turn to Eat: The Story of a Kenyan Whistle-Blower* London: Fourth Estate.

Wu Yanrui (2003) *China's Economic Growth: A Miracle with Chinese Characteristics* London: Routledge.

Yan Xuetong (2006) 'The Rise of China and Its Power Status', *Chinese Journal of International Politics*, vol. 1, no. 1.

Yates, D. (1996) *The Rentier State in Africa: Oil Rent Dependency and Neo-colonialism in the Republic of Gabon* Trenton, NJ: Africa World Press.

Yergin, D. (1991) *The Prize: The Epic Quest for Oil, Money and Power* New York, NY: Simon and Schuster.

Yu, G. (1970) *China and Tanzania: A Study in Co-operation* Berkeley, CA: University of California.

Yu, G. (1975) *China's African Policy: A Study of Tanzania* New York, NY: Praeger.

Zartman, I. W. (1976) 'Europe and Africa: Decolonisation or Dependency?', *Foreign Affairs*, vol. 34, no. 2.

Zeleza, P. (2005) 'Rewriting the African Diaspora: Beyond the Black Atlantic', *African Affairs*, vol. 104, no. 414.

Zeleza, P. (2006) 'The Disciplining of Africa' in Zeleza, P. (ed.) *The Study of Africa: Disciplinary and Interdisciplinary Encounters* Dakar: Codesria.

Zha Daojiong (2005) 'Comment: Can China Rise?' *Review of International Studies*, vol. 31, no. 4.

Zielonka, J. (2001) 'How New Enlarged Borders will Reshape the European Union', *Journal of Common Market Studies*, vol. 39, no. 3.

Zweig, D. and Bi Jianhai (2005) 'China's Global Hunt for Energy', *Foreign Affairs*, vol. 84, no. 5.

Index